To Nigel

best w's

IF

[signature]

and

Shirley

Thompson

NELLIE & WALTER ROACH'S

WALTER – 3, BACK 90 TOWER ST, B.1875, D.1930

b. c. 1894
Walter
m. Hilda
(4)

b.1897 d.1989
Mary Ellen
(Cissy) m. Albert
Sheargold (3)

b.1898 d.1984
Agnes
m. Thomas
Hunt (4)

Leslie
b.1924

R O A C H

SHEARGOLD

H U N T

Nellie   Francis

Bertram
b.1922

Walter was in the
colonial police in
Palestine in 1945.
Later became Chief
Superintendent in
the police force in
Hong Kong.

Frank   Albert   Joan   George
Roach b. 1920 b. 1923 b.1930
              d. Aug
              2001

Joyce
b.1926
m. Leonard
Taylor
1949

Kenneth
b.1930

A partially completed family tree, compiled by the authors from information supplied by Peter Mulroy, John Owen, George and Norma Sheargold, Joyce and Leonard Taylor, Stan Ballard and Pat Roach. This is only designed to show a *particular* section of the family. We have tried to make the information as accurate as possible, but, should there be any unintentional errors, the authors apologise in advance.

FAMILY TREE

MARRIED NELLIE,
B.1873, D.1935

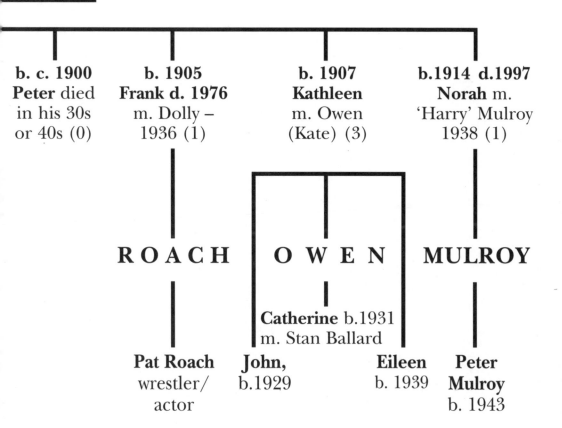

b. c. 1900	b. 1905	b. 1907	b.1914 d.1997
Peter died	**Frank** d. **1976**	**Kathleen**	**Norah** m.
in his 30s	m. Dolly –	m. Owen	'Harry' Mulroy
or 40s (0)	1936 (1)	(Kate) (3)	1938 (1)

R O A C H **O W E N** **MULROY**

Catherine b.1931
m. Stan Ballard

Pat Roach **John,** Eileen **Peter**
wrestler/ b.1929 b. 1939 **Mulroy**
actor b. 1943

b = born; d = died; m = married; (digit enclosed) = number of children, resulting from a particular marriage; 'c' = an approximate number. dec. = deceased.

The following are some of the nicknames that we know about: Agnes was 'Winnie', her husband Tom was 'Bert'. Mary Ellen was known as 'Cissy', Kathleen was 'Kate'. Walter Roach fought at Dunkirk before Palestine, and later joined Scotland Yard.

IF

Pat Roach with Shirley Thompson

BREWIN BOOKS

First published in 2002 by
Brewin Books Limited, Doric House, Church Street,
Studley, Warwickshire B80 7LG

British Library Cataloguing – in – Publication Data
A Catalogue record for this book is available from
The British Library

ISBN: 1 85858 209 1

Made and printed by
Warwick Printing Company Limited,
Theatre Street, Warwick, Warwickshire CV34 4DR.

CONTENTS

ACKNOWLEDGEMENTS

The authors are indebted to the following people, companies and organisations, for their very valuable contributions, various favours and support, which have been of great assistance in the publication of this book:

Relatives and Friends:
Doreen, Mark, and Dolly Roach; Aunt Freda (Robertson), John Bevis and 'Frankie' Roach; Joyce and Len Taylor, Peter Mulroy, George and Norma Sheargold, Stan Ballard and John Owen; Jim White, Eddie Fewtrell, Ronnie and Alison Callow, Dennis Sullivan.

David Thompson – the co-writer's husband, and mother-in-law, Ellen Thompson, (Pat's second cousin). Dennis Wareing and Eileen Wareing, (the co-author's cousin and mother) – for family research.

Robert Knight, for his assistance in *many* areas, and especially those involving computer technology and photography. Andy Townsend, illustrator and fan, aka Hudson Shaw.

Birmingham Residents:
Tom Arneill, Denis and Cynthia Wood, Albert Townsend.

The Canal Chapters:
Architect, Alan Goodwin; former *British Waterways* Chief Architect, and landscape artist, Peter White, M.B.E.; George and Jean Smith; Sam Waller and Graham Wigley of *The Birmingham & Midland Canal Carrying Company Ltd*, Gas Street Basin, (includes *Parties Afloat* and *Camping Afloat*).

Gower Coast People (Evans research):
John and Kaye Beynon, Gary Sheaf, Rosemary Brangwyn, Gill Wales.

Show-business personalities – including several who are friends; their associates and families:
Arnold Schwarzenegger, Steven Spielberg, Sean Connery, Harrison Ford, David Tomblin, Ryan O'Neal, Martin Shaw, the late Norman Mitchell.

The *Auf Wiedersehen* cast: Chris Fairbank, Jimmy Nail, Noel Clarke, Kevin Whately and his wife – Madelaine Newton; Tim Healy, Tim and Shane Spall; Joan Pugh – Gary's mother, and his manager John Harwood-Bee – for contributing on Gary's behalf.

Actresses: Sheila White and Melanie Hill. *Actor/manager:* Ian Sandy. Pat's theatrical agent, Peter Charlesworth.

Our special thanks go to Jan Harlan, Christiane and Vivian Kubrick. We are particularly grateful to Anthony Frewin, Stanley Kubrick's former personal assistant, for his kind assistance in a number of areas, including his guidance in obtaining an accurate profile of the director. Also, for enabling us to obtain special permission from the Kubrick Estate, to publish five stills taken by Jan Harlan.

Vic Armstrong, stunt director, and his wife, Wendy Armstrong; Billy Horrigan and Roy Alon, former and practising stunt men; Mara Bryant and Sharon Lark, on the Bond production team; Roy Button, Director of Warner Productions Ltd.

Sports personalities: Former World, Commonwealth and Indian (Rustom-E-Hind) wrestling champion, turned-actor/director – Dara Singh; Paul Mann Singh; Randhawa Singh; Johnny Hayles, aka *Killer Kowalski*; Mitzi Mueller and her manager/husband, Brian Dixon.

Boxing booths and Fairs: Ronnie and Lily Taylor. Former boxer Thomas Paddy Hallet, aka 'Big Paddy', later assigned by manager Gordon Mills, as bodyguard to Tom Jones, Engelbert Humperdinck, and other celebrities.

Photographers: Albert Clarke, Peter William, Jack Bannister, Yvon Dorval, Nick Lockett; Norman Fletcher of the Victoria Studio, Birmingham, John Landon – Shakespeare Road/Anderton Street photo, John Whybrow Ltd; Tony Smith, the Carlton photographer who took the *Auf Wiedersehen Pet* stills, for the two original series.

Organisations, Institutions and Companies:
Birmingham Library Services: Central Reference Library – Local Studies and Archives, and the Arts, Languages and Literature Department. We are grateful to them for their advice, access to a wide range of records and for permission to publish four Birmingham City Council photographs. Also, Sutton Coldfield Library Archives, and Shirley Library.

The Reverend Doctor John Sharp, Birmingham Archdiocesan Archives, Saint Chad's Cathedral, for advice and access to material concerning the Roach and Wareing families.

Avery Berkel, trading name of GEC Avery Ltd (formerly W & T Avery Ltd); Mike Cooper, Communications Manager for the company; Howard Green, curator of the Avery Historical Museum.

Nick Lockett, Head of Pictures, and Carlton Television – for arranging and granting permission for us to publish a selection of *Auf Wiedersehen* photographs; our additional thanks go to Nick for his photograph of Pat, as Petty Officer Evans.

Rank Gaming Division, for the *Miss World* photograph.

Various agents and attorneys: acting on behalf of Steven Spielberg, Arnold Schwarzenegger, Sean Connery, Ryan O'Neal, Jimmy Nail, Martin Shaw and Harrison Ford.

Publishers, Literary Agencies, and Publications:
Alan and Alistair Brewin, of Brewin Books Ltd.

A P Watt Ltd, on behalf of The National Trust for Places of Historic Interest or Natural Beauty, for permission to include the poem *If –* by Rudyard Kipling. Also for advice regarding the William Blake quotation.

We are grateful to several publishing companies and literary agents for granting us permission to include extracts from the following biographies, in a range of countries:

Sean Connery A Biography, by Michael Freedland, (1994):

The Orion Group, on behalf of Weidenfeld and Nicolson Publishers, for granting us World rights, including distribution throughout the U.S.A.

Sean Connery, by John Parker, (1993):

Victor Gollancz, a division of The Orion Publishing Group Ltd, for granting United Kingdom and British Commonwealth rights to publish quotations. Also, McGraw-Hill Education, a division of the McGraw-Hill Companies, for granting US rights.

Harrison Ford, by Minty Clinch (1987):

The Blake Friedmann Literary Agency, for granting World rights, to quote two extracts.

Stanley Kubrick, by John Baxter, (1997):

Our thanks to HarperCollins Publishers Ltd, for World rights to quote extracts, excluding U.S.A. and Canada. Also to Curtis Brown, for granting North American rights.

Stanley Kubrick, by Vincent LoBrutto, (1997).

Faber and Faber Ltd, Publishers, for granting UK and Commonwealth rights, excluding Canada. Also, Penguin Putnam, for North American rights to quote extracts from the book.

From STEVEN SPIELBERG *A Biography* by Joseph McBride. Copyright © 1997 by Joseph McBride. Reprinted by permission of Simon & Schuster.

The authors are grateful to Simon and Schuster, for granting rights to publish extracts from their publication in the United States, its territories and dependencies, the Philipinne Republic, Canada, and the open market.
Also, to Faber and Faber Ltd, Publishers, for granting UK and Commonwealth rights, excluding Canada.

Thanks are also due to HarperCollins Publishers Ltd, for Worldwide rights to publish extracts from *Men are From Mars, Women are From Venus,* by Doctor John Gray, (1992).

Jessica Carney of L'Epine Smith & Carney Associates, for granting permission, on behalf of his family, to publish Norman Mitchell's 'likeness' in a *Barry Lyndon* photograph.

James Curran, for authorising the publication of an extract from *British Cinema History* (1983), edited by Vincent Porter and himself. This is referred to in Chapter 10 – *Bondage in Pinewood.* The extract is taken from Chapter 12, *The James Bond Films: Conditions of Production,* written by Janet Woollacott, to whom we are also grateful; our additional thanks go to Vincent Porter.
The Permissions Department of Penguin Group (UK) for advice about publishing the extract from Trollope's *Orley Farm.*

Newspapers:
We are grateful to the following publications for allowing us to quote from a range of articles:

The Sunday Telegraph	*The Sunday Mercury*
The Sunday Times	*First Down (American Football publication)*
The Birmingham Post and Mail	*The Birmingham Post*
The Sutton Coldfield News.	

Our additional thanks go to the *Sunday Telegraph* newspaper, for permission to publish observations made by Christiane Kubrick, in an article dated 6 February 2000. The article, entitled *Kubrick's widow finds lost scripts he wrote as a teenager,* was written by Chris Hastings.

FOREWORD

I first met Pat in 1983 at the poolside of a hotel in Juarez, just over the Mexican border. We were there to film "Conan II" in Mexico City. As Conan, I had two fight scenes with Pat. Pat's characters were Goran, the wizard turned into an ape man and Dagoth, the horned monster. The roles were physically exhausting for both of us, particularly with the lighting and mirrors. So, we needed to keep very fit.

In the mornings and evenings Dolph Lundgren, Grace Jones, Vic Armstrong, Pat and myself worked out together in the gym. I remember Pat teaching Vic various boxing techniques. I had my own exercise regime with weights, but was able to give Pat some useful tips. There was a real mutual respect for each other and our abilities as not only actors, but as athletes.

For the role of Goran, Pat had five-and-a-half hours of make-up every morning. They had to pump oxygen into him, to keep him cool because of the prosthetic head he was wearing. A special studio/dressing room was built for him to relax in between shots.

It took eight people to get him into his Dagoth suit. They moved the various body parts from outside with levers. The enormous weight of the suit made our fight scene particularly demanding. It was difficult for Pat to keep his balance. I didn't realize until recently that during one of the fight scenes my sword went right through Pat's costume and nearly severed his head!

I've always enjoyed wrestling tournaments so I arranged for a group of us, including Pat, to visit a wrestling stadium in Mexico City. André "The Giant" was there. He and Pat already knew each other from wrestling tournaments in England. After the tournament, a group of fifteen to twenty of us went to dinner at a restaurant. Pat warned me that André might try to pay the bill. The evening ended with André, weighing 460lbs at 7 feet 3 inches and Pat and myself both well over 6 feet and approaching 20 stone, having a friendly argument about who would pay. The frightened Maitre D' standing between us was thinking to himself, "I don't care who pays – as long as I get out of this alive!" André is no longer with us, but he was the biggest wrestler and an extraordinary champion. As giant, powerful and strong André physically was, is how generous, kind and softhearted he was.

Pat is multitalented. I enjoyed working with him on the movie and I got to know him well during the filming. He is a very strong man and an incredible athlete. He was a great performer, a great wrestler and a great lifter, and now a great author. Pat is also a philanthropist who is involved in the Special Olympics and mentoring others. He tries to ensure that whomever life he touches realizes their potential, and that their dreams are obtainable. I have always valued his friendship.

Arnold Schwarzenegger

If – you can spare a few seconds, when all around you are rushing headlong into this book...

Dear Readers,

This letter is especially for you, from your co-authors, using a format that sets the style for the entire biography. We've varied the type of print to clarify which one of us is 'holding forth' at any given time. My own humble thoughts are in bold print – how appropriate! The 'master of disguise' and subject of this book, has done the gentlemanly thing, by agreeing to have his revelations set out in two kinds of italics, although, God knows, it's the most important part. The exceptions to this are few and far between – and in inverted commas. You might say, if you were being unkind, that our choice of print stands in direct contrast to our true personalities. Oh – and don't be surprised when we slip in and out of conversational mode – nobody's perfect!

Although we have an *Acknowledgements* section, we'd like to say an extra thank you to all of our contributors, who have given so generously of their thoughts, time, experiences and photographs. We hope that you enjoy reading Pat's book, at *least* as much as we've enjoyed writing it.

We have used Kipling's poem, 'If', because it has been a great favourite of mine, and a source of reference since I was quite young. The ideas and philosophy contained within it have been inspirational, in terms of the way I try to live my life. There are, for example, certain aspects of the church, particularly those involving finance, that I cannot agree with; although that's not to say that I'm not keen on God.

In a way, Kipling's poem has become my own 'Lord's Prayer'. Having said that, while staying in America, I experienced one of the most beautiful things I can remember seeing in my life. It was televised on an American TV channel – just before close of transmission one particular evening. A Red Indian on horseback said the Lord's Prayer, using Red Indian sign language; someone else provided

the American dialogue – in the rich velvet tones of a 'voice-over'. But the image
and that particular setting stayed with me: it just hit me so hard; it was one of the
most moving things I have ever seen.
While you are contemplating 'If' – don't forget to be 'aware'.

With our very best wishes,

Shirley Thompson and Pat Knock...

IF – by Rudyard Kipling

('Brother Square-Toes' – *Rewards and Fairies*)

If you can keep your head, when all about you
Are losing theirs and blaming it on you,
If you can trust yourself when all men doubt you,
But make allowance for their doubting too;
If you can wait and not be tired by waiting,
Or being lied about, don't deal in lies,
Or being hated, don't give way to hating,
And yet don't look to good, nor talk too wise:

If you can dream – and not make dreams your master;
If you can think – and not make thoughts your aim;
If you can meet with Triumph and Disaster
And treat those two impostors just the same;
If you can bear to hear the truth you've spoken
Twisted by knaves, to make a trap for fools,
Or watch the things you gave your life to, broken,
And stoop and build 'em up with worn-out tools:

If you can make one heap of all your winnings
And risk it on one turn of pitch-and-toss –
And lose, and start again at your beginnings
And never breathe a word about your loss;
If you can force your heart and nerve and sinew
To serve your turn long after they are gone,
And so hold on when there is nothing in you
Except the Will, which says to them: 'Hold on!'

If you can talk with crowds and keep your virtue,
Or walk with Kings – nor lose the common touch,
If neither foes nor loving friends can hurt you,
If all men count with you, but none too much;
If you can fill the unforgiving minute
With sixty seconds' worth of distance run,
Yours is the Earth and everything that's in it,
And – which is more – you'll be a Man, my son!

Rudyard Kipling

Reproduced by permission of A P Watt Ltd on behalf of The National Trust for Places of Historic Interest or Natural Beauty.

For Ma

Dolly Roach

'Queen of the Gypsies'?

Chapter One –

BIG HEAD

If you can keep your head when all about you
Are losing theirs and blaming it on you...

In my very early days, I got the blame for almost everything, as well as being called 'Big Head' time and time again. So this is where it all started – all sorts of things, some nice, some awful – but that's life. And talking about life – here I am – just about to put in an appearance!

The worn iron bedstead groaned and swayed precariously beneath her. Praying that it wouldn't collapse, Dolly pushed stoically against it yet again, with all her might. She could feel the wall creaking under the strain. The pain was becoming unbearable. She cried out, wondering how much more she could take.

The midwife bounced on her belly, then the beleaguered young woman bounced her off again. The two women repeated the process several times. "I want you to drink this stuff," the midwife said impatiently. She was nearing the end of her tether as she thrust a cup of vile-smelling green liquid under her patient's nostrils. Looking down at the curly-headed young woman sprawled out unceremoniously on the bed, she felt a strong sense of pity. There was no dignity in childbirth – that was for sure!

Dolly's hair was sopping wet. She looked a real fright – and no wonder! Two solid days and nights they'd been trying to deliver this child! The midwife's muscular arms, with stamina to match, were normally more than adequate for even the most irksome of deliveries. But this one would have tried the patience of a saint!

"Tell me what it's for then," laughed the woman, feebly. "You ain't gonna have me put to sleep are you? Because I can't fetch me babby!" She's got spirit, I'll give her that, mused the midwife. Been through the mill, but still ready with a joke. Just as well – she'll need a sense of humour with what's coming to her!

1

"It's to strengthen the muscles of your womb, love," she said, trying to sound as soothing as tiredness would allow, as she applied a cold compress to her patient's forehead. In between spasms, Dolly drank the awful liquid, while the older woman collapsed into a nearby chair. How much longer? She made a mental note to award herself a double-brandy when this was all over. Leaning over she explained hoarsely: "The baby's there sweetheart. You've been two days and two nights. We shall lose him if we're not careful."

When the child finally arrived, he was so heavy that they had to weigh him on an enormous pair of fish scales, suspended from a hook. His head and body were unusually large. He weighed in at a few ounces over $12\frac{1}{2}$lb. Dolly stared at him in disbelief. "I've just never had that!" she gasped.

A few weeks later she was pushing him in a large boat-shaped pram, down Park Road, Hockley, near their home, close to Birmingham's Jewellery Quarter. It was a beautiful summer's day. She crossed over the road, passing Alf and poor little Bridget's second-hand shop.

Francis Patrick Roach, her first-born, was certainly making an impression on passers-by. His abundant flaxen curls, made golden by the sunlight, were packed tightly together like a cauliflower. Little did she realise that in later years, he would have a cauliflower ear! The baby's gorgeous big blue eyes focused intently on everything around him. "Did you see that baby?" people would comment, as Dolly walked proudly by. And it's been like that ever since – one way or the other.

Dolly's parents, Bill and Amelia Bevis, had christened her Doris, but everyone knew her as 'Dolly'. She was one of four children: a 'war baby', born in 1915, in the Scarlet Buildings, Garbett Street, in the Ladywood district of Birmingham. "There was Freda, the oldest – now 91 years of age, then Charlie, myself and Stan, who was the babby – there were two years between us." Speaking of Freda, Dolly said: "She always says, 'I was born in nineteen eleven pence' – 'er never fails to say that!"

Their mother Amelia's family had been water-gypsies, or 'boat people' as they usually preferred to be called. Amelia's life is described in more detail in Chapter 4, which, together with Chapter 5, takes a look at life, past and present, around the canals in the Gas Street Basin area of the city. Amelia's first introduction to the city would have been via this centre of the English canal system.

"Momma had worked all her life," explained Dolly. The two of us sat eating cake and drinking tea in her flat. "Poor mom, she had a sad life; she was separated from daddy, but he used to come and see us and bring us ice cream, off the Italian woman who came on the corner – you wouldn't remember that – in Garbett Street, Ladywood." This street was just off King Edward Road. "Our dad used to come and see us every Sunday and buy us ice cream." An Ordnance Survey map of what was then a newly developed

Ladywood, in the early 1900s, shows many of the streets and landmarks which we refer to, as Pat's life story unfolds.

Dolly, a very warm-natured, affectionate person, continued her explanation: "We lived in this little back house in Garbett Street, and there was Mrs Leach, Mrs Bevis – that's us, Mrs Gill, Alfie Riley and his poor old mom. Mrs Freeman – cocky little Mrs Freeman – funny little bugger she was! Then there was Mrs White and her daughter – nice people – in the corner. We all shared the toilets and the brew houses." Although many of these neighbours have long since gone, they seem to be almost reincarnated, when one discovers a list of these same names on copies of the 1920 and 1933 electoral registers for Garbett Street.

In those days it was completely safe for the Bevis children to play in the yard. "There was nothing to be afraid of them days. You never locked your doors; there were no murders." Dolly recalls that there was very little traffic and there were always children playing in the back yard or street.

Amelia helped her children to get ready for school, before going to work at the local factory. She worked all her life, right into her early 70s, until ill health finally brought her to a standstill, resulting in her death, from pneumonia.

Dolly attended Nelson Street School, on the Parade, near the Sandpits. "We used to go with Maudie Meakin, Alice Robinson, and get there late. We'd always have the cane you know, for being late. They could do with doing it now! And of course I wouldn't cry. The teacher said: 'Hold the other hand out Bevis,' and I had another one!"

Dolly is uncertain about how her parents first met. To the best of her knowledge, Bill's family lived somewhere in Bearwood, a suburb of Birmingham.

There were lodging houses near the Sandpits and the impressive-looking Chamberlain Clock, a local landmark, mentioned again in later chapters. It was restored by Birmingham City Council, and stands again in pride-of-place, in the same spot – at the top of Warstone Lane. Tom Arneill, who lived, in the Camden Street area of Ladywood, as a young boy, from 1941 to 1951, recalls the clock being referred to as *Big Tom*. "It was a good 15 foot high, green with a large face," he explains. "There was a big post office on the corner and the churchyard was lower down." Spring Hill was nearby, continuing up to Summerfield Park, by the library.

Before Dolly met her future husband, Frank Roach, Pat's father, she and Henry Robinson had been courting. Henry and Jackie Broadhurst, who later became a prominent Birmingham business man, were friends. The two men had arranged to meet Dolly and her friend, Maggie, at another Crown pub, the one in Snow Hill. The four of them enjoyed the 'free-and-easies' and concerts there. "I was sweet on Henry Robinson, who lived down the entry in Thistle Street, Summer Lane. He was sweet on me, 'cause I was really something to look at – very smart."

Pat describes his father, Frank Roach, as "A very well-travelled man, 'educated in the university of the world', to quote him." Frank had travelled across Canada by train. "He used to travel the trains in '27 and work the land. What is portrayed in films as a 'bum' or 'hobo'." He killed a man during a bare fistfight. Following a short spell in jail, he was released, because of the circumstances of the fight.

Frank might well have remained in Canada, but the year was 1934 and his 65-year-old mother, Nellie, had become ill. He therefore returned home. She died the following year. Until recently, Pat had never seen a photograph of his grandmother, and only saw a photograph of his grandfather, Walter, Frank's father, a little before that – courtesy of his cousin, Peter Mulroy. Fortunately, another cousin, John Owen, came to the rescue, providing photographs of Walter and Nellie. These can be found in the *Roach Family Album*, which we have put together with the kind assistance of Pat's cousins. Stan Ballard and 'Frankie' Roach also helped.

Dolly recalls that soon after Frank's return to England, the relationship between the two of them took a dramatic turn. "There was a nice crowd of us used to collect at the Crown, Snow Hill. Frank Roach had set his heart on me. Everyone was terrified of him: he was a very powerful man. When the Chairman said: 'Will Henry Robinson go outside?' we said, 'Frank Roach!' So we all went out and there was a big crowd. At that time, it was always a fair fight, and the best man won – no putting the boot in. It went on for a while – they gave one another a belting. Henry Robinson was really gallant. He was known to be useful with his hands. I loved Henry Robinson and yet we never had sex or anything like that."

Matters however, didn't rest there. "Frank said he was going to get him and kill him. Henry worked at the Delta factory and I went and warned him, because Frank was quite capable. And yet Henry and I weren't very serious, but he always loved me company. Always very smart, with a lovely black overcoat and a black Anthony Eden hat."

In 1934, Dolly was just 19, Frank was ten years older. According to Dolly, "He was the model of John Boles, the film star." But Dolly preferred Henry to Frank, who she found too domineering: "I didn't like the way Frank took over."

Dolly was a respectable girl. "Sex wasn't recognised as much as it is today. There was none of that going on before you were married. If you made up, they thought you was a bitch, and I made up – lipstick, you know, and eye-black. Except them that knew me, knew I was a good-living girl – and I was in love with another."

Dolly never met Frank's parents. His father, Walter, had died in 1930 at the age of 55. Nellie died the year before her son's marriage. According to

John Owen, Frank's nephew, she suffered from Parkinson's Disease, in the days before there were drugs available to ease the condition.

To describe Dolly's original wedding day as a nightmare would be a massive understatement! "They were all there to see me – I'm always a last minute merchant – I'm always late for everything. I was going to get married to him and me mate's wedding came just before. Frank smashed my friend's wedding up and because of that I kept my word – and called my wedding off. I thought, I shall have to make myself scarce, 'cause he's going to kill me if I put it off. They said, 'Ooh, there's Dolly here,' and I ran out, and I was supposed to be married within twenty minutes. I was wearing a whole fox and a tail. I was very popular – full of beans. Everybody loved me!

"I was really nice: figure-wise, clothes-wise. So I put the wedding off. And I had to duck-and-dive! He came to the house and he wanted to fight me poor father and everything. Oh he led me a life: I was terrified!"

Surprisingly, Dolly relented and married Frank in July 1936, when she was just 21 and Frank was 31. Ten months later, Francis Patrick Roach was born, which is where our story began. The couple began married life in Park Road, where they had a scrap yard, close to Birmingham's Jewellery Quarter. Frank was what in those days was called a 'general dealer', or less elegantly, a scrap metal merchant.

Life with Frank soon became very difficult for Dolly and her infant son. Pat explains: "I didn't live with him after the age of four, when we parted company. In later years, we became friends, but it was a struggle to be father and son."

Dolly recalls that Frank could be very cruel at times. "If I didn't get the sharp cheese, I'd get a back-hander. But I won the day. He was going to kill me. I won my child and he'd got to pay me 15/- a week, which was a hell of a lot of money, because it was £2. 10s. then."

Despite such difficulties, it is clear that both father and son had a special affection for one another. According to Dolly, although he was separated from his family, Frank 'thought the world of Pat.' In later years, the two of them worked together in Frank's business. The following story, told by Pat, provides a graphic example of the positive side of their relationship:

> *I remember my father used to tell this dramatic story: "I came home from work, and you were lying there and you were breathing heavily – you couldn't get your breath. And your little nostrils were going in and out. And I said, 'He's got double pneumonia! Get him to the 'orspital!'"*
>
> *They must have walked down Park Road, looking for a taxi. Then he tells the story – my father. There used to be a big, long bridge, like where the trains used to go across. They only took it down a few years ago. It was a very, very long bridge. On a dark night, certainly, you'd struggle seeing the other end. And it was a foggy night.*

"And as we walked up the road," he said, "a taxi loomed out of the fog. And it just came under the bridge," he said, "and a man got out, with a moustache and a beard, tall – and he looked like Jesus Christ! And he stood for a second and he paid the taxi off. And as the taxi went to go," he said, "I flagged him down."

At that time, when you think about it, there was no need for anyone to get out of the taxi in that spot, because there were no houses there. There was a graveyard on the one side and the railway yard on the other. There were no houses –they would have been at a distance.

So anyone who would have caught a taxi would have gone to an abode, to a place of entertainment, to somewhere. But not got out of a taxi – in a wilderness. He said the man just disappeared into the fog. He told me that story many times.

"You see, that taxi, arriving at that time," he said, "when I got to the 'orspital they said: 'This child would have died if you hadn't got him here – straight away.'"

That's how he tells the story. That was his claim to fame – me old dad – saving my life.

An even stranger thing about this story is that nowadays, if old Grandfather Bill, Dolly's father, could stand on his grave, and look down the slope to where the bridge used to be, he would actually be looking at the spot where all this happened.

Prior to hearing this story, I had quite naturally assumed that Pat's creativity and strong sense of the dramatic came from his mother, Dolly, who has a very exuberant, theatrical type of personality. But clearly, Pat's father was no mean storyteller either! Perhaps it was the Celtic element in him. His ancestors were from the Ross Common and Galway Bay areas of Southern Ireland. As the story unfolds we learn that at least two of his sisters enjoyed taking part in amateur dramatics or playing musical instruments; in Agnes' case, it was both.

Dolly explained that when she and Frank separated, "I took all my bits and pieces to Maggie, to sell up – I had a 'sell-up' from Park Road." She and Pat moved back to Garbett Street, Ladywood, to live with Amelia for a while.

Pat describes his childhood as a very 'dis-jointed' one. There can be no doubt that he and Dolly share a close and loving mother/son relationship. However, as a child, growing up in what was, at least for a while, a 'single-parent' family, he experienced several traumatic incidents, which were to have a profound effect upon him.

He moved several times during his childhood. In an effort to trace his movements around Birmingham, I asked: "You were born in Park Road, then moved to Tenby Street, followed by Garbett Street? That's the way I worked it out."

I thought it was Tenby Street. But my life was so dis-jointed, so dis-jointed. But don't forget, Tenby Street could still have been in existence and my mother could still have been living there and I was living in King Edward Road – somewhat divorced from the situation. I mean, I don't know.

I always seemed to be living apart from my mother and father – with someone. I remember once, somewhere between the ages of 5 – 7, it must have been Christmas or my birthday, my mother bought me a hat and coat. I think I was living with my Aunt Edna, or someone – at the time.

My father arrived on the scene about the same time as my mother, who had come to see me and presented me with this hat and coat, and I thought it was marvellous. My father just threw it on the fire: I stood there and watched this hat and coat burn on the fire. It was the first new coat that I remember having. I suppose I cried – I don't know. But I remember that very vividly.

Because of the confusion surrounding that period in Pat's life, it perhaps comes as no surprise to discover from Dolly that the aunt he was staying with at that time was not Edna, but Aunt Hilda, Frank's older brother Walter's wife, who had four children. "I was there and poor momma bought the hat and coat for Paddy, because I lived with her. I took it round; she was golden – our momma. I think Frank had come round to sort me out."

Pat was very tall for his age, with big feet. Understandably, people often used to think he was much older than he actually was. Having to cope with being called 'Big Head', was an additional problem:

In the very early days, I remember one time I'd got a hat and it went missing. I came home from school and I'd been crying. My mother said: "You look a bit upset." I said: "The kids have been rude to me at school – calling me 'Big Head'." She said: "Don't take any notice of that." I said: "I've always been called 'Big Head'. Have I got a big head, mother?" She said: "No, don't be silly! Anyway – wear your hat."

So I said: "Oh, all right, but I can't find it – where is it?" She said: "It's in the kitchen, with five hundredweight of coal in it!"

His first school was the one that his mother had attended, years before.

I went to Nelson Street School in the very early days, when we lived in 180, King Edward Road, and Colin Evans lived about three doors up. He was my friend who I used to play with. Titchy Coakes lived at the bottom of the entry, with Mickey Coakes. Peter Price became notorious later in life, went off to America, made his fortune, then came back: went into the car game. I met him as an adult, many years later.

Pat recalls several incidents from that time, the first being the school Christmas party:

We were told to bring a knife, fork and spoon and a small tea plate. I took a big dinner plate. The teacher gave me a slap for bringing a big dinner plate, because she thought I was being greedy. I remember I knicked all the scissors out of the class: about ten pairs of scissors.

Why, I wondered, had he done it?

Because I was a little 'tea-leaf'. And I stood in King Edward Road, trying to sell them at 1/6d a pair. Walked up to them and said: "Hello Mrs – d'you want to buy a pair of scissors?"

They'd probably say: "Where did you get those?"

Yes. I don't know whether I actually sold any though. I remember I'd got a 'Diana' air rifle, which was broken. I used to go out and play with Colin Evans. It was my contribution towards our game.

Colin eventually became a window designer. His father worked for the Austin car factory, and owned a black Austin Atlantic.

I remember one day they wouldn't let me play with him any more, because I was too scruffy.

His mother wouldn't?

Yes, because I was too scruffy. I used to throw the gun over the gate for quickness. I must have been somewhere between five and eight years of age. I lived with my poor old grandmother again – before Shakespeare Road. One time when I went in at night, I'd thrown the gun over the gate and I must have hit her on the head and cut her eye. And of course, that upset me – poor old gran. She became deaf through washing her hair in the canal, or the 'cut' as my mother would call it.

I can remember playing in Anderton Street, just off Shakespeare Road, with Brian Webb, who wasn't my cousin really, we were just friends. But I called him my cousin. I can remember somebody saying something to me, and me saying: "Well, I'm only 10!" They must have thought I was much older.

I remember being at my grandmother's when I was very young. I left home when I was about nine or ten. We were living in Belgrave Road, Balsall Heath. I was going to Hope Street School. I just turned up at my grandmother's. I remember that she said, when I walked in through the door: "Go on, get off. I don't want you!"

I wasn't too happy about my stepfather at the time, I suppose. Somehow or other I cemented myself with my grandmother and went off to Steward Street School.

Many of the houses led out onto the pavement. They played the usual street games, such as Hopscotch and marbles. 'Glarnies' were the king marbles and they also played 'jack stones'.

There was another game called 'Tip-cat', which I've never heard of, but Tom Arneill assures me was a popular game in the Ladywood area, and possibly elsewhere. Pat explained:

> *It's a shaped piece of wood, oblong and cornered at each end. Like a sausage, if you like, but to a point either end: rounded and coming up to a point, so that you could tip it. You hit the tip with a stick and spun it into the air. The idea was to be the first person to reach the other side of the road, or the corner. So what you' do, you'd hit it, up it would go and crack! You'd whack the thing, and go up the street with it. You'd have about three goes at it.*

Opposite Pat's home in King Edward Road was a gravel area known as the 'rec' or recreation area, with swings and roundabouts – although they were often broken – through heavy use.

> *I remember the Ice Rink on the corner of Summer Hill, when the Americans used to come here. We used to ask them for gum.*

"Got any gum chum?"

> *Yes, all the kids used to say that. I went up to one and said: "Please sir, have you got any chewing gum?" And he looked at me like that, and he said: "Well, what a well-mannered little boy you are!" And he gave me a piece of gum – yes.*

Denis Wood, a retired Birmingham millwright, used to go skating in his youth, at the same ice rink; as events turned out, it's an occasion he is never likely to forget! "I was actually across the road from the Palais de Danse when it was bombed. We were skating there on the ice and the blast seemed to lift you up! It was at night. Of course, all the lights went out and we had to scramble out." He helped his friend, Bill Morgan, who, like Denis, was an amateur wrestler, to escort his girlfriend across the Hagley Road and into a shelter off Granville Street, closer to the girl's home. The shelter under *Cruickshank's*, in Camden Street, would probably have been nearer, but they felt safer staying together.

"I got fed up and pulled out," continued Denis. "I had to go towards Five Ways. A bomb had hit *Kunzles*, which was right on the corner. I saw the 'plane strafing around that area and I ducked down. Then all I could see was the line of fire – and a bus coming along slowly – just a driver. So I chased and got on it. It was a 3A bus, and he slowed down by the *Green Man*, in Harborne. I jumped off, because I lived in Harborne at the time. The driver didn't know I was on – I got a free ride! I heard later that a bomb was dropped close by where we'd sheltered. I think it was in William Street – luckily it didn't go off!"

While Denis was making his escape, only a few streets away from the ice rink a very young Pat was taking cover, protected by Dolly and Aunt Freda, in the basement of a Ladywood sweet shop.

> *That was in Garbett Street – Moss's sweet shop. I remember, we used to go down in the cellar. We could hear the "bom, bom, bomb," but we never used to really understand what it was. And I remember, my mother used to stand and sing, and the more the bombs hit, the louder she sang. They were so brave.*

What songs did she sing?

> *(Sings). "Sally, Sally, pride of our alley.."*

Oh, wonderful!

> *And the other one – "On Mother Kelly's doorstep…" (Hams it up)!*

I thought you couldn't sing Pat!

> *I've got a videotape of Aunt Freda, which we made years later – you've got to see it. She and my mother do a double act. They used to do all those songs in the shelters. And the more the bombs dropped, the louder they got – the nearer they got – the louder they sang. (Imitates the bombs dropping again).*

Were you frightened?

> *No, because being young, we didn't quite understand. We used to emerge the next day and see everything flattened. We really couldn't quite understand death. People would get killed. And we'd come up from the cellar and look.*

Weren't any of the neighbours killed?

> *Well, I suppose they were, but we were protected – by our mothers – **they** protected us. They were so brave: just like 22-carat gold. They never talked about people who were killed – in front of you.*

According to Dolly, during the earlier stages of the war, she and Pat were evacuated to Whitegate, at Litmarsh, near Hereford, when the pub on their street corner was bombed. They were living in a little back house in Tenby Street, at the time.

"I was with Frank Roach," Dolly explained. "We used to go to Warstone Lane, under the crypt, when the sirens went, and when they offered for us to go away with the kids to a safe place in the country, I was glad to get away from a mad, violent husband. We were took from one place to another. Poor Charlie, my brother, came to look for us on his bike every weekend – over the months. He *worshipped* Paddy as a babby. He *adored* him, because we were a close family."

Years later, Pat and Dolly re-visited the local pub at Marden, *The Volunteer*, in the area where they had been evacuated, but the place had changed so much, with many more trees, that she no longer recognised it. Amelia eventually moved around the square to live in Shakespeare Road, and Pat lived with her for some of that time.

When Dolly describes Pat's childhood, she makes the point that although he had many neighbourhood friends, he was more like an only child. He later had two stepbrothers, Rickie and Pete Meakin. According to Dolly, Rickie was born the day before Pat's ninth birthday, on 18 May 1946, and Peter in December 1948, when Pat was eleven. "I had my two other sons in 18 months and they were happier children than Pat, because they'd got one another."

There were several periods during his childhood when Pat lived with his granny, but he eventually returned to live with his mother, and immediate family, in Balsall Heath, completing his schooling at Hope Street Secondary School. Former production manager Albert Townsend was the oldest of a family of ten children, who were well known in that area, living in nearby Princess Street. He attended the same secondary school as Pat just a few years earlier, and recalls a rather strict regime.

Hope Street Junior and Secondary schools shared the same campus. "There was one large playground – the junior school was situated in the bottom right-hand corner," explained Albert. "It was a fairly strict school, with multi-levels. The main assembly hall was at the top level. I always remember, the children were assembled in the playground and had to march up to various levels of classrooms. You had to march up the centre of the stairs, but weren't allowed to use the handrail. There were prefects stationed on landings and if you were caught you had the cane or some other punishment."

Although life must have been lonely for Pat, at times, the picture that Doris paints of him is of a very kind-natured lad. "Pat used to fetch me a loaf and run errands. He'd say: 'Shut your eyes mom, hold your hands out,' and put a loaf in, when he was a lad." Had she known that he was buying the loaf? "No. Very kind – loved animals – believed in God."

Was their anyone from Pat's childhood who had been a profound and positive influence, perhaps even providing a role model for him? Initially he was quite adamant that no one came to mind. Then he remembered his headmaster at Hope Street Junior School, Mr. Cooper.

I hadn't got any dinner money – two-bob. He paid it. Oh yes, Mr. Cooper. I saw him many years later at another school. I meant to go back, but it didn't happen. Oh I don't know. It seems like I've been on the road all my life – really.

I think I've said it before. I've never been clever enough to earn a living like other people have – and then just relax. I've always had to work seven days a week and go to work at night- time, to try and survive. I've never been that clever – never have – never claimed to be. Always had to get my head down and do it.

Chapter Two –

NEAR VARNA

If you can trust yourself when all men doubt you,

Desperate to escape the ridicule of their tormentors, the schoolboys marched stoically two-abreast, up the centre of Varna Road. Determination tinged with fear, in the face of such raw aggression, made them oblivious to the dangers of passing traffic.

But the poverty-stricken 'raggy-arses' who taunted them – relatively innocent, post-war fascists-in-the-making – knew no better. All they knew was that these stony-faced kids were different … with their smart uniforms, orderly manner and neat satchels. And for that they were going to be punished.

One rather tall boy hung back, unobserved by his fellow tormentors. Something inside him balked at the intrinsic inhumanity of the situation. But his youth and inexperience prevented him from putting a name to it. As he watched the pallid faces of their quarry, he was struck by their bravery and sheer determination not to be bullied. To retain dignity at all costs … and not be defeated.

Years later, Spielberg was to tell Pat that to his mind, the most hateful symbol in the entire world was that ancient symbol adopted by Hitler – the Nazi cross, or swastika. Such passionate feelings struck a resounding chord with Pat.

My thoughts always go back to how brave those little kids were; I've never quite forgiven myself for that, and my understanding of Jewish people afterwards is that they were so brave. What makes me think about:

If you can trust yourself when all men doubt you

Is that in our ignorance, though we were kids too, we used to shout things after them. It stayed with me all my life, and I've always had a special little thought for Jewish people: about how they'd always been persecuted and how they'd come under fire – and how very stoic they are.

13

One of the things about living in Belgrave Road, Balsall Heath, and going to Hope Street School, was that Hope Street backed onto Saint Luke's Road. The school went straight through the block. Saint Luke's Road, where the Jewish school was situated, was at the bottom of Varna Road. A large Jewish contingent lived around Balsall Heath, bordering on Edgbaston – by Cannon Hill Park and Bristol Street.

As an adult, Pat was to meet many of what he calls the 'Liberal Jewish Crowd'. Tony Green, a good friend of his who he trained with for many years, comes from a family of Lithuanian Jews. He also has a friend whose family name itself, Gurovitch, reminds him of the sheer strength of the race.

At the age of 13, Pat lived at number 92, Belgrave Road, about the third house down from Varna Road – an area notorious for its prostitutes.

My mother, and next-door-neighbours – Mrs Doyle on the one side and Mrs Brown, two doors away, used to take it in turns every evening to go down the passageway at the back of the houses – with a stick. They were rather big old houses – six rooms – with big long gardens and a passageway – not a driveway – down the back.

They had a paper bag and they used to pick up all the contraceptives, so that us kids wouldn't get hold of them and start playing with them – blowing them up as balloons, or whatever!

It sounds like a scene from *Porterhouse Blue*!

They used to take it in turns. My old mom used to try putting them down the toilets – silly old sausage! And of course, they wouldn't go down. So eventually she had to get them all out again and bury them. I think they were scared to put them in the dustbins, in case the dustbin men thought badly of them – thought they were prostitutes! So they got their husbands to dig a hole and bury them.

Albert Townsend's memories of Balsall Heath pre-date Pat and Dolly's by several years, and provide an interesting contrast. "In my formative years," he remembers, "the southern part – Princess Road, Belgrave Road, Varna Road, was primarily a Jewish family area. I used to have a paper round, but also did small jobs on Saturday mornings for the Jewish families, who observed Saturdays as their Sabbath. This included lighting fires in their houses, in Princess Road. We were a Christian family, living right in the middle of a Jewish community." Following in his father's footsteps, Albert initially trained as a sheet metal worker when he left Hope Street School.

"In Princess Road in those days," continued Albert, "every other house was a Jewish house – they were all tailors – or in the clothing industry. One of my neighbours used to have a little tailor's opposite the Hippodrome in

Hurst Street. He'd do a lot of work for theatre people. My wife Beryl, who was a tailoress, used to take her own clothes to him, to have zips fastened and fixed. He was typical of the people who lived in Princess Road, Alexandra Road and Varna Road."

According to Albert: "We used to enjoy Balsall Heath. It was at the edge of Cannon Hill Park and you also had Calthorpe Park. As I remember, it was a very nice area to live in." Pat acknowledges that shortly before he moved there, "It was a well-kept area, with lovely big houses where maids were seen on the steps. Then we moved in," he quips, "and brought the area down!"

Albert recalls: "Saint Luke's School and Hope Street School were almost joined. In fact, if you were walking through some parts of Belgrave Road and Princess Road as a youngster, quite often we used to go through Saint Luke's School to get into Hope Street School, because it was a short cut.

"Although the Jewish families tended to keep themselves to themselves outside of the family group, you could communicate and get to know one or two of the Jewish children, because we were in adjoining schools and used to walk to school from the same area, backwards and forwards. I've got a recollection that sometimes they were almost shepherded to school. They were very guarded; it wasn't easy to mix with Jewish children."

At the age of 22, Albert began working in the Black Country, and on Saturday evenings watched the Turpin Brothers at the boxing ring in Gosta Green, by the Fire Station. "Very often all four brothers would fight on the same bill; because they were different weights, they never fought each other." That same year Pat, who was soon to become involved in the sport, left Hope Street School, just as Albert had before him, at the age of 15.

> My mother said: "Don't work for your father, son. Get yourself a nice job in the factory. Get yourself married to a nice wench. Get yourself a nice little backhouse – about eight bob a week."
>
> It was never me. I could never see myself doing that. And I went to work for my father, who was a general dealer and lived at 68 Hamstead Road. I'll never forget his telephone number. It was Northern 1419.

Dolly's advice, which she gave for the best of reasons, was based upon her own limited experience of life in the Ladywood area of Birmingham. She worked at Bulpitt's factory for some years. Tom Arneill, who lived very close to the factory, at 39, Camden Street, Ladywood until he was ten, from 1941–1951, describes the area as "… very poor – mostly factories and shops."

A large proportion of factories within the Jewellery Quarter made jewellery or badges. He recalls, "There were a few gun factories round there. Bulpitt's made kettles and saucepans. Cruickshank's, for some reason, stocked acids. I think they dealt in metals as well. They were next door to where I lived. I was trapped in between Cruickshank's and Bulpitt's. It was deadly. We had quite a number of cats, because I'm sure most of them were killed off by the acid and what-have-you."

As a young boy, living in Ladywood, Tom heard Dolly Roach's name mentioned. "It was in conversation with other people. Most people knew everybody around the area, because they all travelled the pubs – usually. It was the main meeting place for most of them. Of course my parents were drinkers as well. All us kids used to stop outside the pub and have a glass of pop brought out to them and a packet of crisps, or whatever. Because all of those pubs never had backs or gardens, so you played on the street.

"My parents used the local pubs until they fell out with somebody, or vice versa, then they'd change pubs, then go back again and they were all the best of friends. I've seen a few fights after closing time in the streets. They'd all be drinking together again the next day!"

Dolly used to work on saucepan bases. "Down the hole was a great big power press and you changed that into a saucepan. The machine shaped it." Many years later, Pat was a guest of honour at Cocks Moor Woods Leisure Centre. Several other celebrities attended the event, including Birmingham singer, Maggie Moon, actor, Patrick Mower, and football player, Peter Withe, in the days when he played for Aston Villa.

> *One of the senior directors of the European branch of Rockwell International, which sent rockets to the moon, was sat by my side. We were chatting away for an hour or so, and suddenly he said: "We have just bought the Bulpitt site." And I said: "Oh really, my mother worked on a press at the Bulpitt site," whereupon he didn't speak to me again, all night long!*

What a snob!

> *And I told him that she used to drink pints – I think that upset him as well!*

According to Freda, Dolly often only drank barley wine, but faced with such sanctimonious treatment, Pat decided to 'lay it on with a trowel'! Bulpitt's was bombed during the war. Tom recalls: "The bombs dropped across a diagonal line from Albion Street, from an aerial point of view, where they caught a factory in Pope Street. Also Bulpitt's and the Palais de Danse in Monument Road." The Palais was one of Dolly's favourite venues for an evening out.

Denis Wood's wife, Cynthia, then a young girl of ten, recalls young ladies like Dolly, making their way to the Palais. "You'd see them all dressed up in their long dresses, swishing away! Either walking up the road – or I think there was a tram – which would take them up that way. But I remember seeing all the frilly dresses. I used to think, when I'm grown up I'll be able to go up there. But of course, war broke out, and we never had anything like that then."

She also remembers Bulpitt's, where Dolly, Freda and others worked a full day, divided by a lunch hour. "They used to sound what I call the 'Bull' – a kind of horn – at the factory. If we heard that horn and we hadn't started out for school, we knew we were going to be late. It was morning, dinner-time, then again at night – 'knocking-off' time. They didn't have shifts: they worked set hours. I think it was from 7 to 12. Then they'd have their dinner hour."

According to Tom: "I do feel that I recollect seeing Bulpitt's burning. Just the shells of the buildings remained for us to play in." Freda worked at Bulpitt's too and at French's in Browning Street. She found that jobs were relatively easy to come by, so she and Dolly could afford to change factories if something upset them.

We have included a photograph of the Bevis family outside their home, at 2, back of 78, Garbett Street. Freda was previously married, but eventually went to live with her father, Bill Bevis, in Monument Road. The electoral roll for polling district 313, 'Spring Register 1920', shows him registered as William Bevis. Amelia is listed immediately below. The 'HO' code alongside her name means that she was entitled to vote in both government and local elections, because of her husband's occupation.

Freda recalls that Bill, formerly a soldier in the First World War, worked in a local Cambridge Street factory, which produced motor parts. "Momma used to put his dinner up. That was when they were all right together then. I used to take his dinner in a basin every day." Her father, unlike Pat, was of about average height. She remembers him with great affection. "He was ever so kind to us – he loved us all. He'd got an auburn beard and a moustache – our Paddy was auburn too – from Bill Bevis. I was 'daddy's girl'. He took me around the ladies and that. It was his fault. He had a separation – parted from momma. A sad life she had. He loved me because I was his first-born … and I had auburn curls."

In addition to buying the children ice cream on his Sunday visits, Bill was also a keen fisherman and would sometimes take them with him on his local fishing trips. "He used to win prizes 'an all! Big statue – beautiful!" Freda thinks that they fished at the Birmingham Reservoir, although after so many years, she can't be sure. Almost certainly it would have been, as it's the only fishing area within walking distance. "He brought a big bottle of cider and we seen it off – he di'nt!"

Although the route they would have taken in the 1920s has changed beyond recognition – it would have been little more than country lanes – their destination remains relatively unaltered. The contrast between the grand, in some cases almost palatial houses on the Hagley Road side of the reservoir, and their own impoverished environment, must have been quite awe-inspiring for the Bevis children: like stepping into another world.

The tranquil surroundings and tree-lined banks of this almost boomerang-shaped area of water remain today. Pat has lost count of the number of times he has jogged around the one-and-a-quarter miles of its perimeter, as part of his fitness program. Entering from the Rotton Park Road side, walking through the trees, then looking diagonally right, across the water, the Tower Ballroom can still be seen, towering above the sylvan scene.

Freda describes Bill as "A really kind man." I wondered if he had any other hobbies – apart from fishing. "No, except taking me round to meet these 'ladies of leisure' and all that! And it was the fault of his mate: introducing him to someone – and he went with them. And poor momma knew it, you know. She chucked him out. Now and again she'd look in his pocket for a match, to see if there was any news or letters from this woman."

Pat recalls meeting Bill at Freda's house in Monument Road, years later. It was the first time that the two men met. Sadly for Pat, "There was no thought of him being a granddad at all." A later electoral register, for 1933/44, shows that Bill was still officially living with the family in 1933, and was there for Dolly's wedding in 1936, but it seems likely that he had left by 1940. Freda's name is also listed; born in 1911, she had reached the age of majority the previous year. Around this time, she married her first husband, Jack Egerton. Sadly, he died at Dunkirk: "… blown to pieces in a cattle truck – the 17th June 1940."

In total contrast, Pat's grandmother Amelia was there to support him on most occasions, throughout the course of her life. He returned to live with her in Shakespeare Road, soon after he left school.

I suppose I used to give her about £1 a week – I don't really remember. We lived in the house shown in John Landon's photograph. Almost next to the corner, next to the Callaghan's house and next to Thomas's, the other side of the entry: Mickey Thomas and Margaret Thomas. Next door to them was Georgie James.

Georgie James' dad was a barrow boy and he used to come home with periwinkles and all sorts of stuff and a two-wheel barrow and George and I were sort of gamblers as kids. We used to have a bet on the horses at Billy Lowndes' – a betting shop which was next to the outdoor on the corner, which would be across the road from the Callaghan's.

In the days before televisions were commonplace, George's dad and family had the first television in Shakespeare Road. Being a barrow boy of course, he could afford it. I remember we watched the horses win and we ran up to the bookies and put a bet on. We got away with it once or twice!

You'd have to be running pretty quickly!

> *Well it was only a few yards away. We wrote all the horses out, about six horses' names, and had five bob or half a crown, or two bob on each – I forget. But then we'd dash to the bookie and put the bet on. And he stood for us two or three times, then he wouldn't pay us out any more.*
>
> *But George and I, when it was pouring down with rain, we used to stand in the entries in between the houses and the shelters – the old air raid shelters – even when it was raining. We'd have a pack of cards. We'd cut the cards and whoever had the highest cut would be the winner. The winner would then have the pick of whatever cigarette packets were in each other's pockets.*
>
> *We used to put all our cigarette packets in our pockets. There'd be 'Sweet Afton' and 'Craven A' – all sorts of things. He'd put them in his pocket and if I won, George would hold his pocket open with one hand and hold it against his hip with the other, so that I could dip in. I could never look. I'd have a sort of mooch and pull one out and that was the one I got for winning.*
>
> *Years down the road, I found that he'd got the first ticket pocket that was ever put into a suit of clothes. We always wore second hand gear anyway. But George had something new: he'd got this sports coat and he used to keep his finger over the ticket pocket – the little bastard! So I couldn't get the Drummer Boy or Bullshit Whiffs. He used to put them in his ticket pocket. I was two years without finding either of the two favourites! In the end I found out why – we fell out over that.*

Denis Wood also lived in Shakespeare Road, just ten doors away, but left several years before Pat first lived at number 68 with Amelia. "I went to live down Shakespeare Road around 1933," Denis explained – "by Monument Lane railway station. I lived at number 88." This was a general store and sweet shop called *Woods*, owned by his mother. "The next sweet shop to us was two doors down – *Greens* I think was the name."

Among the whole gallery of real-life characters in this book, the most enigmatic, or difficult to fathom is Pat's father, Frank Roach; perhaps because his personality seems to have been full of so many contradictions. His father, Walter, was one of seven brothers who emigrated from Southern Ireland, probably in the 1880s.

Frank, born in 1905, was the fifth of Walter and Nellie's children. He had two older brothers, Walter and Peter, two older sisters, 'Cissy' and Agnes, and two younger sisters, Kathleen, and the youngest, Norah, born 1914. Norah's son, Peter Mulroy, recalls some of his mother's memories about that childhood period.

The family lived in Tower Street, Newtown, next door to the *Birmingham Settlement* Youth Club and opposite Tower Street recreation ground, both of which remain to this day. Kathleen's birth certificate confirms the precise address as 3 back 90 Tower Street.

Recent research has produced enough information about Frank's family to fill a book. Due to the early split between his parents, much of this information was previously unknown to Pat. With the considerable help of several of Pat's relatives, listed in the *Acknowledgements*, we have discovered missing pieces of his family history. *The Roach Family Album* illustrates some of our findings, and features some family members.

Walter and Nellie, Pat's paternal grandparents, lived just a street or two away from each other as children, in the Saint George district of Birmingham. Nellie was born in July 1873 to Pat's great grandparents, David and Mary Woodcock. The family home was Waterloo Cottage, Bridge Street West, just one street away from what was eventually to be her home, when she married Walter in the 1890s. Both of them were still in their 'teens' when they married.

Pat's cousin, Joyce Taylor, Agnes' daughter, recalls that grandfather Walter was much taller and stronger than his photograph suggests; Nellie, by contrast, was very small, although this was counterbalanced by an extrovert personality. Like their future grandson, they were both entrepreneurs. Walter was a bricklayer, who eventually had his own team of builders; Nellie owned two shops: a tailor's and a second-hand shop. According to Joyce, she could make a suit to measure, simply by 'sizing up' the person concerned! Unfortunately, she had to cope with Parkinson's Disease, from which she eventually died, in 1935.

Walter and Nellie had four daughters and three sons. Family legend has it that there may originally have been fourteen children, but an epidemic caused seven of them to die in infancy. The eldest child Walter, later married to Hilda, was born in 1894. Their son, Walter, became a high-ranking officer in Scotland Yard. We understand that he moved to the West Country on retirement, but have so far been unable to trace him.

Pat's Aunt 'Cissy' (Mary Ellen) was born in 1897. She married Albert Sheargold and had two sons, Albert and George, and a daughter, Joan. George is a boat enthusiast. Shortly after the war, his father, Albert, was Staff Manager at the Theatre Royal in New Street, Birmingham. Mary Ellen's sister Agnes married Bert Hunt and had three sons and a daughter, Joyce Les, Ken and Bert. Pat's creativity was already present in the Roach genes: Agnes enjoyed amateur dramatics; Joyce quoted lines from *The Merchant of Venice*, in which her mother performed at Saint Chad's School. Agnes and her sister Kathleen also played the piano. There used to be regular 'jam sessions' at the Hunt household, with friends.

Pat's Uncle Peter, despite his early death, had a successful army career. Initially, he became a member of the 'Pals', a local branch of volunteers, attached to the Royal Warwickshire Regiment during the First World War.

Kathleen, described by Joyce as, "gorgeous-looking – beautiful eyes and lovely blonde hair," married Alfred Owen, who was originally part of a music hall trio – *Massana, Ronald & Stanley*. They had three children, John, Catherine, (Cathy) and Eileen.

Cathy's husband, Stan Ballard, a former Navy man, who writes poetry, recalls several Birmingham members of the Roach family travelling to London in August 1951, for his wedding to Cathy. He writes: "Catherine and Katherine (her mother) often used to tell me about Uncle Frank, almost making him an idol." Katherine (Kate) also told him that: "… none of her family cared for Alfred Owen, especially Uncle Frank, who had threatened him." Sadly, Cathy died of cancer several years ago.

Norah remembered big brother Frank as a 'tough nut', who particularly enjoyed street fights and was 'always scrapping'. She also recalled him waving goodbye to his two older brothers at Snow Hill Station, as they went off to join the Infantry in the Battle of the Somme. One of the soldiers threw a tin of 'bully beef' into the crowd. It hit Frank on the head, leaving a nasty gash.

In 1923, Frank joined the army, serving in India. He was able to put his pugilistic skills to good effect, becoming regimental boxing champion. When he eventually settled around the Summer Lane area, he was just a stone's throw from his childhood home. Tower Street is one of the streets off Summer Lane.

Dolly recalls: "Pat didn't know his father really, but being a kid, he liked to go and sort it out. He felt grown up, being amongst them. The dealers' time was any time: they'd please themselves when they went to work. They didn't have to clock in at a factory or anything."

Dennis Sullivan, although younger than Frank, was rather a tough character himself, according to Pat. Dennis and Frank, who originally met at an auction, knew each other very well. The following account, kindly provided by Dennis, hopefully gives further insight into Frank's character and confirms the generosity that he showed in helping his friends.

"He was a very strong man and spent time as a lumberjack in Canada. He was also a general dealer when he came back to this country, dealing in scrap metal, machinery, and going to auction sales. Frank spent most of the time, when not busy, in Shay's café. It was called his 'headquarters'. People knew they would find him there. He was well thought of and many a helping hand he gave to friends, down on their luck.

"I met Pat once or twice in the café, with his father, when he was a youth of about fourteen. Later I met him again through my friend, Ray Corbett. His brother Gordon, who died young, was a great wrestling and boxing friend of Pat's.

"Frank also had a knack of telling a few yarns. One that stands out in my memory is about when he was a lumberjack. They had been working many miles from any town and they had not been out of the camp for months. They were told that there was a female group coming – to do a show in the Mess Hall, where they had their food.

"They decided to smarten themselves up, and all showered and put their best shirts and trousers on – anticipating some lovely ladies. He said that he and his pals got the shock of their lives. After waiting, and on their best behaviour, the ladies arrived. They turned out to be Indian squaws – chewing tobacco. It was the quickest move he had seen out of the Mess Hall. As you can imagine, no more concerts were arranged!"

I went to work for my father. I used to get about £4-10s. a week. Dennis was one of the dealers and there was quite a little mob – not a firm – of dealers: a scrap-dealing mob. My dad was so-called 'King of the Castle' – 'Stick of Troach'. They all looked up to him – very much so.

When they were all waiting to get 'weighed off' (going into the nick) 'cause there was always someone going in or coming out, what they used to do was go and see 'Stick of Troach' down at Shay's café in New John Street West, to get sentenced. My dad would sit there with a custard and a cup of tea and say: "Tell me all about it son." They'd say: "Well Frank – well 'Stick', we went at the 'Direct'."

Dennis Sullivan's description of Frank, combined with the incident where he saved Pat's life, in our first chapter, are just two examples of the humanitarian, caring side of Frank's nature. They contrast quite starkly with Dolly, Freda and Jim White's experience of him.

Jim's father, Charlie White, and Frank were friends for many years. According to Freda: "I didn't see much of him. He wasn't very nice to know. He was shouting and a-roaring at me sister, Doris. I went to stop him and he threw me on the bloody floor! I've had this ever since: a swelling on the foot – and it aches."

When asked about Henry Robinson, she comments: "I don't know much about him, but by all accounts he was a nice bloke. Yes. But then again – Paddy wouldn't be here, would he?" Freda describes Pat, or 'Paddy' as she calls him, as a "… treasured and kind nephew." Frank later had a daughter, Frances or 'Frankie', by blonde-haired Adele, whom he met after he and Dolly had separated. Adele used to call him 'Fran'. There is a picture of Frankie in the *Roach Family Album*.

Joyce Taylor remembers two-year-old Pat visiting her family home. "He was very fair, with curly hair and sat by the door – between Frank's legs." Joyce recalls Agnes' comment to Nellie about her brother Frank: "Of course, he's a bit of a darling!" She also heard that, "He was in a fight, the police were after him, and he dived through a window!"

Jim White draws a comparison between Pat and his father. According to Jim, Pat and Frank were both good at giving sensible advice. Jim then goes on to qualify this: "But his father had a very short fuse. In those days – I'm going back many years now – they used to call him the 'Tent Pegger'.

"Apparently, if someone upset him, for one reason or another, he'd go into the pub where they were, buy them a half-pint of beer and say: 'Drink!' The guy would look at him: he'd know he was in trouble, and he drank this half-pint. Then he'd hit him on the top of his head with his fist – bang! You know? Knocked him straight out. Because he was a big man: as big as Pat, I believe. Big … tough. He used to travel across Canada with the loggers and all those people."

Although for the most part, Frank emerges as the 'black sheep' of the family, information provided by other family members such as Joyce, Peter Mulroy, John Owen and George Sheargold shows that most of Nellie's offspring were very respectable. This includes Pat's Uncle Peter, who died in his thirties, and all of his aunts.

The only exception to this, apart from Frank, was his older brother, Walter, who by all accounts, became quite violent. However, as Peter Mulroy explains, prior to fighting in the First World War, Walter was an agreeable man. His change of personality can be explained by the fact that he returned from the war, suffering from 'shell shock', from which, like so many of his contemporaries, he never really recovered.

In the previous chapter Pat revealed that Frank's brute strength had resulted in his being jailed for a time, for killing a man in a bare fistfight, although he was later released because of the circumstances.

My father delivered a devastating blow to this Pollack's heart, when he was lumber-jacking in the Northern Hemisphere of Canada. Ironically, I was able to use the incident in a constructive way in Indiana Jones 2, with my suggestion to Harrison Ford. But that's something we can talk about later…

Chapter Three –

ANY OLD IRON

But make allowance for their doubting too...

The Summer Lane Mob spent half their lives in doubtful situations... in dark entries and on street corners – waiting for fate to give them that one big break. When their future was in doubt, they'd be straight down to Shay's café, to ask my father, 'Stick-of-Troach', for his verdict.

The process known as the 'Direct' was practised by some of Frank's scrap-dealing 'Summer Lane' mob. It was also known as the 'Anthony Hoist' or 'hoist' for short, often pronounced 'iced' in the Birmingham dialect, rather like the American vernacular for stealing – 'heist'. Pat likes to quote one of his father's favourite sayings, about what fate was likely to have in store for some of his Summer Lane friends: "Coffee house, public house, Big House" – the 'Big House', needless-to-say, being prison!

Albert Townsend, although a respectable craftsman, acknowledges: "If you were looking for something shady in those days, you could go down to Summer Lane. The first big shop on the corner of Summer Lane was a tool shop. From there on down there were various properties and what-have-you. Coming from Great Hampton Street, going along Summer Lane, on the left-hand side, a little way down, there was a small but interesting shop. It used to still produce, and have on show, Victorian mantle gas fittings, and I loved to go into it. I remember it vividly. You used to *smell* gas fittings because a lot of them were assembled and tested there.

"In Summer Lane there was such a variety. There were a number of scrap-yards in that area, all on the right-hand side of Summer Lane, for some reason or other, with Great Hampton Street at your back. There were at least two or three scrap-yards together." Frank Roach's good friend Dennis Sullivan ran one of these yards. "It was next to *Dare's* public house," he recalled recently, "opposite *Wheeler's*, the local bookmakers." Funeral horses were stabled nearby.

"The gas fitting shop I'm talking about was a little further down, on the left-hand side of the road," continued Albert. "You could even buy lampposts specially made – an original. The shop was all wooden fixtures – wooden floors. There was a very famous pub on the left-hand side: it's a preserved building; it has a conservation order on it."

For obvious reasons, we'll give two members of the Summer Lane mob fictitious names – Charlie and Pete. Then we'll imagine the two of them standing on a corner in the Jewellery Quarter, by a road junction. Traffic would be obliged to stop at the white line, close to a 'Halt' sign.

A lorry would come down and it would have on it all sorts of things: brass hinges, brass buttons – whatever. Charlie and Pete would stand close to the corner, and as it stopped they'd peep over the top. As they heard the fella – there were no airbrakes in those days – the guy would have a little 'rev' to get away. As he did, they'd spot a bag and just as he pulled away, two arms would go over and they'd lift the bag up. The lorry would drive off from underneath the bag, and they'd just put it on the floor.

The driver would be none the wiser?

No, they'd just leave it there. He'd stand there with his bag at his feet. Another one would come and he'd have another one, or if they thought they'd have it off, they'd probably go to the telephone box, ring up 'Goldie' who used to buy the scrap metal, or 'Clarkie', 'Wardie' – any of the old dealers. And of course they wouldn't know they'd just knocked it off the back of a lorry. They'd say: "Can you send a lorry up to Spencer Street? We've got a bit of gear – a bit of metal." They'd send a lorry up; they'd load it onto the back of the lorry. One of them would go down, weigh it in, come back. Then they'd 'corner up' (share the money).

That was off Warstone Lane was it – Spencer Street?

Yes, round that way. That's what they'd do. It was called the 'Direct'. 'Hoist' being – you know – block and tackle; they used to pull the old chains – that had a hook-on thing. If you mention to your readers, they used to call the old block and tackle the 'Anthony Hoist', or once you'd got it they'd say: "Is it hookie gear?" 'Cause what would happen is that you'd hook the Anthony Hoist on to something, with a chain and wheel, and it would click over and lift. They're all over the world, for lifting things. In a factory they'd have a hook in the ceiling.

So they'd say: "Is it hookie?" (Has it come by means of the Anthony Hoist)? Because the 'Anthony Hoist' was that: called the 'Direct' – the 'Direct Feeding'. So that's where 'hookie gear' comes from.

26

The other thing they used to do was to wear long gabardine macks without belts – straight down. They'd also wear a pair of braces across the shoulders. The Jewellery Quarter was a hive of entries where you used to go up, and there were press shops. God knows where they got the machinery! Little hand presses.

They'd walk up and down these entries. No one would stop them, because people did it all day long. The factories used to put the stuff outside for obvious reasons. They might have a delivery of nickel anodes. Now nickel anodes in those days were 26/- (bob) a pound, long anodes with a hook on – again – 'hookie gear'. They're still used today: zinc and copper anodes. Nickel was the most expensive of what you might call the ferrous or non-ferrous metals.

Non-ferrous have no iron in them?

Right – it's almost a precious metal, but not quite. They used to have cadmium anodes, which were worth a fortune – but not many people did cadmium plating, a lot of people did nickel plating. So what they'd do, they'd walk down these entries, or they'd stop the wagon. There were certain days when they'd pick up the anodes. When they went down to 'bayonets' because the acid would eat them away and redistribute the nickel onto the brass component, what they had left was, you know how when you suck a lollipop, you had a strip left that looked like a bayonet?

They knew that the wagons would pick the bayonets up, even the hooks were actually made of nickel, and they would weigh them back against the new anode and charge them so much a pound. So with a 40- pound nickel anode they'd have seven pound of scrap and charge them for, say, 33 pounds worth of nickel anodes.

But what used to happen was, Charlie would walk around and he'd spot all the scrap – ready to go – ready for the guy to pick up. Or he'd 'clock' the lorry. That's an expression that means not only look, but also 'time' it. 'Clock' is the vernacular of thieves and burglars. If you 'clock' something you time it. Although people sometimes say they 'clocked' someone, they mean 'saw' him. But the intensity of it was that he was 'clocked' for future reference.

The guy would deliver the anodes to a certain point. So Charlie and Pete would go in, pick these anodes up and hook them onto their braces. They would hang down the length of their body.

They'd be so heavy they'd be walking at a slant! They'd have to be very strong.

Because they'd got the straight down gabardine coats, you couldn't see that they'd got bloody great long nickel anodes! They'd got their hands in their pockets and they were through pockets, so what they did was to hold the bottom of the nickel anodes; it took the weight off their shoulders. They'd walk to a coffee house.

Would they have a 'contact' in there?

No, they'd sit down and have a cup of tea

Talk about cheek! They were 'cool customers' weren't they?

Yes, and they'd ring up the guy who was going to buy the nickel anodes, and he'd come down.

Shortly after Pat began working for his father, he met a man who was to have a significant effect upon his future working life. Eddie Fewtrell was a car dealer when Pat first met him; later, he became a highly successful entrepreneur. It was the beginning of a friendship that was to last throughout the years.

With hindsight it was perhaps not surprising that the two men should gravitate towards one another. Pat's own people within his circle – especially his father, had encouraged entrepreneurial skills, from an early age. Eddie was older than Pat and was already quite experienced within the business world of the car trade.

Pat would undoubtedly have learned a great deal, just by associating with him. Both men possessed the steely determination that would lead to success, enabling them to escape their poverty-stricken roots. Eddie had just come out of the army. He and his older brother Frankie had a car pitch called *F & E Motors* in Alum Rock Road. According to Eddie, "It was a place that held 20 or 30 cars, at the side of a butcher's would-you-believe? Just like an entry. Pat used to come down with the occasional car to sell."

Pat's entry into the world of cafés and nightclub ownership began earlier than one might expect. Eddie explains: "Pat was just a young man when I first met him. I remember him quite well, because he used to have a café on the way to Handsworth – *The Fly-over* – by the Hockley Fly-over. I used to pass it every day."

Eddie's pathway to success is described in more detail in Chapter 16, which covers Pat's Birmingham-based business life and subsequent friendships in greater depth. Eddie's transition from car dealer to nightclub ownership began when he bought the *Victory Café* and expresso bar club in Navigation Street.

"There were headlines because a lad was stabbed to death in there. The police closed it up when it was a coffee club. I bought it and turned it into the *Bermuda Club*. Pat used to come in there."

Pat worked for Frank until he was 17. At this point his main ambition was to gain his driving license. As he didn't have his father's support in this, he borrowed Frank's lorry a couple of times – without his permission.

Yes. I went out with Alfie Evans. It was a big V8 5-ton steel-bodied Tipper HOA 276, the number was. Alfie Evans' mom was Lily Evans, who worked at the market; that's a whole episode that we can talk about later – the days of the markets. Alfie and I used to go out and it was terrible to drive – this truck. I went out a couple of times – but my father certainly didn't like it.

In order to pass his test, Pat got a job working on the coal; first at Hockley Brook, working for *Carter, Lee and Pattison's* – part of a conglomerate that gradually increased in size. He then moved to *A. Wall and Company* in Sheepcote Street and worked for Charlie Baylis.

Pat's time on the canals is described in more detail in the next chapter, which also takes a closer look at his grandmother, Amelia's life. Meanwhile, Pat describes what sounds like 'The Test From Hell', but actually proved to be an important milestone along the road to future success.

I went through the driving test in my father's red five-ton truck.

Wouldn't that be too difficult? It's bad enough in a saloon car.

In those days there were no separate kinds of driving licenses. I remember it had no handbrake and I used to have to ride the hills on the clutch with the driving instructor. I remember pretending to pull the handbrake on. When he said to me: "I'm going to shout stop in a minute and I want you to pull your handbrake on," there was no mirror, so he couldn't look to see what was behind us. He had to open the door and look out. So of course, I knew when he was going to shout stop.

When he shouted stop I slammed the break on, but nothing happened, because there were no bloody brakes, were there? It was so funny! He said to me: "Well, if you can drive this, you can drive anything!" Oh, and it had five-ton of rubbish in the back as well. But he let me pass.

How old were you when you passed?

17 years and three months old. I just applied for the test when I was 17. I'd been driving for some time.

There are many other fascinating stories about Pat's days in Birmingham, some of which we're putting on hold until later chapters. But we can't end this particular chapter without mentioning a few more illustrious members of the 'Summer Lane Mob', and recounting two of Pat's 'tatting' stories.

The Chicken Story:

> *I'd just about got my driving license, and the first thing I did was run out and buy myself a car. I bought it off Bertie Barton or 'Limpy Barton' they called him, in Summer Lane. Peter Price bought the pitch off him later on. Limpy left and went abroad somewhere: the 'Busies' were looking for him, the pressure got too much and he 'hopped it'.*
>
> > *So I gave him 14 quid for an old Morris Oxford 14.9, which we called 'Bess One'. We used to go out in it – all the mob from up Sparkbrook, I think it was in those days, Eddie Hart and Johnny Hart, Barry and Mavis.*

Before Limpy had the chance to 'hop it' Pat discovered that the old Morris was 'a pig in a poke'. He happened to mention this to another of the Summer Lane Mob, Darkie Cruise, when they were in the coffee house. Darkie, always a stylish dresser, is hopefully, still alive today and living in Quinton.

> *He's a tremendous character – a guy who got his living by his wits all his life. He's an ex-navy guy who did the Merchant Navy thing during the war. They carried bombs and other armaments on the ship he was working on, so they couldn't have anyone around them.*

Darkie and Pat's father, Frank, decided to pay Limpy a visit – to discuss the merits of Pat's transport arrangements. After taking one look at Darkie, this doyen of car dealers "gave him the 'dough' in about two seconds flat!"

> *'Tuzzie' was the bookie's lookout, outside what was, allegedly, an illegal betting shop. He used to sell newspapers outside Harry Davis' bookmaker's shop – when he wasn't getting arrested. Harry had a big Austin Sheerline 1950 or 52 it was, and a big Austin Princess – beautiful cars. I used to sit and watch them for hours – thinking how much I would love one. I had an Austin Princess in later years. I think we dismantled it and broke it up for scrap.*
>
> > *Tommy, otherwise known as 'TPH', lived just opposite Harry Davis' betting shop and George Davis had another betting shop – about 500 yards up the road. That's how close they were in those days – betting shops. 'Wheeler's' was round the corner and somebody else's around the corner again. Tommy's brother, Duggie, used to bet under the name of 'Biro' and Tommy used to bet under the name of 'TPH' – that was the 'nom de plume'.*
>
> > *Shay's café was just a stone's throw from Tommy's. Tommy and I decided to go out 'tatting'. We didn't call it 'totting' as they did in the Black Country. We weren't 'totters'; we were 'tatters'. I think a 'tatter' was a person who collected what is known in the vernacular as 'tat' – scrap metal.*

There's a saying isn't there – 'old tat'?

Yes. We went out looking for scrap metal. And tatters looked for scrap metal, but if they found something else of value, they wouldn't pass it over, they'd pick it up. So 'tatters' always used to cover big tips.

We didn't do that, we used to go out 'tatting': Tommy, myself and Billy, God-rest-his-soul, he's dead now. He died in the 'nick' playing football. Real fit kid – ex-SAS.

Did he have an heart attack?

Yes – in an open nick. We decided to go out tatting. So we went and bought some balloons and some chickens – small, day-old chickens. 'Mot Nep', as we used to call him, wore his gabardine mack, the one he used to do the 'Directing' – Billy too. Away we went. Took the back seat out of this old 14.9 Morris. We worked one of the most popular areas to work – the Pineapple Estate up Kings Norton Way.

We put 'Mot' down on the corner with a pocket full of balloons and ripped the top off the cardboard box all the chickens were in. Put two chicks in to run around – 'gee-up', in a way. We put Billy down on another corner, with a couple of chicks and a pocket full of mixed balloons. And I went round 'mooching'.

We used to shout: "Any old rags, accumulators, perambulators, and tiddley-baiters." (Repeats this in the gravel-voiced cry of the tatters). "Any old rags? Any old iron? Any rags? Accumulators, tiddley-baiters. Any old rags?" We used to do all that.

I remember that in our street.

The kids used to shout: "How many rags do you want for a balloon?" And we used to say: "Well you'd better go and fetch a handful, then we'll see." The idea was to get them to fetch more and more. Of course, the poor young devils would come out with their mother's coats and all sorts of things! They used to get a right clip on the ear I suppose, later on. We were never around for that.

They'd say: "We want a chicken!" We'd say: "You can't have a chicken." So they'd go and get some more. And we'd say: "Just put that down there on the floor." They'd get some more. The idea was not to let the chickens go, 'til towards the end of the day and the chickens started to flag. Then you'd have to get rid of them before they 'popped their clogs'!

I remember I'd got this little lad chasing me for a chicken, and I kept sending him back for more and more rags. I'll never forget him: a little 'copper-top' he was – little ginger-haired 'copper-top'.

How old was he – eight or nine?

6, 7, 8.

He'd have to have been quite young to have fallen for it.

Oh yes. I'll never forget – he had a slight squint in his eye. If he ever reads the book and he's out there, he's going to come and say hello to me. I've got a chicken for him. I wouldn't give him a chicken. He fetched more and more rags. I hadn't got a chicken to give him. The only two I'd got left were dead! I decided to pick Tommy up. He was stood on the corner with a big pile of rags.

How old was Tommy?

He was older than me: I was only a kid. Then we picked Billy up. He'd got a few rags. Threw them all in the back – away we went. We were all coffee house merchants. Let's stop for a cup of tea; the old transport cafés, you know. We stopped at the first café that we came to. "Three teas, two custards and an Eccles cake" – or a dripping cake. All of a sudden this same little kid came running up: "Mister, mister, I've got some more rags!" I said: "Oh Tom, work him a balloon." But Tom was eating his custard; Billy was eating his Eccles.

So I went out and he said: "I want a chicken." I said: "I haven't got any. Have a balloon." "Don't want a balloon!" "Have two balloons!" "Don't want a balloon!" "Have three balloons!" "Don't want a balloon – want a chicken!"

I thought, there's only one way to get rid of him. I said to him: "Shh, be quiet!" He said: "What's the matter mister?" I said: "Shh, you'll wake the chickens up!"

He'd have a job to do that!

So I opened the boot of the car, and I picked up this chicken. "Shh!" I gave him his chicken – away he went with this chicken. It's haunted me ever since: working this poor little cock-eyed kid with red hair, a dead chicken.

It would be awful when he found out – because he'd been trying for hours!

All you had to do was put it in the stove at night and it would come alive again! It's true! It would warm them up.

Really? No! It had already died!

So there we are – the story of the chicken. If that cock-eyed little 'copper-top' would like to come forward, I'll treat him to dinner – chicken and chips!

The other story, of course, was the one about when we used to go to the Saturday afternoon dance at the Casino.

Any Old Iron:

We used to go to the Casino. We'd got a few quid, so we'd 'do the flash' – flash our money around. I'd have a little dance – in the early days this was, when I was 17. There was a girl in there I used to look at named Mona: a big, tall beautiful girl she was.

We used to talk about the Jockey Club – Duggie Penn and me. The Jockey Club was the scrumpy house down Wheeler Street, called 'The Horse and Jockey'. We could hardly call it that and tell her that we used to go for a glass of scrumpy, so we used to call it The Jockey Club!

Very often when we were in town, we'd go to Yates' Wine Bar and drink Yates' 'giggle water'. We used to call it 'giggle water'. We used to have a schooner of wine for 1/6d /1/9d. Three glasses of that and it used to drive you barmy! Ronnie Callow used to have a drink with us there. Ronnie's in transport now, and doing quite well. He had a spares yard, which I bought off him years later.

I remember it was a beautiful summer's day, and we were tatting up around Smethwick. I forget who was with me.

We were walking up and down the big long entries. The kids were off school – that's why it was a good time to go there. We were shouting "Any old rags, any old iron? Accumulators, perambulators, tiddly-baiters. Any old rags? Balloons for rags!"

I was walking down this entry – and it was boarded. I told this story to Stanley Kubrick, by the way, Ryan O'Neal, Stanley Kubrick, Marisa Berenson, Diana Koerner, Ferdy Mayne, Hardy Kruger.

The reason I told the story was because we were all sitting down to dinner one night and Hardy Kruger, who was to my left, told a story. His best pal was Humphrey Bogart – and he told this story about 'Bogey', as he used to call him.

It just so happened that it went clockwise and Ryan O'Neal picked up the story and told a story about either Jayne Mansfield or Marilyn Monroe. Stanley told a story about someone named Dick, who they all knew and I didn't. Diana Koerner's English was very limited, so they let that go. Marisa Berenson told a story about Lisa Minnelli in Cabaret. Ferdy Mayne, who was a great character –

He's been in dozens of films.

Oh yes – everything. He had a story about John Wayne. Then they all looked at me for a story. Well what did I know a story about? I was trying to hide behind my pint of bitter actually. I thought, oh my God! I hope they don't ask me to tell a bloody story!

They all looked at me for my story and I shuffled and buried myself even deeper into my pint of bitter. And Hardy took up the story again. I suppose I was excused because I was just a nonentity really, among all those stars. Hardy had a story about Betty Bacall, O'Neal told one again about either Mansfield or Monroe – he did both – I forget which way round.

Stanley Kubrick told another story about the same guy – Dick – Diana Koerner passed again. Marisa Berenson told another story about Lisa Minnelli; she didn't seem to like her very much – but that's just my opinion; they did 'Cabaret' together. Ferdy Mayne told a story about someone else. Then it all settled on me again

Only this time you couldn't wriggle out of it – you'd gotta tell something!

All of the stories were somewhat embarrassing: about Mansfield's enormous bosoms, Monroe's bosoms. Dick's something-or-other – I forget what it was! It emerged that 'Dick' was 'Tricky Dickie', Richard Nixon, by the way. I'd got to choose an embarrassing story – so I went back to tatting.

I was walking down this entry – I told the story about the Casino. Hardy Kruger said: "I've been to the Casino." He'd obviously been there, I don't know why.

Was it a gambling place?

No, it was a Mecca Dance Hall, right opposite where Lewis's used to be; that square where they put the toilets downstairs.

By the Minories?

Right. The Steelhouse Lane side of the Minories: as you come out of the Minories, turn right. I said: "You'll appreciate this story because it's cinematographical." They all looked at me and they shuffled – thought it sounded interesting. I told them about being a rag-and-bone man. Stanley said: "A rag-and-bone man!"

It was certainly different, wasn't it? They wouldn't have been expecting it!

Hey listen, Kirk Douglas' dad was a rag-and-bone man. I think he was a Lithuanian Jew. He was a rag-and-bone man. I admired him when I read his book – because he admitted it. One of the things I hoped was that I might perhaps meet Kirk Douglas, make a film with him and talk about his dad. But of course as the years went on, I hoped I might meet Michael Douglas and talk to him about his granddad. It would be lovely to talk about that sort of thing. I was really rather thrilled that I wasn't the only rag-and-bone man in the film business!

They all laughed about 'any old iron'. As I was walking down it was boarded and as the boards are put together, they leave slight slits. So as I walked, I got a cinematographical picture of these two ladies in bikinis, on this very lovely afternoon – lying sunbathing.

I was quite empty-handed and decided to peer over the fence, to get a better look at these two scantily clad young ladies. And to make it genuine, I shouted: "Got any old rags missus?"

And – like – they believed you!?

As I peered over the fence – it was Mona: I'd blown my cover!

What had you told her that you did?

They thought we were 'Jack-the-Lads' – racers, gamblers. Never told her I was a rag-and-bone man! You can imagine Humpty Dumpty sliding down the fence can't you? Melting down the fence instead of falling off it? Well this was a new version of Humpty Dumpty: I melted.

And hoped the ground would swallow you up?

And very quickly disappeared. Well, the next time I went to the Casino I thought: oh God, I hope she's not here! So I peeped in, couldn't see her anywhere, no sign. I had a right good look. No, she wasn't inside.

So I spotted a little bird and had a dance. When I got round by the orchestra, the guy that ran the orchestra – I must try to remember his name – I used to teach him judo at one stage, years afterwards. As I danced past him, the band struck up 'Any Old Iron'.

Oh lovely – she'd got there ahead of you!

Yes there she was – hiding! And from then onwards –

They played 'Any Old Iron' every time you walked in!

It soon becomes apparent that, despite having his head shaved recently in aid of two charities, Pat is a man who is attractive to women. Also, that notwithstanding the 'Big Bad Pat Roach' image, carefully stage-managed to promote his wrestling career, the *real* Pat Roach is considerably more complex.

Four aspects of his personality combine to produce a very heady cocktail. The first and most obvious of these is what several of his friends, including Ronnie Callow, refer to as a 'strong' personality. Some of them view this strength in the sense that Pat exudes the self-confidence of a man very much at ease with himself. Ronnie sees it as the ability to "… think things out well, before he acts on them." Added to this however, are three other ingredients: shyness, sensitivity, and a tremendous openness to new ideas and experiences – an endearing combination!

Pat's cosmopolitan career has resulted in his meeting a host of tremendously varied, frequently very attractive individuals. However, what has become abundantly clear, during a very wide-ranging series of conversations, is that the woman who has had the most profound and long-lasting effect upon him, is the one he met years ago in Birmingham, when he was a relatively inexperienced teenager.

> *We were just kids, eighteen years of age. We used to go to Laura Dixon's, above Chetwynd's the tailors, at the bottom of Hill Street in Town. We were a bloody nuisance: Alfie Evans, Harold Evans, Tommy used to come sometimes, a couple of other guys. Little Vince Turner – always turned out smart little Vincie Turner. I was always a scruff – but there we are! And we met a few girls from time to time, I suppose. One particular time, in the nicest possible way, between us we met a couple of sisters named Pat and Doreen Harris, who lived out South Yardley way.*
>
> *I think Alfie fancied both – so did Harold. I think everybody did: they were both very beautiful girls. To cut a very long story short, I finished up courting Doreen, who I later married, at the age of nineteen years, which was 45 years ago from today – something like that. The day we went to put our banns in, I used the same big red V8 Tipper truck, which I'd already passed my test in, with a load of rubbish in the back. I got Doreen up into the seat somehow, and we went to put our banns in, in the big old red truck.*

Roy O'Neal, a fellow dealer, was Pat's 'best man'. The couple were married in 1956, at Broad Street Registry Office in Birmingham, then moved in with Pat's grandmother, Amelia, in Shakespeare Road, Ladywood. Amelia died unexpectedly, just a few months later, so unfortunately was never able to see her grandson.

> *When my poor old gran died, they moved us into a back-to-back house in Stoke Street, in Ladywood, where Tricorn House is now, I believe – within a stone's throw of the canal. Stoke Street of course was off the back of Broad Street, a hundred and fifty yards from Gas Street Basin. We lived there for a while and after about a year, Mark was born.*

Although Dolly and Doreen's mother never met, Dolly explained that Mrs. Harris worked all the way through her illness. "Doreen's momma had cancer – in the early days. She brought four of them up and worked with a bag on her side – on a power press. I said, 'Your mommy deserves a platinum medal, covered in diamonds'; a sad life."

Doreen inherited her mother's hard-working disposition, and later ran her own farm, independently of Pat. With some assistance from Mark, and an ex-wrestling friend of Pat's, she fed 300 pigs, and looked after 60 calves and 30,000 chickens.

Doreen's always been very been fond of my mother – very close to her. She's a hard worker, a good provider and tremendously loyal over all these years. As the book progresses, you'll see that I was a hardworking person too. But if you're in a marriage, or any sort of relationship, it always requires a partnership. Doreen has given me total support all the way through my life. Without her, in the early days, nothing could ever have happened.

Further grief lay in store for Pat and Doreen, when they discovered that their newly-born son, Mark was deaf. The family moved from Stoke Street to a house in Melbourne Avenue, which they bought from Eric Barber. Shortly afterwards they moved again, to Middlemore Road, Smethwick, where they had an unbelievably-low two per cent mortgage off the Metropolitan Camel Works. In true entrepreneurial spirit, they turned this third home into a coffee house and later a fish-and-chip shop.

When we did it up, we were scraping all the bits and pieces off the doors: it turned out to be some woman's brains! The guy who lived there had killed two of the women in his life. When we were scraping the door down, there were bits of bone and stuff on it- oh yes!

During this period, Jimmy White and Pat started a one-armed bandit business, and had about thirteen cafés altogether. "He lived in one on the Hollyhead Road, with his wife Sylvia and the two kids, and I lived in Middlemore Road, with Doreen and Mark. We had cafés on Hockley Flyover, and one in Blackheath, next to the old Bingo Hall." A third was in John Street, on the corner of George Street. Pat would often travel around the country for sports fixtures.

On the domestic side of my life, my wife, in my particular case, put her time in, at home and waiting for me, while I was on the road, and being content that eventually, I came home. Her loving care within our relationship meant that it didn't matter how long I was away, I never had any worries or aggravation about my wife: I knew she would always be there, and that Mark had a stable home.

Doreen also ran one of the cafés. As Pat and Jimmy systematically acquired their string of cafés, they installed one-armed bandits. Meanwhile, Mark was attending the Deaf School at Barnes Hill, in Northfield.

The poor little devil had to go miles and miles. As things got a little better for us, and as Mark used to have to get up at six o'clock every morning to get the coach, I said to Doreen: "Go out there and buy the nearest house, opposite the school." There was a house right opposite the main gate. I think we paid £2,760 or something; that's where we lived for quite some time. We moved from there and that's where she and I parted company. I signed the house over to her, I think; Mark would probably have been about 5 years old. So from 1962 onwards, we were separated.

It was always lovely to come home to my boy. I was away that much, my boy once said to his mother, when he was older: "Where was my dad when I was little? Where was my father?" He saw so little of me; he was out to school and I was up and gone and away.

In an attempt to alleviate the problem, Mark would occasionally travel abroad to visit his father on film sets. Despite the fact that Doreen and Pat were separated, Doreen travelled with Mark on these occasions.

Quite simply, we have a handicapped son, who can't travel by himself: he's deaf, he doesn't speak. Mark and I have always been in close contact, and we've always been a sensible separated family about things. So when Mark came to see me, his mother was the natural person to bring him.

During discussion with Pat's fellow actors on *Auf Wiedersehen Pet* about the undoubted problems of trying to combine family life with a showbusiness career, Chris Fairbank made a particularly apposite comment: "It's never right – that's the only constant thing about it – whatever the scenario – it's not right; there's something that causes a problem. Whether it's working away from home, not working, working on and off. It's not conducive to family life at all. But I don't think that there's a *blueprint* for a harmonious/ conducive anything really." Nowadays, Pat tries to redress the balance with his young namesake.

I've got a little grandson, Patrick Mark Roach, who I'm very proud of. I try to spend as much time as I can with him. I sometimes try to talk to him about serious things, which I think he'll need to know later, but he's probably a bit too young yet. He's seven-and-a-half now, so he's not quite ready to retain the information. What he's into right now is play games and things. He's a new light in my life – and really rather wonderful.

Chapter Four –

AMELIA

If you can wait and not be tired by waiting...

A dark-haired gypsy child waited patiently for her mother, on the muddy canal bank. In the distance she could hear raised voices – followed by a scream...

Lucy Leach, her next-door neighbour, stood in the doorway. "Read me cards Bevis!" she exclaimed. Amelia was thought to be psychic: able to look into the future – with special powers. She could also read palms. From time to time she would give Lucy Matilda a reading – or other neighbours, friends and relatives – if they made a special request for her to do so. People said that she had the 'sixth sense' of the gypsies.

Later, she replaced the cards in her special lacquered box, then gazed out of the window for a while. No sounds entered her private world. She had been deaf for many years, from washing her hair in the canal. Gestures and lip-reading were her means of understanding the world around her. Amelia devoured the information on each page of her daily lifeline – the newspapers – reading them from cover to cover.

She sank down into her favourite chair with a cup of tea. The reading, as always, had left her feeling exhausted. As she half dozed, her thoughts drifted back to a time when a Romany curse had hung over her. A mere slip-of-a-girl she had been then, with a mane of bluey-black hair cascading down her back, and an uncertain future ahead of her. The curse had been put upon her because she had chosen to marry Bill Bevis, instead of one of her own kind – a cardinal sin in her gypsy world.

Then suddenly time moved back further still. Until once again, she was a fearful three-year-old child, staring dismally down at what appeared to be a bundle of untidy rags at the side of the muddy towpath ... but she had known that it wasn't.

A figure disappeared as quickly and silently as it had come, over the low wall at the side of the canal, and from there into the undergrowth. She stood there, paralysed with fear, for what seemed like an eternity. Eventually, with tears streaming down her poor little face, Amelia summoned up the courage to bend down and touch her mother's lifeless hand. It was stiff and cold.

At the inquest, it was decided that Amelia was too young to give evidence against her mother's killer. There were no brothers or sisters to comfort her. Kindly Grandfather Jackson took her under his wing. From that day onwards, she followed him everywhere. Such memories had been stored away for years, confined to the darker recesses of her mind. But every now and then, when she least expected them, they would re-surface...

Apart from Granddad Jackson, Amelia had no family to care for her, no mother to hug or comfort her during the trials and tribulations of childhood; no brothers or sisters to play with, fight, or confide in. Such are the legacies of childhood, that this was later reflected in the fact that although Pat and his grandma were close in many ways, he never once received a hug from her, and is unable to remember her doing so with other family members.

The Birmingham canals became Amelia's family, and a working day-boat her home. Dolly is able to recall a few details about her mother's canal childhood. 'Millie', as Amelia was often referred to, was a 'love child', probably from within her own clan. She came from 'real gypsy' stock, of casual farm labourers and peg-makers, rather than tinkers.

Theirs was a fairly basic, un-named, horse-drawn boat. It had a low cabin, providing adequate shelter from the rain. Leading a horse, and working the boat through locks, was part of her everyday routine. They had two or three regular countryside stopping places en route. In her teens, when Grandpa Jackson was probably no longer around, Millie worked on boats in Gas Street Basin.

The canals became their livelihood. Throughout her life, despite her earlier trauma, she felt a strong affinity with them and her experiences within this early environment shaped many of her later attitudes.

As the grandchild of a boatman, Amelia's life in the late 19th, and early 20th centuries, revolved around yards. Even though she worked off the canals, they'd have yard frontages. Pat recalls that in later life she often talked about renting a yard, but she'd want to rent it cheaply and would never consider paying rates.

Another legacy of her gypsy background was that sometimes she would slip into 'backslang'. This consisted of splitting syllables to confuse people, then reversing words – very useful when her forebears were arranging a private deal! For example, she described herself as being 'dlo' (pronounced 'deelo') which was 'old' spelt backwards. "TFEL at the renoc," would mean: "Turn left at the corner." The Birmingham dialect would sometimes distort this even further, so that 'renoc' sounded like 'renic', thus obscuring, to an even further degree, that 'renoc', if an 'r' was added, was simply 'corner' – spelt backwards! When Pat gives other examples of 'back-slang' or 'half-chat', as it's sometimes known, it sounds like a foreign language.

Amelia had a normal speaking voice, so her deafness may have developed during her childhood. Nevertheless, she reacted differently to things around her and had a different sense of timing. When she had a family of her own, they adopted the habit of shouting, so that she might hear them more clearly – but they were never certain that she could.

Such a background produced a hard-working, very independent individual, despite her disability, who seemed to have exerted considerable influence upon those around her. She was also someone who had, by all accounts, suffered a great deal in her emotional life. The Bevis family photograph indicates a friendly woman with a forthright, spirited nature, a fact endorsed by various members of her family. Conversely, our photograph of a younger Amelia, shows the more wistful, reflective side of her nature.

Eking out an existence on the Birmingham canals at the same time as Amelia, was a young boy by the name of Thomas Henry Smith. Born in Pickford Street, off Fazeley Street, Digbeth, he ran away from home at the age of eight, and worked on the old working or 'cabin' boats – the kind that were lived in.

The canal company depot of *Fellows, Morton and Clayton* was just across the road from Pickford Street, in Fazeley Street. This company expanded considerably. One of their modern-day depots, now used as offices, is situated at Sherborne Wharf, in the Birmingham canal complex. The fact that the canals were in such close proximity undoubtedly influenced young Thomas' decision to make them his livelihood.

Unlike Amelia, who married early, Thomas didn't marry his future wife, May, until he was at least 30, and she was 28. Almost 80 years later, I visited the Sherborne Wharf home of their son, George Henry Smith, at the kind invitation of himself and his wife, Jean.

Having spent 43 years working on the Birmingham canals, George was able to provide a unique insight into the boat people's way of life. "I first came to live by the canals when I was four years old, in 1931. I lived there for a few years. I went to school from there and I even started to work from that house, in the old Crescent." A treasured photograph shows his parents, Thomas and May, at the front door of their canal cottage in Gas Street, during the 1940s. The same house is now part of the *Tap and Spile* public house. A second photograph, taken by the author, shows the identical spot, almost sixty years later.

George attended Saint Peter's School, off Broad Street, where the International Convention Centre now stands. "I started to work about three months before I was 14. I had permission to start to work with my father as a boatman, with the old horses. I carried on until just before the war finished, then resigned from the waterways and went to work elsewhere. I was away nearly five years, during which I had various jobs.

"But when I came back it was all nationalised of course. We moved into Gas Street in 1942. My mother was worried about the house, when my father died in 1949, so I came back to work for the waterways, as a boatman, and did various other jobs."

George transported bricks, clay and coal for the different depots, through Cannock and around the canals, from various places. There were different companies. "Birmingham Canal Navigation, were the engineering side of the canals. They kept the canals open in the winter and repaired."

Peter White, M.B.E., former Chief Architect for *British Waterways*, played an important advisory role in designing the master plan for Gas Street Basin, featuring the *James Brindley* pub, the subject of our next chapter. A 'polymath', or man of many talents, he also painted scenes, showing various aspects of the Birmingham canals, during the 1950s and 60s.

Peter has very generously allowed us to include photographs of his oil paintings, as excellent illustrations for the Birmingham canal locations, featured in this chapter. The paintings were exhibited on 22 November 1991, as part of Peter's exhibition entitled *Two Canal Cities* – Venice and Birmingham – which was opened by the Italian Ambassador. This is the first time that they have actually been published in a book.

Speaking recently at his Cornish farmhouse, Peter explained: "When I was walking the Birmingham canals at this time, in the early 60s, I was on my own. There were dead dogs in the water – and oil. It was a very forgotten land, I suppose. But one that had lots of worries for me, because I saw how easy it would be to ruin it and how important it was to conserve and refurbish it, in a way which didn't over-stifle the simple vernacular. Any fool can ruin a place like that; it's much more difficult to decide what you *shouldn't* do."

He has been involved with canal conservation for thirty years. "From the mid-60s, I lived on board a narrow boat in Gas Street Basin, then moved into a canal cottage in Gas Street – Number 42. I was working in Local Government when I was spotted by Sir Frank Price – a great 'Brummie'. He persuaded me to go and work for *British Waterways Board*. I was the first architect to be hired on the canal – it's quite humbling to say really – since Thomas Telford!"

In 1970, following Peter's success in regenerating Birmingham's canal environment, Sir Frank said: "I want you to do this over the whole country." Subsequently, Peter set up an organisation within *British Waterways*, which placed greater emphasis on culture, heritage, conservation and regeneration. "I was in London by then, working on over 2000 miles of canals – trying to do the 'Birmingham Trick' elsewhere. It was a marvellous challenge – and a privilege." He ended up 'Chief Architect, Design and Planning Manager', and was eventually awarded the M.B.E. in recognition of his considerable achievements.

"From humble beginnings I went to work in London," he recalls, "then set my office up on the Oxford Canal, at Hillmorton, to be at the hub of the canal system." He set up 'Waterway Environment Services' with a staff of approximately thirty, including architects, historians, landscape architects and ecologists. "We helped change the *culture* of *British Waterways*. Not just me – obviously – but my own work and that of colleagues too."

George Smith remembers playing with the canal children, as a child. "Me living where I did, I was always put with the boat children, because they could learn off me – the school ways – and things like that. The canal children used to go to certain schools, where they happened to be.

"There was St Thomas's on Bath Row, which has gone now of course, St Peter's and Nelson Street." The latter was right in the middle of the area where Pat was born. In our opening chapter his mother, Dolly, described Nelson Street School, which her brothers and sisters also attended. It seems likely that Amelia may have too, although we can't be sure; unlike George's father, she was certainly able to read and write.

"When my father got married, me mother learned him to read and write. That was the old 'boat people'; but you give them a penny short in their change – they'd know!"

Although we can never know exactly what life was like for young Amelia, growing up as one of the boat people, George Smith's knowledge of their way of life fills many gaps. Having befriended some of them at school, he had first-hand experience of their living conditions.

"Very, very hard – believe me!

"Winter was harder still," recalled George. "The canals don't get frozen half as hard as they used to in those days. During the early 40s to 50s I've been breaking ice at fourteen inches thick!"

George took Pat and myself on a trip, to show us the difference between the two canals. As he steered the boat, he recalled: "All the boat people I knew were hardworking. I mean, Ada Morton was a girl of 12 years old. She used to come to school. When she wasn't at school she used to have to help with the boat."

There were warehouses in the old Cambrian Wharf including a sugar warehouse. He moored his friend's boat alongside the same spot – where the *Pot and Firkin* stands today, while the three of us had a drink. "The sugar warehouse was here," he elaborated. "She'd carry a huge bag of sugar on her knees, using two hands – carry it along the boat – for the hoist to take it up into the warehouse – at 12 years of age." I could almost imagine poor Ada performing the whole exhausting routine – 70 years ago!

"She used to 'hop-scotch' it along the boat: lift up one knee then drop it, and she had muscles like balloons!" Not surprisingly, some boat people became crippled as they aged; it was almost an occupational hazard.

Both George and Peter remember an old boatman known as 'Chocolate Charlie', whose real name was Charlie Atkins. "He used to come to Birmingham periodically, when I lived in Gas Street, as a young man, early 40s – during the war years." Charlie later moved into Top Lock Cottage, featured in one of Peter's paintings.

According to George, "Everything was short – food in general. But Charlie took the raw chocolate to Cadbury's – that's how he got his name. He sold me half an old brown carrier bag full of raw chocolate, every time he came through. You'd want some new teeth after you ate a lot of that!"

Before the WVS began to supply school meals, during the Second World War, the school morning started at nine, breaking at mid-day. George explained: "The canal children went home for dinner – the same as us. We had to be back there for a quarter to two. We finished at half past four."

According to Birmingham Reference Library information, the only working boats based in Gas Street Basin these days provide charter and public trips; most are privately owned. Sam Waller and Graham Wigley run *The Birmingham and Midland Canal Carrying Company*, which includes *Parties Afloat* for boat trips. Joseph Brace, who I originally contacted before Sam, runs *Second City Cruisers*, with Mark Nicholls.

George explained: "The campers are about, owned by *Camping Afloat*: the old working boats converted. They've got bunks in – a full kitchen – all the amenities. They're mostly for students. There are hire boats for family holidays. We have just one boat come through here every month, loaded with coal, which is sold along the canal." Graham Wigley explained that, by a strange co-incidence the name of this coal boat is *The Roach* and even more strangely, its owner is John Jackson – the same surname as Amelia's grandfather!

Broad Lane, or Pig Lane, as it was known in the early 1900s, was sufficiently rural to have stables for canal horses. "Fellows, Morton and Clayton, as well as the depots they had in the old Crescent Wharf where I lived, had one at Fazeley Street and an extra stables at the far end of Fazeley Street from town – Liverpool Street; they took about 20 horses.

"I can remember when I was a lad, that if the boat people who worked for Fellows, Morton and Clayton hadn't got a suitable horse at the stables – they only used to cater for six horses at the Crescent Wharf where I was – they used to go up to Liverpool Street and fetch one back. They used the horses mostly for locks and horse-drawn boats.

"The 'upper-crust' of the boat people lived on the canal basin, worked for a company, and were known as 'Number Ones'; all expenses would be paid by the company to such families – for the use of their horse and boat. There were two distinct classes: those without a horse would be provided with one by the canal company; whether they had to pay to hire them I don't

The Roach Family Album

Pat's paternal
grandmother,
Nellie Roach

Paternal grandfather,
Walter Roach

Pat Roach

John Owen (cousin)
Kathleen's son

Kathleen Roach (aunt)

Frank Roach (father)

Catherine
(Cathy - cousin)

Stanley Ballard,
(Catherine's husband)

Frances Roach (Frankie)
Pat's step-sister

The Roach Family Album

Norah Roach (aunt)

*Mary Ellen Roach
(aunt 'Cissy')*

*George Sheargold, at
3 years of age (cousin)*

Peter Roach (uncle)

*Agnes Roach (aunt)
Joyce's mother*

*Joyce Taylor
(cousin - neé Hunt)*

*The Hunt Family (1951)
At 62, Eastwood Road. Pictured from left to
right are Bert, Joyce, 'Pop', Agnes and Les.
Ken is behind the camera.*

*Photo's included in this section are published
by permission of Pat's cousins, John Owen,
Joyce Taylor, Peter Mulroy and George
Sheargold. Pat's stepsister 'Frankie' Roach and
Cathy's husband Stan Ballard, have also given
their kind assistance.*

Garbett Street, back of number 23, c. 1905. Just a decade later, the Bevis family were living in the same street. BY PERMISSION OF BIRMINGHAM LIBRARY SERVICES. PRINTED BY JOHN WHYBROW LTD.

The Bevis family, 1935, outside the family home at 2, back 78, Garbett Street, Ladywood. Pictured from left to right are Bill, Freda, Amelia, Dolly and Charlie. Stan, the youngest brother, is absent from the photograph, as he was in the army. BY PERMISSION OF FREDA ROBERTSON, (SECOND FROM LEFT) - PAT'S AUNT.

Hope Street Junior School football team 1947 – 48. Pat, centre back row, wore Dolly's old shoes, they couldn't afford boots. Headmaster Mr. Cooper, back right, provided an important role model for him.

Paternal grandparents, Walter and Nellie Roach. Pat probably inherited their entrepreneurial skills via Frank: both ran small businesses. BY PERMISSION OF PAT'S COUSIN, JOHN OWEN.

Frank Roach at his scrap yard in Hunters Road, with his 1952 CA Bedford van. A Forerunner of 'Steptoe and Son' perhaps? BY PERMISSION OF HIS DAUGHTER, 'FRANKIE' ROACH.

Aunt Freda, born 1911: "I was daddy's girl. He loved me because I was his first-born … and I had auburn curls." BY PERMISSION OF CHARLIE'S SON, JOHN BEVIS

Freda and William Robertson on their wedding day, taken outside Birmingham Registry Office, 1942. BY PERMISSION OF FREDA ROBERTSON.

Dennis Sullivan and Frank Roach were friends for many years. This photograph, sent to his mother from India, was taken just before Dennis went into Burma. BY PERMISSION OF DENNIS SULLIVAN.

Dolly on the beach c 1950. She wrote her address on the back, 92 Belgrave Road, Balsall Heath. An additional note reads: 'Singing "Hey Dolly" on my old accordion!' BY PERMISSION OF DOLLY ROACH.

Family group, taken at Margate, c1949. From left to right: Pat, and Nellie (Charlie's wife). Pat's cousin John, seated next to the tiger's head, is held by his Uncle David. On the tiger's back is Charlie - Pat's favourite uncle. BY PERMISSION OF JOHN BEVIS.

Pat's grandmother Amelia, seated at her desk. Her Romany background enabled her to read palms. Dolly describes her as: "Tall and slim with bluey-black hair. She had amber eyes – not brown – unusual they were." BY PERMISSION OF JOHN BEVIS.

'Sisters': two of Pat's aunts, (Frank Roach's sisters) Mary Ellen and Kate, in their twilight years. BY PERMISSION OF GEORGE & NORMA SHEARGOLD.

Junction of Shakespeare Road and Anderton Street, Ladywood, 5 June 1967. Pat returned to live with his grandmother Amelia, at 68, Shakespeare Road. Their house was second from the far corner – with two boys playing outside. BY PERMISSION OF JOHN LANDON – (LADYWOOD COLLECTION).

Narrow boat yards – BCN: The artist, Peter White, M.B.E. was a former Chief Architect for British Waterways. According to Peter: "The height of the wall, between the bottom of the sill and the eaves, is seven feet; a boat bottom has been turned sideways and made into the walls of these buildings." The brick structure was the forge, for ironwork. QUOTATION & PAINTING BY PERMISSION OF PETER WHITE.

Back of Broad Street – early BBC Radio Studios (before Pebble Mill): Peter describes this scene as: "A romantic Bruges - which nobody knew about!" Amelia and her grandfather would have hauled up in this area for the night, when they delivered their goods. Icknield Port Road was another convenient stopping point. QUOTATION & PAINTING BY PERMISSION OF PETER WHITE.

Top Lock, Farmers Bridge: Two lock-keepers looked after Farmers Bridge – George Norris and Bill Oakley. Top Lock Cottage, on the right, was 'Chocolate Charlie's' home. Peter managed to save and restore 'Kingston Row' cottages, on the left: "From that small beginning was founded a whole policy of change." QUOTATION & PAINTING BY PERMISSION OF PETER WHITE.

Top Lock and Cambrian Wharf (one of Peter's favourite scenes - enshrouded in 60s fog): "The iron bridge on the left was restored and the gas lamps were re-introduced as replicas." George Smith recalls Ada Morton working on this actual site: "She'd carry a bag of sugar along the boat, for the hoist to take it up into the warehouse." QUOTATION & PAINTING BY PERMISSION OF PETER WHITE.

Old Turn, looking towards Gas Street and the Unitarian Church. As its name suggests, this was a turning point for narrow boats. "The Lucas works are on the right. The signpost saying 'Wolverhampton, London,' and so on, is a replica." On the left are early premises of Mitchell's and Butler's brewery. QUOTATION & PAINTING BY PERMISSION OF PETER WHITE.

Well-equipped interior of a long-distance narrow boat (turn of 20th century): Peter's intricate painting includes lace-edged plates, polished brass, and decorative bed- knobs. "The matriarch is sitting in the 'bed'ole'." The semi-circular table served the dual function of cupboard door and fold- down table, around which family life revolved. QUOTATION & PAINTING BY PERMISSION OF PETER WHITE.

Longer prospect of Gas Street Basin (looking towards the back of Broad Street). By the mid-19th century this region had become the heart of the national canal system. Between the ages of 17 and 20, Pat worked in three different locations, around this particular area. The narrow boat on the far right was Peter and Paula White's home, for several years. QUOTATION & PAINTING BY PERMISSION OF PETER WHITE.

Farmers Bridge Locks - (looking up, towards Top Lock): George remembers having to unlock the gate at the top of Farmers Bridge, to access Cambrian Wharf. The key had to be borrowed from the lock-keeper's office. Nowadays people can just walk through - a situation which particularly pleases Peter. QUOTATION & PAINTING BY PERMISSION OF PETER WHITE.

George Smith's parents, Thomas and May, at the front door of their canal cottage, number 16 Gas Street, during the 1940s. There were 3 storeys, with 2 rooms on each floor. BCN canal number 34 was above the front door. The mother dog was 'Toss' and her son was 'Prince'.
BY PERMISSION OF GEORGE SMITH.

A second photograph, taken by the writer, shows the identical spot, sixty years later. The Smith's home is now part of the Tap and Spile public house. PHOTOGRAPH BY SHIRLEY THOMPSON.

George took Pat and Shirley on a canal trip. He moored the boat alongside the Pot and Firkin, former site of the sugar warehouse, where they stopped for a quick drink.
PHOTOGRAPH BY SHIRLEY THOMPSON.

Canalside architect, Alan Goodwin, with Bobby Browns night-club in the background. In Amelia's day this building was the stable block for donkeys working on the Worcester and Birmingham Canal. PHOTOGRAPH BY SHIRLEY THOMPSON.

*Canal-side architect Alan Goodwin, standing on the Worcester Bar, in front of the pub he
designed, the James Brindley. The 'hive of activity' behind him reflects the pub's popularity.
PHOTOGRAPH BY SHIRLEY THOMPSON.*

GAS STREET

NEW PUBLIC HOUSE
GAS STREET BASIN
BIRMINGHAM

Gas Street Basin is the major
junction at the heart of the
English Canal System and has
fallen into dereliction over
many years.

As part of a major rejuvena-
tion connected with the
proposed National Convention
Centre, British Waterways
Board is promoting the new use
of land surrounding the basin,
of which this project is a
part.

The commission was for the
joint clients British Waterways Board and Bass Mitchells
and Butlers Ltd, with both of
whom we have a close liaison.

The brief was for an exciting
new pub, but to a design which
would be sympathetic to traditional canalside buildings.

This project is currently
awaiting planning permission.

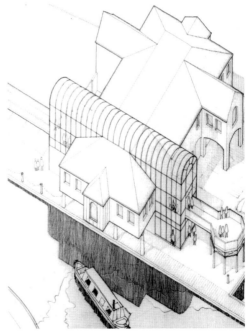

*Isometric view of the James Brindley and description of the project brief. The pub opened in
March 1986. BY PERMISSION OF ARCHITECT, ALAN GOODWIN.*

The original old flour mill site of the Brindley, taken in the 1940s by George Smith. A modern day view would show the old Central television studios in the background, and the Holiday Inn above it. BY PERMISSION OF GEORGE SMITH.

Modern-day photograph of the same Brindley, site taken from the opposite side of the canal. The green lucam, or hoist cover, overhanging the path, remains a integral feature.
PHOTOGRAPH BY SHIRLEY THOMPSON.

know." We don't know whether Amelia and Granddad Jackson owned their own horse; they may have hired it.

"Fellows, Morton and Clayton were one of the biggest users of canal traffic in the country. They'd have depots all over the country. They used to build the boats at Saltley, just outside Birmingham. They'd also have repair yards, and another boat building place at Bull's Bridge, London."

George's wife, Jean, spent the last 11 years of her working life in the canal offices where he was – at Camp Hill. In the old days there were different firms, like Leonard Lee (Pelsall) Ernie Thomas (Walsall) T & S Element, coal carriers of Gravelly Hill, under Spaghetti Junction, Sammy Barlow. They were all 'day' boats: pick a boat up in the morning and go.

The people next door to George were caretakers of the old church in Broad Street. "When I first moved there, there was a cottage on the side of the lock, which is now a café. That was occupied, but I don't know anything about them. Then there were the Dances next door. The *Opposite Lock* was amalgamated with *Bobby Browns*. It used to be the old stable block for donkeys – on the Worcester and Birmingham Canal."

The canal in Birmingham was the second to be built, the first being the Bridgewater Canal in Manchester, also by James Brindley. The Birmingham Canal and Gas Street Basin, otherwise known as the Worcester Bar Basin, opened in 1769 – one of the oldest – the BCN. Gas Street took its name from the *Birmingham Gaslight Company*, whose premises it once included.

Brindley built the canals to bring coal from the Black Country to Birmingham. It was very difficult to build them – because of the Birmingham Plateau. So they needed plenty of locks. He followed the contour of the land.

In 1824 Thomas Telford rebuilt Brindley's canal, as it had become totally inadequate. He described it as 'little better than a crooked ditch', with almost no towing path and serious traffic jams. They had to build basins all around Birmingham, where they could unload the trade onto boats, then deliver to the factories and bring the finished goods back by rail. By the mid-nineteenth century, Gas Street Basin had become the heart of the national canal system.

George used to accompany parties of schoolchildren along the canals. "The teacher was there and I'd tell her a bit about the canal life and when the canals were built – what they were used for."

George would explain that when he began working for the waterways in 1940, the wages were 19/2d a week in old money, the equivalent of 91p today. "I used to get a shilling pocket money, which bought my cigarettes for the week. When I worked with my father, his wages were £2-50p a week. He was a boatman too."

He'd show the classes his collection of miniatures, of which he is justifiably proud. "I've got a miniature 'buckby' can – boat people used to have two on each boat. They carry two to two-and-a-half gallons each, so depending on the size of the can, four or five gallons of water, for drinking and making the tea.

"The boat people used to get their drinking water where they stopped off. Wherever there was a tap, they filled their cans up – usually by locks and stables. There wouldn't be time to stop for provisions; by the time the can was full, the boat was on its way down the locks."

George explained that shopping would be done whenever they stopped at night or sometimes in the early morning. "There were various stopping places on the canal where they used to stock food and provisions for them. They'd be further out – probably in the rural areas – for fresh food there'd be nearby farms – very basic. Depending on the family, I think it was mainly bread and soup. For vegetables they'd go out in the country; they'd see a field of potatoes and they'd go and dig a couple of buckets up – something like that. It was rather a rough way of life."

Having lived on a narrow boat himself, Peter White regards Amelia's lifestyle as privileged, in comparison with alternatives, such as factory work. "When you poked your head out of the boat hatch and you'd sampled the 'great outdoors', it was hardly confined. They could listen to Nature and see the wild flowers, and listen to the birds. If the boat people had a contract that took them out into the countryside, they were kings of the industrial world."

George recalls: "Some of them would keep their barges really smart, painted and decorated with roses and castles. There was one particular family that I knew very well – the Powells. There was Jakey, Charlie, and another brother and sister. Jake, was my favourite mate – one of the boat people.

"There were the Tulleys – I think they had eight children. The Shaws were two brothers – Jack and Joe; they used to come to the same school – Saint Peter's. And then there was – I shouldn't say this really – what we used to call the *Rack Hang Gang*, a family who looked as though they'd never had a wash. That was the type of life they used to live.

"There were two lock keepers who looked after Farmers Bridge. They'd be there when I used to go round to play with the boat children. They were two old chaps – well they were old to *me*. There was old George Norris. He lived in one of the old lock cottages at the top of Farmers Bridge, at Cambrian Wharf." Photos E and G of Peter White's paintings show a top lock at Cambrian Wharf and Farmer's Bridge Locks, respectively.

"The other one was old Bill Oakley. You had to unlock the gate at the top – you can walk through now – into Cambrian Wharf. I went down this one day to see Jakey – I'd heard he was in – I'd seen his brother. 'Jakey's in,' he said. 'Top of the lock at Farmers Bridge.'"

The gate was locked. One of the boat children was going in with a key. They had to borrow the key off the lock keeper to get through the gate. "I went by the lock office, over the bridge and down the other side, and who should be on the gate but this George Norris? 'What are you doing here young Smithy?' he said. I said: 'I've come to see Jakey.' 'You ain't going over there,' he said.

"He let me go in the finish and see Jakey before he left."

In the 1940s, Tom Arneill was living in Camden Street, a short distance from George's canal-side home. He knew the section of the canal towards Monument Road swimming baths, and used to watch the bargees travelling along it. He differentiates between 'bargees' and 'boat people', as both terms were used at the time. But generally speaking, we have used the words 'boatman' or 'boat people', because we are advised, by both Peter and George, that these are the terms preferred by the people concerned.

"There was a slight difference between them – between those who had a barge or a narrow boat," Tom explained. "Most of them were 'bargees' – because they used barges. They were transporting heavy goods like coal, metal, cement, and things like that. A lot of them had horses and used to walk them along the tow-path. Unfortunately, in Monument Road, the towpath finished at the bridge, so we used to help to bring the horse over the top. Then they hitched the horse back up again, the other side of the bridge."

There were no stables in Monument Road, as far as Tom knows, because there was nowhere to moor up for the night. Instead, they were located around the Gas Street Basin/Sheepcote Street areas. He remembers Icknield Port Road as another stopping point, because he used to go down to the coal yard, opposite *Landon's*, the bathroom place. George confirmed that the name of the coal merchants, who Pat also knew – *Ashford and Sons* – remains on the side of the house.

> *I remember old Ashford: he had an old blue Bedford, and wore a trilby hat. He was middle-aged when I was a young kid of 17. They were 'posh' coalmen who'd been in the business all of their lives. They had special customers and only sold high quality coal. I used to look up to them.*

In Tom's experience most of the boat people were from the Black Country: from areas around Wednesbury, Wolverhampton and Tipton. He describes them as: "a breed of their own, who very rarely mixed with anybody else. They used to say hello, but they never allowed us on to their barges because they were private: they lived on them.

"My father worked for the waterworks, in Waterworks Road," explained Tom. "He was a 'gangerman' who maintained the big black pipes that ran alongside every bridge and carried water. They used to have spikes, to stop the kids climbing onto them."

Keeping broadly within the same geographical area, but moving swiftly on a few years, between the ages of 17 and 20, Pat shovelled coal from a barge, and also from trucks, in three different locations. He recalls the first of these, which was in Hockley:

I walked into Hockley Brook and said to a fella: "If I become a coal man can I learn to drive?" and he said yes. I took up driving from there with the L-plates on. I used to drive around wagons with 3½ tons on them – 70 bags weighing 1cwt each. We used to shovel, tap the trucks, shovel, bag, weigh, stack, then carry them off and tip them out. When I was 17 I went on to straightforward coke loading. I was doing like 21 ton a day on my own.

The second wharf, run by Carter, Pearce and Cutler, was in Stanmore Road. A. Wall & Co. actually owned the premises. There were two directors: George Dyas and Bill Eaton.

The third and final location was a wharf on the corner of Great Tindal Street, St Vincent Street and Browning Street. While working there, he made the unexpected discovery that his grandmother, Amelia, had been born in a canal cottage, just a 'stone's throw' away, in Sheepcote Street, right next to the café where he had breakfast each morning. The exact site, opposite the back entrance to Symphony Court, is now boarded up – the café sign barely visible, behind the boards.

Later I changed to a smaller company. Charlie Baylis I worked for, at Sheepcote Street. I still know his two sons – Charlie and Johnny. We knew each other well; we became friends years afterwards. Johnny runs a garage now, up in Bearwood. I met the daughter; she was always into horses and dogs – out Bromsgrove way somewhere. But Charlie was a lovely little man – little bright Toby Jug face – Charlie Baylis. Used to wear a trilby hat – yes, pleasant memories of old Charlie. I've since discovered that George Smith knew him too.

We were up in the morning – crack of dawn – and finished early – one o'clock. Then I used to go to the old Casino Dance Hall, Wednesday afternoons or go to the races. We'd start at five or six o'clock in the morning. We sometimes used to have to light a fire to thaw the bags out, because they were all frozen up. Because the bags were always wet, they'd freeze up and we couldn't get the coal into the bags. We'd have to thaw them out. It was a terribly hard job.

Well I knew quite a few older men who did it. There was old Monty – 60 odd. There were a lot of older guys over 60 who used to do it – they were as hard as nails (repeats this). Did it all their lives. They became tough; never caught colds. Oh we were soaking; wringing wet nine o'clock in the morning – soaked right through to the skin. And we carried on all day long. It never bothered us. I used to get two shillings a ton – two bob a ton to tap a truck, bag it, weigh it, load it, unload, then deliver it.

We have gathered a wealth of interesting information about the canals – enough for an entire book. But we've had to settle for just one more chapter – the next – which takes a closer look at the regeneration of Gas Street Basin. Meanwhile, Pat brings our chapter about Amelia to its conclusion.

Amelia Bevis was 72 years of age when she died. She was laid off where she worked and I think she died soon afterwards, from double pneumonia. It's always double in my family! I lived with her in Shakespeare Road, Ladywood. It sounds like a lovely address, doesn't it? But it wasn't, it was not a nice area – you'll see from the photograph. She used to go to work every morning – about eight o'clock. And she never listened to a radio, because she was deaf. She was never sure of the clock, so she'd go and stand on the step and watch people walk by, and remember what time they walked by.

She'd see Mr. Hardy across he road and she'd shout: "What time is it Hardy, is it a quarter?" And he'd nod. Or "What time is it Simmonds, is it twenty?" And they'd nod. She knew what time it was by the time they were going to work. If they were in a hurry she knew they were late: she knew it wasn't 'twenty to' – it was 18 or 17. Or it wasn't 'a quarter'; it was 12 or 11. That's what she did – she stood on the step every morning.

Think back as far as you can and then describe her: tell me what she was like then.

I'd be eight or nine years of age. She was 5 foot 6, very slim – I think she still had dark hair when she died. Yes, gypsies had good heads of hair for some reason. I think it's because – I don't mean this disrespectfully – they don't wash it so often. That's what I honestly believe. I don't mean it disrespectfully at all.

She was always lending money to the family. Stan used to borrow money off her – I think everybody used to. She used to like a bet and was an avid reader of the paper because, obviously, she couldn't hear the radio. There was no television. She used to read the paper from end to end: all the obituary columns!

And everybody knew her really well?

Oh everybody knew her, yes. And the way she'd go to work with the shoes she'd got on and the bunions sticking out the side – poor old Amelia – poor old Gran.

Chapter Five

BEYOND BRINDLEY

Or being lied about, don't deal in lies...

Choosing the name 'James Brindley' for the Gas Street Basin pub, was not so much a lie, as a misnomer, because that part of the canal was probably built by Telford.

James Brindley was born in 1716, the penniless son of a poor Peak District labourer, with little schooling, but a genius for all things mechanical. He was so successful that 270 years later, his name was chosen to herald the dawn of a new Canal Age in Birmingham.

A photograph taken by George Smith in the 1940s, shows the original site of what is now the *James Brindley* public house. The part of the building on the right-hand side, which projects out over the water, is the lucam that was carefully preserved, and remains as an integral feature of the pub. A comparison with the second photograph on this page, a modern-day view of the same location, illustrates how the site has been totally transformed.

In the summer of '99, I visited the *Brindley* with the innovative architect charged with the responsibility for designing of it – Alan Goodwin. Seated at a table alongside the canal, we discussed the history of the pub, opened in 1986. Since that time it has become a significant landmark in the development of Gas Street Basin, representing as it did, the first major step in the re-vitalisation of the heart of the Birmingham Canal system.

He worked for various firms from the 60s onwards, including James Roberts, and designed the tower with the large revolving restaurant, often seen against the Liverpool skyline. In 1983 he started his own practice. Since then he has worked on 65 pubs in total, many of which were built, including several *Jefferson's* projects, the *Barley Mow*, Studley, *Timberdine Farm*, Worcester, and others too numerous to mention. Primarily, these have been 'new-build', but include some refurbishment projects and alterations.

Alan explained: "The *James Brindley* was the first new building in Gas Street Basin – the site was derelict, more or less, all the way around. The warehouses had gone when I first came here. Some of it was brick-paved and some of it had granite sets, but it was just used as a surface car park – for years and years." On his *List of Projects*, it is described as a 'New build – 2-level city centre pub'. Our illustrations contain one of Alan's original drawings, accompanied by a description of the *Brindley* project. We are particularly pleased that he has given us permission to publish these, for the first time.

According to Alan: "Bass wanted a pub here and British Waterways owned the site and I think they still own the freehold. Unusually, Bass took a 99-year lease on this; they normally like to buy the freehold. As soon as we started building the pub, the plans were developed for the other buildings around us and for office blocks. These next door started to be built just after."

The canal arm remained under Bridge Street, but was full of rubbish. There was warehousing on the other side, but no bridge. The main canal originally ran under the road, but that had been blocked off, so a false bridge was built on the arm of the canal. They also found a leak in the side of the canal, close to where the pub was to be located.

As we watched the bustling scene around us, Alan elaborated on the *Brindley's* design. "If you notice on the side where the arm is, there's what is really just an artificial *lucam.*" A lucam was used to cover a hoist, for hauling up sacks of corn. Originally, it would overhang the canal, so they could haul sacks up, out of the barges.

Alan recalled: "The brief was that British Waterways would only let this site go, provided that they could have a say in the design. It all had to happen very quickly, so for days on end, I was just designing and re-designing it, and running between Bass and British Waterways – in the evenings. Going to the Chief Architect's house – of Bass, and Peter White's – the Chief Architect of the Waterways, 'til in the end they both agreed on this design. It had to look as though it had something to do with canals – hence the brick arches.

"Peter White was particularly keen to have this vaulted roof on here; that was a bit of a fashionable thing at the time – these new glass arcades were coming in. So we just put that straight down the middle. It had to have pitched roofs, and be made of red brick and slate, because buildings by canals usually are, although I notice the ones next door aren't. The aesthetics were – it had to be in the Victorian vernacular, with the appearance of having always been a canal side building.

"The brewery's own Architects Department made various attempts at clarifying the brief; BWB found them a bit too fancy – they wanted something plainer. Finally, although I already did work for the brewery and I'd done quite a few pubs, Peter White said, 'Why don't you get Alan on this case?'

"I think he appreciated me as a designer, and thought that I could do that. Before that and since then I've done quite a few canal side buildings. You know, converting old warehouses into dwellings, and that sort of thing."

Before designing the pub, Alan researched the work of James Brindley, with some assistance from Peter. A versatile architect of many year's experience, he has since worked on similar projects, including a new canal side pub at Leamington. Like the *Brindley*, he used pastiche to make them look as though they've always been there.

Alan explained that the pub had another prototype name beforehand. "I think it was just called *Gas Street Basin Pub.*" The brewery chose the name *James Brindley*: rather a misnomer. "As I understand it, the part of the canal on which it stands is probably by Telford, rather than Brindley. I think that the one on the other side of the Bar is probably where the James Brindley canal was. The name has serious associations with the canal. It's just that perhaps *Thomas Telford* might have been more appropriate."

In an *Evening Mail* article dated 30 January 1986, Nigel Hastilow announced that a pub 'named after James Brindley – the early canal pioneer' was due to open in March 1986. It would be the first stage of a redevelopment scheme and included offices and 54 canal side flats. He quoted Doctor Bill Brookes, then secretary of the *Gas Street Conservation Association*, who said that they were concerned about the security of the 18 residential and working narrow boats that were moored there.

They also objected to the building of the 30-storey *Hyatt Hotel*, overlooking the basin, on the grounds that 'the 104-metre high triangular tower of reflecting silver glass was out of keeping with the Georgian and Victorian architecture of the canal basin.' Despite these protests, building went ahead.

During the time that the James Brindley was being constructed, the office building started alongside, together with work on the *Hyatt Hotel*. Despite being built at the same time, Alan recalls that the *Brindley* was completed first, in approximately 26 weeks.

"Another thing about the design is that it's unusual to have two-storey pubs. They don't normally work because people won't walk up and down staircases: they like them all on one level. But in this case, because of the street level, where you had to have the public entrance, and the canal level which was a storey below, it was actually designed as one room above another, which is the way it is today. I think it has always been successful since it was first built. Its location is pretty central now, it's a good location, whereas when it was first built it was surrounded by dereliction really, but it seemed to take off, right from the start.

"People would actually go to it. Previously it was what is now called a 'destination' pub. That means that it relies upon people walking or driving to it, rather than passing trade. But now, because of where it's located, and because of what's happened around it, it's both a 'passing trade' and a 'destination' pub.

"It never has been a 'theme' pub – it was never intended to be 'Ye Olde Oak Beams', or anything like that. Though in fact when the interior designers got at it, they did try to make it a bit 'folksy' inside, rather than being classical as it was. But then interiors of pubs change every five years or so: that's just wallpaper really – they keep changing the carpets and wallpaper and stuff. So essentially it's like an engineering building, rather than a cottagey building.

"As you noticed off the street, where we walked in, there's actually a footbridge, so underneath there's a storeroom – you can walk under there, into the car park. Every building around here had to be restored, because they were all derelict. Where the Hyatt stands there was a little café on the corner there: I think it was a 'greasy spoon' called the *Appollonia*." Pat remembers the café, which was owned by a Greek Cypriot, and the popular *Rum Runner* nightclub, which remained on the same site for several years.

"The buildings on Broad Street, with the *Merchant Stores* lettering in them, were part of the Broad Street frontage, so that was the back of the shops." As Alan spoke, I could see right through one of the large windows in these buildings, and out into the Broad Street traffic beyond.

He explained that the Worcester Bar and the paving were restored at almost the same time as the *James Brindley* was built. They put some new wrought iron signs there as well, and added a new bridge, involving very skilled casting techniques, to make it look authentic.

"It was patterned off another bridge, further up the canal. There's one behind the arena, I think it's that one." Alan later identified the copied bridge from a Broad Street Tunnel photograph, as the one that the pattern for the footbridge was taken from. It's a traditional 19th century pattern. Looking at the same photograph, he recalled: "The building on the left, at the top, is the old brewery. There used to be a little passageway through here, I think it was called Shakespeare Passage or something like that. There was a little antique shop on that corner there, which was stuck onto the side of the Crown: it was demolished before the church."

Later, we drove past the Crown Pub, Broad Street. Alan's architectural drawings for its re-design, in 1991, can be found in our illustrations. He explained: "The yard of *The Crown* pub in Broad Street, apparently called *Edwards* now, and the back entrance on the I.C.C. is where the church once stood, on the bridge over the canal, in Broad Street." This was the Church of the Messiah, where Chamberlain taught Sunday School.

Travelling from the *Brindley*, and reaching our second stop, the *Round House*, where canal horses used to be stabled, we drove down under the archway, off the street level, into the car park – formerly the yard for the horses. Much of the cobbled area remains. We were now almost alongside the canal, adjacent to *The Fiddle and Bone* pub, Sheepcote Street, the very street where Amelia was born.

Alan described the *Round House* as: "An amazing building … a whole series of arches, built around a curve. The building above is like a horseshoe shape. These are the vaults where the canal horses were kept." Cars were parked inside the archways of this unusual landmark. A ramp, with granite sets led straight up and out towards the pub sign and the road beyond.

At this point, looking out across the back of the canal that comes into Birmingham from Smethwick – the Staffordshire and Birmingham Canal, Alan explained the two principal reasons why railways were always built close to the canals – almost alongside.

"There were engineering reasons, like being as level as possible and following contour lines, so that they didn't have gradients. But the other reason was that it was easier to go on to land that had already been compulsorily purchased for canals, by Act of Parliament. It saved having a new Act of Parliament each time they wanted to build a line, if they could already follow a canal line."

Development of the area is still not fully complete, but 16 years on, most visitors would probably agree that a substantial effort has been made to integrate the waterway with its surrounding elements. There appears to be something for everyone, from walks to entertainment.

The canal environment of old warehouses, wharves, locks, bridges, canal side cottages, towpaths and pubs has undergone a tasteful metamorphosis, creating a pleasurable, relaxing environment. For those requiring a more stimulating experience, there are conveniently – situated theatres, concert halls, art galleries, narrow boat cruises and restaurants of inspired design.

Amelia loved canals, but it goes without saying, that if she or Grandfather Jackson were to return today – or even James Brindley, the Derbyshire-born designer of 18th century canals, they just wouldn't recognise the old place!

Chapter Six –

THE BUDOKAN

Or being hated, don't give way to hating...

I'd never 'give way to hating', or be at the front when it came to fighting, although my friend, Eddie Hart enjoyed it. He used to 'put the nut' on them – head-butted them. One particular day a bruiser came to the crowd and he was a bit on the big side. It wasn't my thing. I was never a brawler or a tear-away.

*I confronted this big guy that wanted to get involved – this big guy with a bent nose and I just 'straight-lefted' him and 'right-crossed' him and down he went, and I was overly thought about, because I could put up a fight. That one occasion was down Halesowen – we used to go down to Halesowen Town Hall and make a nuisance of ourselves and – we **were** a nuisance.*

Pat's Aunt Freda remembers that long before his introduction into the world of judo, he was a sociable boy, who excelled at sport. His very first training sessions, a habit destined to last a lifetime, began at secondary school in Camden Street, Spring Hill, Birmingham. On returning to Belgrave Road, he transferred to Hope Street School, featured in Chapter 2.

You may recall that between the ages of 17 and 20 Pat worked on coal haulage, at various wharves in the Hockley and Sheepcote Street areas of Birmingham. This proved to be a beneficial form of weightlifting in itself, and a means of maintaining fitness. Although his fellow workers came in all shapes and sizes, the job required considerable strength.

I can remember carrying a bag, in the early days, and saying: "Cor, there's a big lump sticking in my back!" And the fella I was walking up with said: "I'll show you how to get rid of that lump." He did a sort of forward twist with his head, that moved the bag off his back about six inches, and as it came down onto his back, he pushed the lump back into place. So he actually straightened the bag up off his back: they used to bang it flat with their own backs!

Pat became British Judo Champion and also won boxing trophies. His wrestling debut was in Tamworth in 1963. Millions of television viewers used to enjoy watching their sporting heroes throw each other around the ring. From that time to the present, Pat has continued to entertain the public in this fashion, although unfortunately, British wrestling matches are no longer televised.

The *Mick McManus Wrestling Book* by Charles Arnold, published in the 1970s, contains an entire chapter about Pat's wrestling exploits. The author chronicled his outstanding achievements, one by one, including the fact that Pat followed his father into the boxing ring for a while. He became a professional boxing protégé of Jack Solomons, but eventually realised that he preferred wrestling.

Jim White recalls: "One of Pat's friends, Gordon Corbett, was a professional boxer. I used to go up to the gym and they'd be pounding away at each other. He was going to go professional, but for some reason he didn't take it up professionally: the boxing game is hard." In his early 20s, having returned to work in his father's salvage business, Pat became an admirer of the TV wrestlers and decided to 'learn the ropes'.

> *I used to go to Leicester, under Jack Taylor, although we were never really taught very much: you had to find out for yourself. Alfie Kent first introduced me to wrestling. He was the Midland Area Wrestling Champion and lived just a mile away from Erdington. He was a good friend of Randolph Turpin's and took him all round the circuits when he was boxing. I've met Randolph a few times, on the shows.*

News broadcasts on *Carlton Television*, and *BBC 1* for the West Midlands, on 1 December 2000, covered the sale of Turpin's famous Lonsdale Belt. Fortunately, it was bought by businessman Tony Baker, a friend of the Turpin family.

The belt was subsequently displayed in Turpin's hometown of Leamington Spa. Pat was present at the auction, and was interviewed on both channels. In the Colin Pemberton interview for the *BBC*, Pat said: "Of course Randy, towards the end, was just a little on the deaf side you know; people used to mistake it for all sorts of other things."

One of the fascinating aspects of Pat's sports career, is that despite an abundance of the physical attributes required to make a successful fighter, he has never enjoyed fighting for its own sake. Yet from a professional standpoint, he has taken particular pride in achieving excellence in not just one, but several disciplines. On this scale, such a variety of allied skills become almost an art form: a celebration of the talents that he was born with, and worked so hard to develop. True to character, Pat takes the more modest, down-to-earth view:

I didn't really choose sports as a career as such: I drifted into it. I was always very tall and somewhat swarthy. People would comment: "Oh, you want to be a rugby footballer, or boxer, or wrestler – or whatever it was." If you're a man you are interested in combat sports. I saw a little niche there where I could earn a few quid.

I suppose it's all part of my aggressive nature. I've been described as a 'driven man', so it could well be that it was part of the fact that I'd got all this energy to expend. On a one-to-one basis it's obviously far more demanding, I would have thought, than team sports – wouldn't you?

Arnold's book reveals that Pat's wrestling prowess resulted in his being hired as *Miss World's* bodyguard. The lady in question was *Miss Peru*, winner of the 1967/68 contest. During her visit to Birmingham, Pat was her escort. Having stopped to speak to someone who'd hailed him, he found himself locked out of a Birmingham ballroom – with *Miss World* inside. He shouted and banged on the door, but to no avail. Finally an attendant inside called out: "If you don't push off *Miss World's* bodyguard will be called to deal with you – and he's a big fellow!"

George Smith, the canal boatman featured in Chapter 4, was one of many fans who used to watch Pat wrestling on television. "When mother was alive, she died in 1978, her Saturday afternoon treat was watching wrestling on the television. She used to watch all the wrestlers; she knew them all by name. We used to watch Pat and Mick McManus. There was a glamour boy – Jackie Pallo – blond he was and slim." George remembered Pat's famous *Brummagem Bump*, which involved lifting his opponent about nine feet above his head – then slamming him down.

In an *Birmingham Post* article, from February 1981, Pat described his famous manoeuvre: "I get my opponent in a state of exhaustion and then lift him above my head and let him fall … it must be a nine foot drop. That's when the crowd go really wild." Conversely, when the *Gentle Giant* used to give judo lessons, it was a regular occurrence for a little boy of three foot to throw him.

You quickly realise that if you go on television it makes you popular, and if you're popular, it's a 'latch-lifter': that's a terminology that I use quite a lot – a 'latch-lifter'. It was another way of life.

Pat's philosophy was also reported in the local press: "I do my exercises and keep healthy as a way of saying a prayer, a thank you to my God, whoever he is, certainly a greater being."

In the course of his career Pat has made personal appearances at various sporting and Keep-Fit events. One of the more unusual examples of this took place in February 1981 at the *Birmingham Post & Evening Mail Boat &*

Caravan Show. A fashion show was staged in the *Pinelog Theatre* at the *National Exhibition Centre,* as part of a *Keep Young and Beautiful* health club scene. Pat's role in the proceedings was to appear on stage from time to time, giving weightlifting demonstrations. But this was a demonstration with a difference: the 'weights' in question were model girls!

Several sporting friends have enjoyed training with him. Just one example is City wrestler-turned actor Johnny Allen, who joined him in a training session some years ago, while filming the *City* series for the former ATV television company. Once British and European Junior Heavyweight, under his ring name *Farmer Johnny Allen,* he was photographed jogging with Pat and commented: "Filming is very taxing, so when I'm in Brum I like to meet Pat and exercise with him." According to Pat, although he was in a heavier wrestling class than his friend, "Johnny gave me a severe thrashing."

Pain, it would seem, was never a problem for Pat. Jim White, his former business partner and fellow judo expert, revealed that Pat taught himself to absorb pain by sticking needles into his body. In Charles Arnold's book, Jim described this type of pain absorption as 'fantastic', recalling that his friend once used a false flame-coloured beard, held on with small safety pins and … "thought nothing of inserting a four-inch safety pin through and along the front of his neck." It's quite a relief to know that the beard Pat has since sported is entirely his own!

Such practices can have their downside. During a yoga exhibition in New Zealand, Pat had a rather embarrassing moment: while he was passing pins through his face and neck, an official fainted; the next chapter contains an hilarious description of the incident.

He sometimes appeared in *World of Sport's* wrestling slot. During the 1980s, 6 foot 4 inch Pat weighed in at 19 stone 3 lbs and had a 51–inch chest measurement. He continued to combine sport with acting commitments saying, "Wrestling has been very kind to me in the past." This had the added advantage of keeping him in peak condition for film roles, such as the six-minute fight sequence with Sean Connery in the 007 blockbuster *Never Say Never Again.*

On Saturday, 28 January 1984, he featured in a contest with fellow heavyweight Tom Tyrone, in *World of Sport.* This coincided with his new role as 'Bomber', the West-Country bricklayer, in the introductory series of *Auf Wiedersehen Pet,* which was destined to make household names of its leading actors. Chapters 14 and 15 are devoted to the series, and the more recent careers of members of the cast. The programme was a completely new departure for him.

Pat considers his most memorable sporting television appearance to be the one against the ex-British heavyweight champion Billy Joyce, because he was, "… outwitted, out-thought and out-wrestled!"

He first met Jim White, in the late 1950s. During an interview, Jim recalled their years together, including Pat's meteoric success with judo and other sports. Readers may recall that Jim's father, Charlie White, and Pat's father, Frank, were friends long before their two sons met. Charlie used to drive a motorbike and sidecar.

> *He'd often drive to my dad's place at 68, Hamstead Road. It was just up the road from the original tollgate, and my father knew someone who remembered it as such. It's a beautiful black and white building today – run by 'Focus Housing', I believe. Old Charlie would come in, wearing a great big leather coat. He'd take his false leg off, and there'd be a big lump of cheese in it. He used to hide it in there during the war!*

Jim did his national service, which included working on radar for REME. He left there to work for *Birkets Air Services*, at Castle Bromwich Aerodrome for a couple of years, as an aircraft electrician. Like his friend, Jim is also a multi-talented person. As a teenager, he won a scholarship to study art in London – no mean achievement in those days. Unfortunately he was discouraged from taking up the offer. In addition to other practical skills and his expertise in judo, Jim is also a chiropodist.

He explained: "I was living at Pig Hill Farm, as it was originally called, in Queen's Head Road, Handsworth, and ran an Auto Electrician business from there. Pat would often call, buying and selling to me through the business. I asked him to join the club because he was so athletic and very strong. He eventually did and we went down to Kyrle Hall with him and started practising judo. He started off great as a novice and flew through, right up to the Brown Belt level. I'd probably been doing judo for two to three years by then. He learnt very quickly, and was very fast on his feet; he's got a long reach and long legs."

> *We were a load of old scruffs – just living in our judo suits, or judogi, as we used to call them. We got up early every morning, practised in the Dojo all day, and never got out of our suits. We'd even throw a tracksuit on over the top, go out, eat something – then come back. We were forever trying to talk in old-style Japanese, taken from a book that must have been at least thirty years old. It was written by a European who'd studied in Japan, E.J. Harrison – a Fifth Dan in judo.*

Jim showed me a card; the final entry was his Black Belt award. It can be found in our illustrations, together with similar cards belonging to Pat, begun just a few months afterwards. Jim explained: "This was my original card when I joined Kyrle Hall – Birmingham School of Judo – run by Frank Ryder, and these were the cards you were issued with. You started as a novice. As you can see, it's like an identity card.

"It gives the colour of your eyes. There's also a photograph, name, and address. – everything; there's even a forefinger print, so you can't cheat! On the other side of the card it's got all the grades, the dates you got them, and what-have-you; they were signed by Ryder, the Black Belt holder, and a witness. So you had three witnesses to make sure that you got that particular grade." Kyrle Hall eventually closed down, for building reasons associated with Aston University. So Jim opened a new club in Queen's Head Road, the *Budokan School of Judo*. Pat helped him to run it, in a large pre-war gymnasium, already on site; built by former weightlifter Ernie Underwood, it had a lower half of highly durable angle iron and an upper half of glass.

"I *believe* that Budokan means *Black Knight* in Japanese. I needed mats when we bought this gymnasium. Pat knew someone who sold us about three hundred old mattresses. We put them down but needed a cover. We paid a huge amount of money for this enormous tent canvas, with eyelets all the way round, stretched it over these old mattresses and it became a proper mat area."

Eventually, the club was demolished. The site is now occupied by modern housing, with Murdock Grove at its centre.

I was 21 when I got my white belt. I got awarded a Black Belt. I think I won the British Championships at Leicester – Humberstone Gate.

"It's a long time ago, but I would say it didn't take Pat much longer than a year to get his Black Belt. I took a year and I think he was probably aiming at that as well. After a short while I couldn't beat him anyway, because he soon picked it up. Eventually, they get to know your style and your favourite throws. If you get the bug you become fanatics. Nothing can stop you! You just go on every night at all times, you know? He got the bug as well."

This meant that Pat could anticipate what Jim was going to do. During the same period, they were also running cafés – the judo having started first. They gave regular demonstrations for many people, around England, as judo experts.

According to Jim: "We'd go there just to see if we could beat them. We'd get fed up, because when you get used to someone in judo, you get to know their style. So to prove yourself you'd got to find someone who's better than you. You learn their tricks, and eventually build right up, until not many people can shift you."

Being a definite 'non-expert', I asked about the colour sequence for judo belts and how the system works. Jim came to my rescue: "It starts off with a novice, who has a white belt with a red tab on the end, so others know not to try anything stupid on them. Once they think they know, they take the red tab off and become a White Belt.

"When they reach a certain standard, they go to a Yellow, followed by an Orange, Green, Blue and eventually a Brown, which is the end of the Kyu (pronounced 'Q') grade. From then on in, they struggle away to get their Black Belt, which is a 'Dan' grade. 'Dan' is Japanese for 'master' or 'teacher', or something similar, whereas 'Kyu' means 'pupil'.

"There are 10 different grades of Black Belt, but it doesn't show them on the card, because you're not expected to get them anyway. I was offered Second Dan, which I refused because I didn't think I was good enough, but I shouldn't have done, because nobody's good enough anyway! Pat got his Black Belt and First Dan at 22 or 23 – very early. In those days, people usually took years to reach that stage; he flew through it – same as I did myself." Inevitably, the system may have changed in some respects since then.

Jim's judo career lasted about 16 years, as he was obliged to stop, because of a serious wrist injury. He remembers Pat winning the British Championship at Humberstone Gate, Leicester, and another in London, at the London Judo Society, Brown Belt (Kyu grade) adding: "… it's a hard thing to get – the championship." He also recalls the time when Pat won a national championship in Barry, South Wales. The venue was situated close to an airfield.

"It was at Saint Athens, across the Menaii Bridge. There's a story attached to that as well, which Pat can tell you. We stayed at the Barry Hotel. I think he won the Kyu grade championship there as well. I'm not sure. It's a long time ago and I've drunk a lot of beer since then!"

Jim and Pat's careers were heavily influenced by their long-time photographer friend, Jack Bannister, although he later moved, and they lost contact. Jack practised at the *Budokan*, from time to time. Pat commented recently: "Although he was graded elsewhere, it was great that he brought the additional knowledge back to us."

I asked Jim whether one of the reasons he and Pat became such good friends was because they were both into pugilistic sports. He replied: "Well we never fought because he'd kill me and he knows that, you see." When I mentioned this to Pat, he felt that Jim was being modest about his own skills.

Despite its unfortunate name, Pig Hill Farm has quite a history! Jim's father, Charlie, bought it during the Second World War. Jim explained: "It was thought to have dated back to at least 900AD, and was owned by William Murdock, during the 19th century, the man who invented a way of using gas. It was the very first place in the world, as far as I know, that had gas pipes put in, which was iron mixed with silver – to stop it rusting.

"It was eventually split into three houses: one was the stables – my father's place – which was quite nice when it was converted; then there was me living in the next house, and Underwood lived in the far one. It was off Queen's Head Road, which runs down the bottom of the hill. At the bottom of the hill was Black Patch Park. My father also had a café on the corner of Queen's Head Road." Pat recalls that the actual address of the farm was 62/64 Queen's Head Road. An Ordnance Survey map of the area, shows the farm's location.

"In the back yard of my father's area was a very deep water well that was falling in. He discovered some footings going down and then a tunnel went off and came out near *Avery's*. It was an escape tunnel apparently. In those days we used to have 'footpads', the equivalent of today's muggers. For reasons of safety, people would scramble down the well and into this tunnel and then escape somewhere outside – near *Avery's*. It was the only building in the area.

"In the back door of the house they had this little thing that you opened, and looked through a grill before you opened the door. It even had an Elizabethan priest hole – behind an inglenook, with a little slot. You had to take a panel off the kitchen wall to get in. When you got into the 'hidey-hole', you could look to see who was in the room. "The horses were used for pulling carriages up and down Soho Road. In those days Handsworth was a very posh place. So the stables at the farm were where they kept the horses and carts.

"At the time Pig Hill Farm was very isolated and the only place within sight was the 'nick' across the valley – Winson Green Prison. There were no other houses, only fields." Ironically, the farm would have been quite close to the building where we were actually conducting the interview – at Jim's chiropody practice on Villa Road. "Yes – only up the valley. Looking across the valley, you saw Black Patch Park – where all the gypsy encampments were. There was a lake there in those days, but now it's all filled in as a park."

Pensioner Denis Wood recalls the park as it was, in the 1930s. "They used to hold a fair – by the railway bridge that crosses the road. We'd see one or two fights there. Someone used to stand up and challenge people in the audience."

Many years later, Pat did *precisely* that, as a young man, on various shows around the country; his days as the 'man on top' are described in Chapter 16. "I witnessed that happening too," explained Denis, "but I'm going back 70 years. My interest was just being allowed to watch from the corner, kind-of-style. I wasn't in any position to judge, as I would do now." He was living in Icknield Port Road, which runs into Dudley Road, then Monument Road.

We decided to investigate the link between the *Budokan* and *Avery's* further. Mike Cooper, the company's Communications Manager at Foundry Lane, Handsworth, told me that the BBC have previously made a programme about the Soho Foundry, presented by Rory McGrath. At his suggestion, Jim and I visited Howard Green, who had been with *Avery's* for over 61 years, including ten years as company curator. We were very fortunate to benefit from his expertise, regarding the firm's history. Nowadays the company is known as *Avery Berkel*, a trading name of *GEC Avery Limited*.

According to Howard, although they are no longer used, there is a 'honeycomb' of tunnels beneath *Avery's* – formerly the Soho Works. He has also heard of a passageway that supposedly led from the foundry, up to the Queen's Head Road. Originally, the tunnels would probably have been alleyways or passageways. Howard provided several relevant photographs, including two types of tunnel, and various maps: some can be found in the illustrations.

After consulting two booklets, also provided by Howard, entitled *Soho Foundry* and *The Avery Business,* it emerged that in 1895, 'The firm of James Watt & Co, with Soho Foundry, its machinery and stock-in-trade, was sold as a going concern to W & T Avery Limited. Total covered area 220,000 sq. ft.' Murdock, mentioned by Jim White in connection with Pig Hill Farm, died at Sycamore House, Handsworth, aged 85, and was buried in Handsworth Church.

One has to be very careful, of course, to distinguish between established facts and conjecture. For example it was rumoured, that at one time, there were passageways linking the houses of the three Soho industrialists, Boulton, Watt and Murdock; it's certainly an attractive notion, and would have been very convenient for the three gentlemen concerned! Maps of the area, dating from that time, show that linking the three houses would have been quite feasible.

We would like to pursue these investigations about the connection between the farm and the foundry in greater detail. It now seems that Pig Hill Farm was the farm building that had existed for centuries on the same rural plot where Sycamore Hill House was later purpose-built for Murdock, and that both buildings housed gas flues for Murdock's system of gas pipes. A photograph shows the remains of gas flues, discovered when the house was demolished in 1927. Jim was present when a substantial group from the *American Gas Board* visited his father's property, to view this historical site. Sycamore Farm, located on the map below Alexandra Road, was a separate property.

I asked Jim to describe the positive and the negative characteristics of Pat's personality. "As you say, it's very difficult, because Pat is a character anyway. He's got a *terrific* sense of humour. But also, he can be a bit over-powering. I remember him once, demonstrating a headlock on a friend, at a café we had at the top of the hill here; he nearly broke his neck. In fact, the guy flaked out. Sometimes, he doesn't know his own strength; he didn't do it on purpose.

"But there were other times. There was some club on the Stratford Road where a crowd of Scotsmen tried to upset the place. Pat and his friend, who died in a car crash, George Cullen, were drinking there. It was George's club; he and Pat were defending the place. They literally fought their way back into a yard and a cellar, or an outhouse or something. They couldn't get through the door because there was only one door. And Scotsmen, when they're drunk, aren't the easiest people to talk to!" Pat explained that this was the *Oyster Bar*, 100 yards below where the *Talk of the Town* was situated, in Sparkhill. The club is described in more detail, in Chapter 16.

"But there you are – he can handle himself. He's not scared of many people you know – Pat! I think he's pretty fair. He's certainly intelligent, because he often used to give me advice about things that you never even think of, you know. He's a great thinker." Such personality traits are, in some ways, similar to those used by people describing Pat's father, Frank.

"I think he's done so well, considering he never really had a good education," commented Jim.

Like all friends, Pat and Jim sometimes argued. "I'd say: 'Pat, you don't know what you're talking about!' He'd say: 'I bloody do!' It was never serious. But other times, we'd roll around laughing at some of the things he did! He's a very funny fella. He can be very amusing." Then he provided a wonderful quote: "I would say there were only two perfect people ever. They crucified one – and Pat Roach was left! I won't say anything about Pat. Don't forget, after we went our separate ways we still kept in touch. But there are so many things that happened to him after that; he's had another life.

"If he gets a bit angry people will just shut up and leave it, instead of talking back to him. They get a bit scared of him and, let's face it, why not? He was a tough guy, or he is – I don't know. I think that maybe in some cases he may not have let people have their say. But there again, he may have had good reasons for that."

Jim expressed the view that, as with many relationships, if someone's only known a person for a while, it's often on a more superficial level. "It's just a thought. So many people know him that they all say: 'Pat Roach is my friend.' And they tell me stories about Pat, and I think – you don't know what I know about him – I was with him for years and years.

"I think they like to say that they know him because he's a famous guy. I mean, I live in Tamworth now, but all the women round there love Pat Roach. They don't know we know him, because I never mention him – because it looks as if you're being big-headed. They say: 'That Pat Roach is a lovely fella. Remember that episode in *Auf Wiedersehen Pet?*' and things like that. They used to love all that: it was a good series, wasn't it? But I couldn't really say that Pat had anything bad about him. I wouldn't have been with him as long if he did.

"I'm sure that there might be a few people who he may have made enemies of. You can't get to the top without making a few enemies. So, yes, I always found him great – no problems. We had our ups and downs now and again – but who doesn't? I think that Pat, generally speaking, is a good guy. He's very intelligent. You can't argue with some of his arguments, because they're so near the truth, you've just got to shut up."

An *Evening Mail* article dated Tuesday May 20 1986, *'Bomber's touchdown'*, described Pat's entry into the world of American football. *Auf Wiedersehen Pet* had finished its TV run, and 20-stone Pat made his debut, that day, for the Birmingham Bulls team at Alexander Stadium, Perry Barr. The Bulls were in Britain's top ten in the British American Football League.

The next big match, against Walsall Titans, was reported in the sporting paper *First Down*, 31 May 1986 edition. His weight and fitness made this an ideal sport for him. The paper carried a photograph of him, bearing the caption *Bombs Away*! The article reported that Pat helped to 'bomb the Walsall Titans into submission'. The team went on to represent Britain in the Euro Bowl Competition in Holland that August, but Pat didn't take part. At one time, he wrestled on TV, made a film, and played American Football – all within the space of a week!

In an article entitled *Me and my Body* – *Mail* Wed. 26 July 1989, Pat, in company with models and gymnasts was asked: "What is the secret of health and fitness?" Ms Murray, the journalist, commented: 'He looks in good shape for his age, whatever it is – you do not argue with 6ft, 4 and a half, 19-stone Pat when he fixes you with a warning gaze and says "over 21." '

At that time, he did 500 Japanese free squats every morning, sometimes followed by a run. Weight training, and a few bouts of wrestling each week, and avoiding alcohol, were also part of his fitness program. The article continued: 'His local is more likely to be the cake shop. "I might have a couple of apple strudels and lemon meringues, then I'll go over toThorntons."'

This chapter just wouldn't be complete without including Pat's glamorous wrestling friend of at least 20 years standing – Mitzi Mueller. Nowadays she describes herself as 'a lady of leisure'. A publicity brochure describes her as 'the undefeated British European solo Ladies Champion since 1975.' She has appeared all over the world in places such as Turkey, Italy, Belgium, Sweden, France and Switzerland, and was a noted competitor in tag team wrestling at major venues around Britain and on the Continent.

Pat and Mitzi, whose real name, as opposed to her stage name, is Patricia, travelled the same British wrestling circuit together, for about ten years. Wrestling had always been in her blood. As a young child she was often to be found amongst the spectators at the ringside, watching her father – the wrestler known as *Gangster Pat Connolly*.

For three or four hours every day, her father taught her the wrestling skills that would eventually pay dividends. In 1963 she became a professional wrestler, at the tender age of 14.

"He made me work very hard. I think he was a perfectionist. He said: 'You're going to be the first female wrestler in this country, and I'm going to be proud of you' – and he was." The idea of being one of the first women wrestlers appealed to her competitive spirit. "We didn't have much publicity in those days. I mean, what we could have had now would have been tremendous. So it just went on hard work."

> *Mitzi Mueller, as far as British wrestling 'gels' go, was undoubtedly Britain's Number One all-time female wrestler. She was very beautiful, and I'm sure she still is, had a very nice figure, and could do the job. Usually, you find if someone's got a terrific physique or figure – or they're very beautiful or handsome – they're usually lacking in some other direction. What gets them by is their beauty, or handsomness, their figure or their physique.*
>
> *In Mitzi's case, she had it all. She had lots of, to use a common term, 'bottle'. She had the common sense and the aptitude to keep the boys at bay – in so much that she was held in respect; which is very difficult, if you can imagine, for a woman who's travelling with a load of guys, to do. She was held in a great deal of respect.*

"When I started," explained Mitzi, "there were very few women wrestlers and nobody thought that we could take the knocks, so it took a few years to become established. I had 27, 28 years wrestling. I always looked forward, never looked back. There never seemed to be enough time for me. Because I was born a few years too soon I think. I could have been a millionairess!

"The male wrestlers didn't think we could do as good a job. But I said to them, 'Well, just give us a chance, and at the end of the day if you think we're not doing the job, then come along and tell me.' But by the end of the day, they came along, watched the wrestling, shook my hand and said: 'Well done!'"

She continues to be very well known in the wrestling world. "If someone mentions Mitzi Mueller, they all know me." She quotes just one example among many: "There was an old promoter in Dudley, Lou Phillips; he'd ask me to appear in his shows almost every week." A photograph shows Mitzi and Tina Starr, sporting *California Dolls* sashes.

Mitzi has happy memories of touring with Pat and the other male wrestlers, "who were all nice and friendly to me. It was such a fabulous time. I can never remember Pat eating much food, actually. He always used to be having – I think it was – Complan. It's like dried food. He was always very health conscious. Always."

I asked her about their week's tour of Scotland. "The mileage we travelled was unbelievable – if we'd been paid by the mileage it would have been tremendous. The other thing I particularly remember happened in Ireland. Our mini-bus broke down, and we weren't too far from the hall we were going to. The next thing, an old farmer with an open-backed truck offered us a lift, and we were sitting in the back with a load of cattle. And Pat said: 'I'll never forget this for as long as I live!'"

Of Pat the sportsman she says: "He was one of the best, to be honest with you. He was so professional. He was training every time you saw him: he would never sit still, you know; he was always on the move. I called him the *Gentle Giant*. I didn't think he *really* wanted to hurt them that much. I knew he had to win; he was like myself."

The saying 'The child is father of the man' springs to mind here. The opening part of this chapter described how Pat was never the aggressive type: he never picked a fight. He enjoyed it from a sporting point of view, but he wasn't confrontational or aggressive with anybody – unless he had no alternative.

Mitzi has first-hand experience of this: "He enjoyed doing what he did, but when he hurt his opponents you could see it in his face, that he didn't like hurting people: he always thought about others first. When you see some of the American wrestlers, they seem to enjoy inflicting pain. Pat didn't go out intentionally to break arms, or anything like that."

What was her experience of him at a person level? As this is a 'warts-and-all' biography, she was free to say exactly what she liked. "I've never heard him say a bad word about anybody. He's the sort of person you could confide in – he could keep a secret. There are no warts as far as I'm concerned. As far as I'm aware, there are no skeletons. He treated me with genuine respect." On the other hand, it has been the writer's experience of Pat, and others who've known him for some time, that he often speaks quite bluntly and directly, and won't 'suffer fools gladly'.

Mitzi met her husband, Brian Dixon, a promoter, when he refereed her. It was a memorable introduction. "I was lying down on my back, on the canvas. Brian was counting me out, and stepped on my long blonde hair. I went to stand up – it was really painful, I can tell you!"

Mitzi is multi-talented, with additional careers as actress, recording artist and media personality to her credit. So how did she manage to achieve such success? With regard to wrestling, "It took about a good ten years. You never stop learning – don't let anyone tell you otherwise! I wouldn't believe anyone who tells me that you don't get nervous before going into the ring. I always got embarrassed walking in – nervous."

She would make a grand entrance, sometimes to the accompaniment of her own recording – *Let the Girls into London Town*. This is a really catchy 'rock' number, with a chorus: *Mitzi Mueller the Queen of the Ring*. Despite initial nervousness, she put the adrenaline to good use: "Once I was in the ring, the only person I saw was my opponent."

According to Mitzi, the main quality that a woman needs, to succeed in the wrestling world is, "Having respect for yourself. Although it was a male-orientated world, you'd have confidence in your ability to do the job." In addition to that, "my father was always there with me – he was very supportive, and cheering me on."

How did she deal with the situation where she often travelled in mainly male company? "As you know, men are men, they'd be talking and swearing. I'd give them a 'ladies look'. Usually I'd be the only woman on the coach. Because it was something I wanted to do so much, I made sure that it didn't stand in my way. I never tried to be 'one of the lads', although some women wrestlers did. What always helped was that quite a lot of the wrestlers of Pat's generation, and before, knew my father."

Pat, it is rumoured, can still be found wrestling, to this day. It's hard to find a sport he hasn't tried – including broad sword fighting! He has had many intriguing experiences abroad. In the following chapter, he relates some of these, together with further tales about friends, and other sports personalities.

Chapter Seven –

ALL THE WORLD'S A STAGE

And yet don't look too good, nor talk too wise…

The Master of Ceremonies certainly looked very good, in the tradition of most M.C.'s throughout the ages, as he strutted about in his bow tie, shiny-lapelled DJ and – let's hope – the rest of his suit. The New Zealand audience had come to see the spectacle of me wrestling Johnny da Silva; their M.C. was equally determined to milk the situation for all it was worth! In offering sound advice to the audience, he obviously thought he was 'talking rather wisely' – at this stage of the game.

Chapters 4 and 5 were both concerned with canals. This chapter and the previous one are also a complementary pair – but this time the theme is sport. Chapter 6 was mainly about Pat's sports career and associated friends in Britain; this present chapter describes a selection of his sporting experiences abroad. But I'm leaping ahead of our story. I'll disappear for now, and leave Pat to explain; after all, he was the one who was actually there …

I used to do this thing about pins through my neck. The M.C. said, before the start of the match: "Ladies and gentlemen, Pat Roach will now perform his, whatever, by inserting pins through his neck and into his head." He asked for volunteers from the audience and stressed – "Please do not come up here if you're of a nervous disposition, if you're pregnant, or if you're squeamish."

As the volunteers ambled up, he said: "You're not squeamish? We don't want you fainting. Is there anyone else? We're getting all ladies – there aren't any men – they're all scared!"

They got some more women up, until they had six. "We don't want any more, we don't want you all fainting together – we'll be in a terrible state – carrying them out! Pat will now do this thing about pins in the neck.

"Now ladies and gentlemen you've all heard me say – and I'm saying it to each one of you now – are you sure you will not – are you sure? O.K. Right. Stand there in half a circle. Now, here's the pin. Is it sharp enough? Oh yes – O.K. What did

71

you say, Pat? Oh, Pat said this one's a little bit blunt – it's a little bit hard to get through." Suddenly you heard: thump! And he'd fainted! All the women he kept talking to – and warning – had to pick him up – maybe he was pregnant!

During a visit to Japan, Pat spent some considerable time with a Japanese family, who were fans of his. Having admired his wrestling, in true Japanese fashion, they invited him back to their home. His judo background, and a particular interest in their culture, helped him to feel at ease with them. He also spent time with a Shinto priest, learning the squatting exercise, and a considerable amount of philosophy. I was surprised to learn from Pat that the Japanese originally acquired the art of judo from the Chinese.

When Japan took over China, they formed a Kimmu government, which, loosely translated, means 'government without arms': they didn't allow the Chinese to have any arms at all. So this particular government invented unarmed combat – they invented 'judo' – that's how it came about. The Japanese took it off them. They got the prospective teachers each to learn something special.

They went out among the Chinese and learned these different things, brought them back and formed 15 different throws: three hand throws; three hip throws; three sweeping foot throws; three throws committed with one side turned to the ground – 'yoko' – which means 'side'. The final one was 'metsa' – with your back to the ground; 'wazza' means 'trick'.

During their *Budokan* days Jim White and Pat had already learned about the Japanese way of life, from a book by E.J. Harrison. Its author had been a Fifth Dan in judo, and one of the earliest Europeans to have studied in Japan. It included a lot of Japanese terminology. The Japanese family who befriended him were trying to learn English, and Pat attempted to speak Japanese with them, although it was often difficult to discern what was actually being said.

I'd be saying something like: "Have I said the right thing?" And all they'd ever do was smile at you, show their stainless steel teeth and say: "Hai!" sharply, which means "Yes!" They used "Mushimushi," when they answered the telephone. All you thought you ever heard in Japan was "Hai" and "Mushimushi." So it seemed as though they'd just use those two words – and smile at you!

The thing was, the lady of the house would make an effort. They'd bring me out a plate of rice – specially prepared Japanese food. They'd sit down and eat some chips – like they'd been westernised; the chips were terrible!

You've got to humour the foreigner!

Yes, and you could see that they were just absolutely short of heaving – almost fetching them back up! They'd eat bread and butter and have all these things to please me. And I'd eat Japanese food: it was good stuff!

They must have liked you – to do all of that for you.

They were great; Japanese are wonderful hosts. I would compliment the chef – the lady of the house – on the food. I'd attempt to say how nice her kimono was.

In English, or Japanese?

In Japanese. I'd say to her son afterwards: "Did that sound all right?" And he'd say: "Hai, hai!" I didn't know at this time that they'd say yes to anything, out of good manners. It turns out that I'd say, "You're a very fine cook," or something like that. The book that I learned from, by E.J. Harrison, was probably 30 years old, so he'd learned the old Japanese.

There are about five different languages in the Japanese culture, within the family. The emperor and the empress would each have a language of their own. The head of the house would have a language. A woman would never speak the way a man spoke; therefore she would never speak his language. When you think about it, it would be as if you and I spoke different languages.

Because of the manners – the culture of the times?

The children addressed people in different ways, according to the way each person was supposed to be approached; approaching the father was different from approaching the mother, and so on. So I would pass a comment in old Japanese, and the equivalent translation would be: "Stap me vitals, you're a mighty fine wench!"

Did you slap your thigh as well!

Exactly! Short of slapping my thigh! She'd look at me...

Like someone from another planet!?

Everybody else would disappear under the table, to hide their reactions, as though they'd dropped their chopsticks! Or rather, the knife and fork, because of the food they were eating. So they'd got a good excuse! I'm thinking – what clumsy so-and-sos they were, not thinking that I was 'dropping my chopsticks'.

73

From having people around him collapsing on the ground with laughter, we move on to more high-flying pursuits. Pat's fascinating career, has taken him to the four corners of the globe and back; some of those journeys provide entertaining stories in themselves. Later in the chapter we hear about a particularly hair-raising aeroplane flight in Asia. But the one form of air transport that he avoids whenever possible, is anything involving light aircraft.

When I was in South Africa I got friendly with a family too. A guy called Willie Grov'e- pronounced Groovay. The English equivalent would be Billy Groves.

Like 'Jacques Verte' in French, would be Joseph, or John Green?

*He took me up in his aeroplane: oh my God! I nearly died – it **terrified** me! When I came down, I'd been holding the seat that tight, I'd got a bloody great groove – pardon the pun – in my arm, that was in there for a week; it wouldn't come out – I'd bruised myself. I was terrified! He wasn't doing anything clever; he must have known that I'd have died on the spot – he just went up and down. So much for 'don't look too good'!*

Did you teach Jim Japanese?

We thought we were learning Japanese – we all tried together. When you go to Japan and the Japanese are talking to each other, you won't understand anyway – because they speak their version of English. It's rather like Jamaicans speaking English. You get two Kingstonians speaking English – from Kingston, Jamaica – and it's patois: although it's English you won't understand.

One of the highlights of Pat's international sporting career was during the 1970s, when he was invited to wrestle with Dara Singh, the great 'Rustom-E-Hind' – 'Champion of India'. Dara was a very well respected wrestler for many, many years. He wrestled some of the greatest sportsman, including Billy Robinson and Lou Thez. The fact that Pat was considered a worthy opponent for the champion was a tremendous compliment.

I wrestled him at the Vala Bhai Patel Stadium – I've got the posters here – great big posters, there was one 'lack' of people: one hundred thousand people – a lot of people!

It must have been a massive place!

Tremendous. He was always very much a gentleman – a very clean wrestler, very strong – talented.

Where was the photograph of you and his brother Randhawa taken?

At the Vala Bhai Patel Stadium, in Bombay.

Were the fights 'stage-managed'? Did you know what was going to happen, in advance?

No, the only thing that you could guarantee was that you were going to be spit upon – by the crowd! As you walked out of the ring they always used to spit on you and throw stones at you. There was all that business about their man versus yours.

Did that depend upon whether you won or lost?

No. Win or lose they always used to spit at you anyway. (Gives a mock demonstration of this)! I used to put my dressing gown over my head – or my towel – if they hadn't stolen it by then!

Who generally won out of the two of you?

Dara was definitely the top man. His brother, Randhawa, wasn't quite as good a wrestler as he was. He was a little on the light side.

You and Dara were both heavyweights?

Yes, Randhawa was too. I wrestled Randhawa up in Guhati, which is a restricted area. The first time I was up there, I'll never forget, I sat in the front of the aeroplane where there was more knee room. While we were flying, the whole of the front partition of the 'plane fell in – it scared the life out of me! Got to Guhati and they wouldn't let me in, because you'd got to have a special visa. It was something to do with being on the borders of a very restricted area. I went back, got the right visa, then I went up again. This time I sat in the same seat – in the front – next to Johnny Hayles. I said: "You know, the last time I made this trip the whole front partition of the aeroplane fell in."

John Hayles, aka *Killer Kowalski*, explained that the flights he and Pat took within India, to Guhati, were in two stages: an *Air India* flight from Bombay to Calcutta, followed by the flight to Guhati in a World War II Dakota plane – hence its poor state. History was to repeat itself – this time a plastic partition collapsed on John!

The first time I ever flew up there we hit some bad turbulence – and the 'plane was absolutely full of Muslims. During the turbulence, I remember looking round and seeing the airhostess on her knees, and she crossed herself, so she was obviously a Christian, not a Muslim. It terrified me – seeing this girl cross herself in the 'plane.

Dara had taken a different plane to the fight destination – perhaps he'd taken the Dakota flight before, and knew what was coming! From sport, Dara made the transition into the Asian film world. This was helped considerably by the fact that the North Indian wrestling fans provided him with a captive audience. His first film – *King Kong* – in 1962, was directed by Babuhai Mistry, the 'king of special effects'. It marked the beginning of a highly successful acting career.

Most of his films did very good business for him. Some that warrant a mention are: *Rustom-E-Baghdad (1962), Rustom-E-Rome (1963), and Rustom-E-Hind (1965). Also, Aaya Toofan, Sher-E-Watan, Shankar Khan, and Balram Shri Krishnan.*

Dara produced several Punjabi films, the first being *Nanak Dukhya Sab Sansar.* He gained respectability as an actor by making special appearances in RK films *Mera Naam Joker* and *Dharam Karam.* Manmohan Desai cast him as the hero's father in *Mard*; Amitbah played the title role. Updated details about his film career, verified recently by Dara, can be found in Appendix A, together with an additional section about him.

His screen roles tend to be that of the strong man, but, as the writer can verify, in real life he is a mild-mannered, very perceptive person. Nowadays his work tends to be mainly in television serials. I was privileged to interview him during an engagement-packed, ten-day visit to London, in July 2001, culminating in a special invitation to be 'Chief Guest' at an Asian Festival in Greenwich, four days later. He provided some interesting insights into his experiences with Pat, combined with an up-dated account of his film and television career. Returning to Pat's tour of India, when he and John Hayles 'touched down' in Guhati, more testing times lay ahead. Here he recalls one of several occasions in his life when he 'diced with death':

When I was in Guhati, wrestling Randhawa, I got stabbed.

By one of the audience? Had you won?

I think I probably did – yes. As I was coming out of the ring I felt like a (claps his hands suddenly). Almost like a slap at the side of me. I'd got this thing over my head to protect me from the spitting. If I'd been wearing my dressing gown I might not have got stabbed, because it wouldn't have come through the gown.

I walked for a little while. I remember saying to this big bearded Sikh who was walking in front of me: "Hey, I've just been stabbed!"

Like you do – yes!

We walked out and got into a dressing room. I told the guy in there. He said, "You must have walked into the gate or something." I wrapped this towel round my waist and got into my tracksuit bottoms.

Was it pouring?

There were just big lumps of jelly.

Ugh! Couldn't they see it?

I've still got the stuff from the Medical Centre somewhere: I'll try and find it. They couldn't get me out because there was rioting outside. They were lhati charging and using tear gas. They finally got me out in an armoured truck!

Was that a typical wrestling scenario over there?

*Well, it **was** India. I was with Killer Kowalski again. They took me to the Medical Centre. I remember looking at this room. The operating table was mucky, and stained with blood. The fella told me to lie on the table! By this time, the blood was like lumps of jelly!*

Oh God!

You could lift it up in your hand! It was in lumps at the side of me. I remember thinking: I'll never see old England again! I looked around the room. There was this glass instrument cabinet with tall doors. The kidney-shaped bowls and medical instruments were all tarnished.

I bet you were worried about the instruments they were going to use on you. You'd be thinking – I'll catch something from that!

The white towel was full of blood. I gathered my senses at one time, which seemed to suggest that I was losing them. I looked up and was suddenly conscious that they'd all followed me in from the wrestling! There was a fella there, leaning on his Raleigh bike – I'll never forget, because when I was a kid, I had a Raleigh bike.

They probably though of it as being another part of the show! They'd paid their money and they wanted to see the rest of the spectacle Pat!

It was ever so funny – they were all looking. By now I was stripped off. I'd just pulled my clothes off. All this blood was still pumping out of me!

Suddenly, there was a bit of a kerfuful– and they dragged a fella in off the street who'd drunk the local brew – and poisoned himself. They just left him on the floor there – vomiting and vomiting! They called it 'jungle'; we used to drink it – or 'country'. It was the equivalent of about two-bob a bottle. We used to put 'coke' in it, so that it looked like whisky – and then pour it, and then put more coke in it. Big Bill Varna was there.

John Hayles has provided a photograph of Pat and himself arriving at Bombay airport. He gives this version of events: "I wrestled there several times, but with Pat two or three times. I do have a huge poster advertising a world championship between Dara Singh and myself. Pat is also on this bill. I later wrestled Dara Singh for the World Championship, about two years later in Fiji and I have the bill advertising that too. Pat and I had a lot of trips abroad together, Japan and Germany just to name two countries.

"All that Pat has mentioned concerning the stabbing at this venue is well described. I don't know what was worse for him, the stabbing or the medical attention. We laughed for many a year following this, mainly about the Raleigh cycle in the 'operating theatre'."

John mentioned Germany as one of several countries where they have toured together. It is undoubtedly one of Pat's favourite wrestling venues. His German adventures, together with many other friendships he has made over the years, during international wrestling tours, would fill several chapters. But that will have to keep.

Chapter Eight –

WRESTLING WITH KUBRICK

If you can dream and not make dreams your master
If you can think and not make thoughts your aim…

Who would have dreamt *that a person like myself* (laughs) *an ex-rag-and-bone-man – a coal merchant – entrepreneur-come-what-may, would work with someone who was such a master of his craft, as Stanley Kubrick?*
    Many actors would give their right arm to have worked with Kubrick – as I did – and not just once – but twice.

If you can think and not make thoughts your aim…
I used to call him 'boss'. I think he found it amusing, for some reason.

As this chapter unfolds, the reasons for the rapport between Pat and Stanley become clearer. They worked together on two films. In *Clockwork Orange* Pat had a very minor role, while in *Barry Lyndon* he played the more substantial role of Toole, the bullying sergeant.

Despite his many talents, Kubrick had a reputation for manipulation and control. His friend since the Bronx days and fellow film director, Alexander Singer, explains this trait. "… control is the essence of cinematography. Control is also the essence of what filmmakers are about, they want to control the universe."

In *Stanley Kubrick A Biography*, published in 1997, John Baxter gives examples of vitriolic exchanges between Kubrick, and observations about him – some more favourable than others – from his actors. Gene D. Phillips, in *Major Film Directors*, refers to the friction between Kirk Douglas and Stanley, when they worked together on *Spartacus*. As the star and producer, Douglas, combined with the scriptwriter and executive producer, was in a powerful position. Phillips explains that it was the only film over which Kubrick did not have complete control. This strengthened his resolve to maintain artistic independence in all future films.

Vincent LoBrutto's biography, *Stanley Kubrick* reveals a hitherto unknown side of the director. Through many interviews with those who knew him both privately and professionally, he shows a much more amenable and sensitive person than the image often portrayed by the media.

Pat is a great admirer of Kubrick, but in terms of personality is very much his 'own man'. However, in common with actors such as Steven Berkoff and Philip Stone, his professionalism enabled him to remain unflustered, and to meet Stanley's exacting standards.

Early in life, Pat encountered people who were adept at manipulating and controlling situations. His dominant father was a case in point, with some of the 'Summer Lane Mob' and his stepfather coming a close second. Despite the stressful nature of such experiences, there were three positive outcomes. Firstly, it taught him to 'empathise' with other people – a rather overworked term these days, but in this case appropriate – to put himself in their 'shoes'. Secondly, he developed a certain degree of emotional toughness or detachment. He also learned to adapt by playing his own 'mind games', when the situation demanded it.

Pat's infectious sense of humour, described by Jim White as 'terrific', was one of the personal characteristics that proved particularly useful. Combine this with an inordinate capacity for hard work, which would please Kubrick, and an almost uncanny instinct for making a quick-fire assessment of an individual's personality, and you are well on the way to discovering some of the factors that have contributed to Pat's success.

During an interview with the writer, Pat's friend and fellow actor, Kevin Whately, explained this talent for diffusing situations very succinctly: "In the nicest possible way, he looks for people's weak spots and winds them up about them – in a very good-natured way. He has a huge laugh; we'd be helpless with giggles for a lot of the time." Pat's account of his relationship with Kubrick indicates a subtle and slightly more complex version of this approach.

> *He used to smile when I called him 'boss'. My interpretation of that, from what Stanley said to me, is what I think he was all about. I may well be wrong. As people comment, he was a very complex person.*

What exactly do you mean by that?

> *On a Kubrick set things could be described as ' very tense' – I'm sure they were. But I think that Stanley had what, for want of a better term, could be called an 'Achilles heel' of humour; where if you reached him, or if you reached his Achilles heel, you could break him down very easily – and he would smile. I think I just found that little niche, where it was.*

Roger Caras, who worked for Columbia Pictures, told Piers Bizony, "Stanley's secretive, a very private person. But he has a really wonderful sense of humour when he's relaxed with some – and, of course, he has this absolutely insatiable curiosity."

British critic and writer Gavin Lambert, Stanley's assistant and friend, also confirms Pat's observations about the director's sense of humour, in relation to a scene in *Barry Lyndon*. He describes it as: "his wicked, humourous side coming out. "There's a lot of that character in Stanley. Not the defeated Barry, but the fuck-the-world Barry." It's possible that the rapport that Pat sensed between himself and Stanley could have been due, not only to the fact that the two men shared a sense of humour – but, more importantly, because it was of a similar type!

> *Perhaps it was also my attitude towards the film industry. I never considered myself an actor, and it wasn't until I got with the 'Auf Wiedersehen Pet' boys, that I learned anything really about acting. I was always professional about earning money, of course. I never saw myself as the sort of person who would work without good remuneration: I don't want to give the impression that I wasn't professional **that** way.*
>
> *I got on well with everyone; we all trained together; I used to do people's backs and legs. David Tomblin, the First Assistant Director, was a tremendous person; he helped me get into the movie and to learn the business. I was probably more relaxed about what I was doing all of the time – that may be what it was, because I was possibly one of the few people who **was** relaxed, in his presence.*

He may have taken his cue from you, in that sense. It was probably quite a relief for him to adopt a more relaxed approach, albeit briefly.

> *Yes, perhaps it was reciprocal. Bear in mind that I used to walk around the set, quite often, with Tatum O'Neal on my shoulders; she'd be drinking a cup of tea and wearing my tricorn hat! I suppose there was some sort of rapport or endearment between Stanley and myself.*

During his schooldays Stanley was no academic. Like certain other highly creative individuals, mainstream schooling failed to recognise and promote his special talents. At Taft High School he was considered to be an under-achiever, with less than acceptable grades in Dependability, Courtesy and Cooperation. Later, he mastered those skills. Motivated by his art as a film director, he developed great strength of character and leadership qualities.

As LoBrutto explains, he also commanded great respect from those who worked for him. Boxer Vincent Cartier said of him, "He commanded respect in a quiet, shy way. Whatever he wanted, you complied. He was a very sincere, low-key person. Some geniuses boast about themselves, but he doesn't."

Baxter describes Jack Nicholson, Kubrick's star in *The Shining* as 'a warm but wary admirer'. Malcolm McDowell, who starred as Alex De Large in *A Clockwork Orange*, 'the archetypal hymn to urban violence', in the 1970s, said of Stanley, "If he hadn't been a film director, he'd have been a General Chief of Staff of the US Forces. No matter what it is – even if it's a question of buying a shampoo – it goes through him. He just likes total control." Kubrick admired McDowell's acting abilities, having seen him in *If*. He is quoted as saying that had Malcolm not been available he probably wouldn't have made the film.

Central to Kubrick's unique genius for creating films lay painstaking talents for choreography and attention to detail, combined with an acute insight. Images of Roald Dahl's BFG spring to mind – *The Big Friendly Giant*, as he trawls the darkened streets, collecting dreams and trapping them in bottles. Film directors, however, are on the manufacturing side of the 'dream' business. Genius or otherwise, superimposed over anything they may wish to create is the inevitable overlay, or colour filter of pre-conceived ideas of the world, which every viewer brings with him. So no two viewers ever see *exactly* the same end product. The creative process, when it combines with any branch of the media, inevitably becomes more complex; no wonder it takes a genius to excel!

> *Stanley's ideas reflect how **everybody's** mind works; he's telling you – in this case me – that he knew how everybody's mind worked: he had an insight. Stanley was involved in every little thing: he never handed anything down to anyone – he did it all. He **was** a genius, and having spoken to me, as you have done, over several months, you must realise how a lot of my philosophies are in there.*

Kubrick was born into a largely white middle-class area of the Bronx, on 26 June 1928, the eldest son of Jacob Cubrick, aka Jacques E. Kubrick. The family was sufficiently wealthy to live in a house, rather than an apartment. His parents were both children of Austrian immigrants and had two dissimilar, opposing personalities. Recent studies show that such a combination of parents is more likely to produce a genius, rather than two highly intelligent parents within a harmonious relationship.

Buying the expensive film rights for *Clockwork Orange* reduced the budget for everything else, particularly casting. Having already decided that Malcolm McDowell should play Alex, Kubrick cast some of the best British actors in the caricature roles, who were keen to be involved. The full cast list, as with *Barry Lyndon*, can be found in Appendix C.

Two exceptions to this were people who became celebrities, but at the time were 'unknowns' – at least as far as acting was concerned. The first of these was David Prowse as Julian, the body building nurse to a crippled Patrick

Magee. He was demonstrating exercise equipment in Harrods when Kubrick spotted him. The second was Pat. A Birmingham newspaper article later reported that Stanley recruited Pat for *Orange* after seeing him in the wrestling ring.

> *The first time I came across Dave Prowse was when we were both in 'A Clockwork Orange', although we never really met. Later, I attended a dinner for the retirement of the Sports Editor of the Sunday Mirror, where I did a wrestling thing and Dave did a weightlifting demonstration, which I was very impressed with.*
>
> *Thirdly, we both auditioned for an Italian bar of chocolate commercial. I got the job, with Julian Chagrin who was a mime expert. That was about it. Dave was British Weightlifting Champion at the time. He was too pretty. They wanted someone big and ugly like me for the job!*

According to Pat, Dave holds seminars and, at the time of writing, the two men continue to meet annually at wrestling meetings. In a *Sunday Times* article, celebrated sci-fi writer, Arthur C Clarke CBE, a great admirer of Kubrick's, and the scriptwriter for *2001*, described how he returned to London in 1999 to the National Film Theatre, for a special print of the film, as a tribute to the director.

Baxter describes Kubrick as "… a man both sensitive and ruthless, petulant and generous, who adulates reason, but whose films can reflect the wildest excesses of passion, and who above all is ruled by a relentless need to place his personal vision on screen."

In a *Sunday Telegraph Newspaper* article by Chris Hastings, 6 February 2000, Kubrick's widow, artist Christiane, expressed a different view of her husband. "Stanley is so gentle, such a shy and sensitive person." She refutes the accusation that her husband was a recluse or an ogre. "He just wasn't very keen to talk about himself or his work to the media. Stanley always thought that his films should speak for themselves."

While researching a documentary, she recently discovered substantial screenplays dating back more than fifty years, written by Kubrick during his teenage years: keepsakes rather than actual projects. They include crime thrillers and war movies and are significant because film historians and fans have previously only been able to access a limited amount of the director's recorded work.

Of *Orange*, Christiane says: "It is undeniably a very powerful film which does contain some violent scenes." She qualifies this, however, by explaining that such scenes are: "stylised and in context. I think it is a very good film."

Pat recalls the experience of working with Stanley on both films.

I gleaned a lot from speaking to him at great length. He used to meander over to me and we'd chat. People who worked with him would actually leave him alone if they saw that he was engrossed in conversation with someone – because he didn't want to be interrupted. If he didn't want to speak to you, he wouldn't: he'd be doing something else.

A Clockwork Orange, made in 1971, was Pat's first experience of working in films. He had little to do: "… just stand around: I was little more than an 'extra'. They sang a hymn in German – and I reacted to that." One of the stills, taken on set by Christiane's brother, Jan Harlan, shows Pat in his role as a bouncer at the Korova milk-bar, which is the opening scene of the film. Alex and his gang are drinking Milk Plus, surrounded by models of nude women. John Baxter describes this scene as being 'suffused with sex'. It was one of three sets that were built inside a warehouse, located just a few minutes away from Borehamwood. Among the other actors in the photograph is a young Warren Clarke, now of *Dalziel and Pascoe* fame, who played the role of Dim.

In Anthony Burgess's novel, upon which the film was based, written when the author mistakenly thought that he had a brain tumour, he gives no precise details about the Korova. Kubrick and his young set designer, John Barry, created a 'temple to sexual consumerism'.

The unfortunate thing about movies is that things get left on the cutting room floor – which is what happened to some of the stuff that I did; they always shoot forty minutes too much. If you haven't got an important part, which I didn't have, this could substantially reduce the time that you actually appeared on the screen.

Did you have any idea when you were working on the film that it was going to be such a significant landmark?

The truth has to be, no I didn't. Because I've always been of the opinion that we're 20 years behind America, I could foresee that there would be some kind of different recognition of the film, but could never foresee that it would last that long.
I thought that like all films, it would just be around for a while – then cease to be in demand. I don't think anyone could ever have predicted its longevity.

Kubrick's films are full of symbolism. According to Baxter, 'Sex in Kubrick's films is never between loving couples. Rather he explores, as did Mickey Spillane, the furtive and violent side alleys of the sexual experience: voyeurism, domination, bondage and rape.' Pat took all of this in his stride:

84

The eroticism, of course, is part of all our lives – is part of everything. The giant penis was merely an extension – pardon the pun – of Cat Lady. What is Cat Lady? A 'pussy' – being American vernacular for a woman's vagina. So there was this hidden message about the giant penis and the pussy. And those who could see it saw it.

*For those who didn't see it, it didn't matter. There was, in Kubrick's movies, **always** a second, or even a third dimension, in what you looked at. As with Spielberg: you could look at Spielberg's movies, and every time you watch one, you realise that there is a little more to be seen – if you look – hard and long enough, with enough varying interest in what you're looking at.*

Alex Singer, after shooting stills for one of Kubrick's earlier films, *Fear and Desire*, described him as "an absolute perfectionist". The perfectionism was "an obsessive thing, and has nothing to do with commerce." Perhaps that's why Kubrick made so few films? Years later, Pat discovered at first-hand, by watching the master at work, "the amount of care that went into every shot."

One of the most impressive things for me was when Marisa Berenson was in the bath, and she had a lace thing over her upper body, so that you didn't see her semi-naked. It was the most beautiful thing, because there's nothing more beautiful – is that the right word? Alluring – is that the right word? Than a sexually, partially clothed woman – and Kubrick captured that.

That's like his approach to *Lolita*, isn't it – tantalising?

I never saw that. That for me is more appealing than just the naked form, although I appreciate the naked form for what it is. But sexually, there's much more allure in the semi-clad body.

Kubrick favoured the visual side of cinema, as opposed to dialogue: "If you have them by the eyeballs, their hearts and minds will follow." 2001: A Space Odyssey proved a defining moment in futuristic films.

The voice-over became one of Kubrick's favourite narrative devices. Alex provides the commentary in *Clockwork Orange*. In *Barry Lyndon*, Michael Hordern's Narrator gives a weary but articulate rendition of Thackeray's thoughts.

Stanley abandoned the use of Cinemascope and developed his own equipment, including a wheelchair with an adjustable seat, for smooth, low-angle tracking shots in tight corners. Eventually this became a common option for camera operators. Pat explained: "There's no such thing as a second unit shot with Stanley!"

85

Warners released *A Clockwork Orange* in New York just before Christmas 71 and in Britain on 13 January 1972. Kubrick retreated behind the high gates of Abbots Mead, emerging only to go to Borehamwood. For more than a year after its release, the film continued to excite comment and controversy on both sides of the Atlantic. Early in 1974, Warners and Kubrick privately agreed to withdraw it from distribution in the UK, but to make no public announcement of the fact. It was allowed to quietly fade from sight. This secret agreement didn't become public knowledge until 1979. Following Kubrick's death, it was re-released in cinemas, nationwide, from 17 March 2000.

Pat played a more demanding role as Toole, the bullying sergeant major, in *Barry Lyndon*. The film, made in 1975, has a theme found in most of Kubrick's best work: that human error often results in unfulfilled goals. In both *A Clockwork Orange* and *Barry Lyndon*, the principal character appears in all the main scenes, while the supporting cast revolve around him – rather like satellites around the sun.

Jan Harlan, Stanley's brother-in-law, and Executive Producer of *Barry Lyndon*, has kindly allowed us to use some of his stills. One photograph worth a special mention shows Pat with Stanley's daughter, Vivian. It is a perfect illustration of a point made later by Kevin Whately, that Pat relates particularly well to children.

As with all Kubrick films, *Barry Lyndon* is based upon an existing story, with photographic elements such as composition, space, depth and light holding centre stage. Through his main character, Redmond Barry, played by Ryan O'Neal, W.M. Thackeray's tale, an autobiographical account of an Irish rogue's life, unfolds. We follow Barry's progress as a soldier, deserter, gambler and lover. He climbs the society ladder, only to descend once more to petty gentry.

Stanley produced a basic 243-page script, discarding some of Thackeray's most outrageous coincidences, and introducing many linking scenes – some of them eccentric. A good example of this is the 'Big Man/Small Man' scene of Toole versus Barry. Pat explained that when considering Kubrick as a director, it's important to define the parameters within which he was allowed to work. "In *Barry Lyndon* I was allowed to do my own ad-libbing. In reality, this meant 'doing your own thing', within the realms of what Stanley wanted."

Ken Adam worked on production design, albeit with some reluctance. He was concerned that Stanley's approach might stifle the instinctive part of his own creative process – "something you can't intellectualise."

Stanley would have preferred every location for *Barry Lyndon* to be within driving distance of his home. In the autumn of 1973, however, he was obliged to begin filming at Ardmore Studios in Ireland, near Dublin, because Thackeray's story was partially set in Ireland, and there were more authentic 18th century houses available.

So how did your role fit into all of this?

Well, as Barry's flicking over all these potatoes – doesn't want to eat them – Toole can see what's going on, and decides to make fun of him. He says something like: "Isn't that to your satisfaction?" Lyndon doesn't say much, so he says: "Give him a basin of turtle soup and a napkin!" (In a mock-cultured voice). Of course, it's not funny, but everyone has to laugh, because if they don't laugh they get a thump off him.

Why did you use that cultured tone of voice?

It wasn't Toole's natural dialect, because he was a lout; he was 'speaking posh'.

Being sarcastic?

Yes, and as he does this, he laughs at his own joke, looks around to make sure that everyone else is laughing at it, there's one of the soldiers sitting by the side of Barry Lyndon, who whispers out of the side of his mouth: "Ask him about the old fisher-woman." (who was his wife – who makes him do something).

He repeats what the soldier says – shouts the insult at Toole, whereupon Toole jumps up and the fight's on! Everyone gets in a big circle and they pair off. They go into this fight scene. When one of them falls back into the circle, it momentarily becomes bottle-shaped.

In *Stanley Kubrick – A Narrative and Stylistic Analysis*, Mario Falsetto, Associate Professor in the Department of Cinema, at a Montreal University, gives a detailed analysis of the director's major films. He describes Pat's red-haired, brutish character and emphasises the importance of the hand-held camera, rapid montage and close-ups in this fight scene, as devices for communicating Barry's momentary sense of freedom.

Pat, as one of the two protagonists, is able to give a firsthand account of events. Given the opportunity, Professor Falsetto would probably have been delighted to hear his version of the proceedings.

I held the camera first of all in my right hand, and then threw long left-hand jabs, which Barry would have ducked. Then we'd change hands and I'd hold the camera in my left hand – a little higher – to do the right-handers. Then Stanley cut into the left and rights. So the camera appeared to be fighting Barry Lyndon: it actually had arms!

Roy Scammell, who was only up to my shoulder, was brilliant at the job: one of the foremost stuntmen in the business – Chairman of the Stuntman's organisation or union. For a whole week he and I – and credit to Ryan O'Neal – he used to come with us, ran for miles and we did press-ups. We used to do about a seven-mile run. 70 press-ups were about as many as I could do. O'Neal could do a few more than me. He was a good runner – and boxer too. He was very fit. Obviously, without making excuses, I was never a 19-stone runner – there's no such thing!

O'Neal's abilities as a sportsman were not always apparent from his screen image as the hero. Baxter found that he portrayed Lyndon's naivete well, in the earlier stages of the film, but described the more debauched side of Thackeray's character, as 'beyond his powers'. However, through training with the star, Pat discovered another, more 'gutsy' side of O'Neal.

He was very much into boxing at the time and was 'game as a pebble'. He could throw a punch, and knew what he was doing. We ran through the fight, for a whole week – Roy and I, where we threw these punches, did this, did that. Of course, we knew that scars and cuts would appear – and to cover the fact that it was a bare fistfight, our fists would get bloody, and fists against teeth – all that sort of thing. We even talked about scars, because it was a bare fistfight. Not many people know about this type of fighting.

Stanley's wisdom in providing ample time for Ryan and Pat to become better acquainted resulted in a trust and mutual respect, which survives to this day. This proved crucial for the fight scenes that were to follow.

When it came to standing there and throwing punches at each other – a 19 –20-stone man throwing big right-handers at you – you've got to have a little bit of confidence! I mean at one stage, Ryan hit me 'fair and square' crack! He stood and looked at me – you know? I mean, Harrison did the same thing – stood and looked at me!

But I just went on as if I hadn't been hit at all, because I didn't want to spoil things for the camera. That actual blow didn't mean anything, because, funnily enough, that was at a time when I went back into the crowd, and they threw me back in. Then he sidestepped me and gave me a last big punch – which he hit me with. I went down from it: it was the finishing punch.

Pat may initially have been offered the role in *Barry Lyndon* because Kubrick preferred to use reliable actors he'd previously worked with: a less time-consuming approach. Patrick Magee, Leonard Rossiter, Philip Stone and Steven Berkoff also fell into this category.

Stone, who played Graham, identifies nerve and patience as two essential prerequisites for Kubrick actors. "You've got to keep calm – no use losing your 'bottle'. He seems to know with the inner eye exactly where he's going."

Berkoff, who played Lord Ludd, explains, "Kubrick was articulate and communicated with everybody. He would encourage people. He wasn't dictatorial, dogmatic, aloof, he was a human being." Whilst conceding that he was slightly obsessive, he adds, "he was deeply human about his work, about his actors and totally accessible." The more minor roles were chosen by proxy, using a video.

> *I think Stanley must have asked for me, and I saw James Liggat who interviewed me for it and did the video. I just did the one recording. He said: "Do you want to do it again?" I said: "No, that's it – send that." Then I got the job.*

I wondered how Pat had felt, after meticulous planning and practise, when Stanley told him that Toole would never land a blow? I was particularly curious after reading Gavin Lambert's account of Stanley's "battery of psychological games." These have included "abrupt changes of mood during filming, or the demand for some enigmatic or obscure change to the script." Sounds familiar. I couldn't help wondering whether Stanley had employed similar tactics in Pat's case!

Why do you think Stanley didn't warn you in advance about the outcome of the fight – or did he not *think* to?

> *The thing about Kubrick is that once he picks you for the job, he knows that you can do it – otherwise he wouldn't have picked you. So there's a 'Catch 22' there. Having done so he then says to the stunt co-ordinator: "Roy, show me what you've got."*
>
> *The stunt co-ordinator, in his opinion the best, showed Kubrick what he had – having been picked by David Tomblin, who is the best. They had picked me – in their judgement, the best person for the job – looking, as I did a little on the 'big bully' side. Then they said: "Here's the man you picked; this is what he's going to do with your man." Stanley just shook his head and said: "Well no, he isn't. Toole does not land a blow. Our Barry Lyndon is a scientific, deep-thinking, fighting machine."*
>
> *In fact, he deflates the bully quite easily. Sure, I still threw all the punches, and still did all the movements, but Barry's head wasn't there: he wasn't on the receiving end. So in actual fact, nothing was wasted. I couldn't believe that it would work on a serious note – but it did. The more time I spent with Stanley – I was there quite some time – the more I grew to appreciate and respect what he was doing.*

LoBrutto explains: "When Stanley approached something he demanded to know all the choices before making a decision. It was his way of sending the message that he was in charge. Stanley didn't like to answer questions that he didn't want to answer just yet – in fact, he liked to be the one that asked."

In conversation with LoBrutto, Gay Hamilton, who played Barry's cousin Norah, described the frustrations of filming the Irish dance scene between herself and Leonard Rossiter, as Captain Quin. "We did it perfectly many times, but Kubrick continued to shoot take after take. I think he was letting us do it until we were doing it carelessly, like we'd been doing the dance all our lives." Philip Stone refers to this unrelenting method of Stanley's as "looking for the x-factor."

He used Leonard Rossiter in the film as a very serious person; it was the first time that I'd ever seen Rossiter in a very serious part. He plucked him from all the comedy he was known for and in 'one wave of Kubrick's magic wand', turned this comedy actor into a very serious, un-likeable character.

In *Reggie Perrin*, because it was a comedic 'send-up' of a serious situation, you could see a little of the serious side of him.

Possibly, I never thought of it that way. I always saw it as a comedy situation. Then, when you see Rossiter playing Quin, it was just tremendous; he really turned him round. Seeing the end product of a person that I'd spoken to. Not fully appreciating it at the time, but realising afterwards how very special Stanley was.

One particular practice session gave the *Garda* a few headaches, but provided Pat with an entertaining story afterwards!

The funny thing that happened was that we were working on an industrial estate or park that had just been built. Stanley had a massive wardrobe there; he dressed many, many hundreds, probably thousands, of people.

We were practising the fight scene and I was beating Roy Scammell, who was only up to my shoulder – knocking nine bells out of him and battling. All of a sudden, two Garda cars screamed up and came to a halt. Out jumped these two policemen, because somebody from one of the offices had reported a fight!

Of course we were doing it on the grass, outside the unit. As they were running towards me, I turned round to the policeman and shouted: "It's OK officer, the little guy gets his own back in just about..." As I said "just about", Roy started to go into the second sequence, where he ducked my right hand and then threw some punches into my stomach and I went "Ooh!" Came forward, left-crossed and straightened me up; threw another right-hander and proceeded to knock nine bells out of me.

By this time, the policeman had taken the last eight paces, the fight had completely turned round, from me battering the little guy, to the little guy getting his own back. As he arrived at the scene, the policeman broke into a broad grin and said: "Ah well – that's all right then!" Then stopped and watched the little guy continue to knock nine bells out of me. At the end of it all, when I was flat on my back and knocked out, they all laughed, clapped and cheered, jumped into their cars – and went.

Pat broke his toe on one of the line of pegs that was set out. At one stage some of the grass was painted green. It took about two years and two major shutdowns to make Barry Lyndon. It seems to have been a stressful time for many of the crew. According to John Baxter, Ken Adam became very ill.

I only worked on it for four months. The story was, at the time that Stanley spent his entire budget just on the wardrobe, preparation and research – that's the first time that he shut down. There were at least two heart attacks during the filming.

It was such a beautiful, beautiful film. It mesmerises me when I see it – although possibly I should have used another word. 'Barry Lyndon' is a film that, unless you've seen it, you can't quite grasp what I'm talking about. It was the first film where they ever shot a scene past the flame of a candle, without the glow of the flame interfering with the shot. Kubrick imported a special lens from the German 'Zeiss' company, originally developed by NASA – for photographing the instrument panel of a spaceship.

*In that movie, we walked onto French guns in exactly the same style as the British army did it. It's the most **amazing** experience you could have – taking the place of the person in front of you, who's gone. You've got to try and imagine someone shooting at that red line of soldiers – through smoke – and never seeing it change! Because if you hold two sticks up, in a perpendicular position, 20 feet away, you would hardly know that one wasn't just six inches in front of the other: you wouldn't know that they weren't level. So what happened was that the guy behind stepped into the man's position when he fell – and I experienced that, in that film.*

Baxter considered the film to be a prime example of Kubrick's view of 'a world under rational control'. Had you any idea, when you were making the film, that Stanley was trying to achieve that kind of effect?

No – not at all. You only saw the perfection of what Stanley was doing at that particular moment.

So you didn't know what the Game Plan was? Just the section you were doing?

Yes. At one stage, he had something like 400 men in a line. He wanted them to all step forward at the same time. They spent days trying to get them to do it, because when they beat the drum in one particular place, the sound would carry at a different level, and they couldn't get the lines to step forward at the same time.

91

So in the end they arranged half a dozen guys, with sticks held at 12 o'clock, and they all watched a guy, stood behind the line, who dropped his stick. As he dropped his stick, they dropped their stick and the whole line stepped forward. So it was a reverse focus thing – their cue was really taken behind them.

After three weeks, Hardy Kruger took over the role of Captain Potzdorf, from Oskar Werner. He is a Prussian who blackmails Barry into becoming a spy. Pat and Hardy became good friends.

We had the same sort of 'triangle' together. Hardy wasn't into training, or anything like that. He knew that I was going into Germany and that I liked Germans. We talked about Germany a great deal. He talked to me about Bogart and Bacall, who were his best friends. We went to a cinema in Ireland one day. We paid 2/6d each to sit upstairs in a cinema and we'd bought identical macks. I think I left mine there. It's a very hard thing to do – find clothes to fit me – off the peg. The film that was on was 'The One That Got Away'. He was the star of the film and no one even recognised him! We just used to be together – talk together.

Pat explained that Hardy lived in Kenya. Sadly, he eventually died. I wondered what type of person he had been, in 'real life'.

He was a 'loner' – very serious and intent on the German thing during the war – about the Nazis. He felt very badly about the Jewish thing. It was so many years ago. We talked about various things. He was very quiet – a very focused actor.

Was he, perhaps, a bit of a perfectionist?

Everyone who worked with Kubrick had to be. They had to be able to 'produce the goods', because they weren't around that long. No big deals about Hardy: we were just friends for that particular time. We just exchanged a few stories. He was very interested in the fact that I'd wrestled all over Germany. We talked about Berlin, Dusseldorf, Hanover – all over. I've got friends there – in Hanover, and have kept in touch with them for over 20 years.

During interviews, several people mentioned the intensity of Kubrick's eyes, particularly during discussion. In LoBrutto's book, Jonathan Cecil describes them as "searchlight eyes".

There's no doubt that he had very deep brown piercing eyes, but they never disturbed or perturbed me in any way at all. Collectively, what mesmerised me was the end product of what I saw.

While filming *Barry Lyndon*, the director invited Pat to the dinner party that we mentioned in *Any Old Iron*. So much for Stanley being a recluse and unsociable!

> *It was in the hotel. Stanley had a house there, in Ireland, which was very heavily guarded, because of death threats. I was invited to sit round the table. He told a couple of stories about this fella named Dick, who later turned out to be Richard Nixon. I think I used to make them laugh, because I'd tell them stories about what I used to do; and tell them the truth about things. They found me amusing – telling stories about wrestling.*
>
> *Godfrey Quigley, the Dublin actor, played Captain Grogan. The two of us had some great boozing sessions together. He was a big theatre man. I worked with Leonard Rossiter again in the film of 'Rising Damp'. We used to exchange a lot of funny stories. He liked to talk about the wrestling; he'd 'take off' the walks of all the wrestlers, and we talked about Big Daddy, Giant Haystacks, Kendo Nagasaki. I was Oliver Reed's favourite wrestler; Leonard's was Wayne Bridges – he thought that he was a fine athlete. He used to watch wrestling a great deal.*

In September 1974, the private press reviewed the film. Several critics attacked the graphic stillness. LoBrutto, however, provides a contrasting picture: "Kubrick's loyal coterie were glad to see him back." He quotes several published letters. "Stanley Kubrick: Proof that there are living geniuses." Another referred to him as "... a cinematic Shakespeare. And I think he knows it." He was also described as "the most innovative person to touch motion pictures since Thomas A. Edison."

Barry Lyndon received several Oscar nominations, and won for art direction and cinematography, best adapted score and best costumes. It was one of Warner Brothers biggest box office grosses internationally, but not in the United States. However, according to LoBrutto, "... reevaluation has positioned *Barry Lyndon* on international best films lists."

At the age of seventy, Kubrick began to receive tributes, including life achievement awards, medals, doctorates, master classes and honorary Oscars.

A fitting conclusion to our chapter on Kubrick, and Pat's association with him, could not have presented itself in a more timely fashion. On Sunday evening, 9 April 2000, BAFTA awarded him a posthumous British Academy Fellowship, which was received by Christiane. She couldn't resist making the point that, had he lived to see such a day, running true to form, he would probably have asked someone else to accept it!

Fifteen months later, in July 2001, Christiane and her brother, Jan Harlan were in Los Angeles, touring the film festival circuit. On this occasion, however, they were there to promote their *own* film: *Stanley Kubrick: A Life in Pictures*. The film's purpose is to dispel the negative images, and show the accessible, loving side of Stanley. Shortly afterwards, it was televised by *BBC 2*, on three consecutive evenings. Pat has no doubt about Stanley's generosity.

> *Stanley called me into his VW Combi one day and said: "What are you doing afterwards Pat?" I said: "Well I don't know. I'm going to Berlin to wrestle, and then I'm going to LA." Whereupon he said: "Where are you staying in LA? I'll make a couple of calls for you." I told him I was staying at the Flamingo Hotel, on Ocean Boulevard – and thought no more of it.*
>
> *Sure enough, all those months later, he was true to his word. Stanley was a very sensitive person, contrary to what some people might say. He'd made the phone call and put me in touch with the feature film casting director at Burbank Studios – Alan Shane – a prime example of the type of man he really was.*
>
> *He also put me in touch with the best agency in Los Angeles. That went pear-shaped because the guy he got in touch with was leaving the agency and setting up by himself, but is now the biggest agent in Hollywood. But Stanley still took the time to do that. He was a **very** sensitive man. I owe a lot to him.*

Returning to the present, Kubrick's 90-page treatment of Brian Aldiss's *Super Toys Last All Summer Long*, was recently taken over by Spielberg, who was ideally place to do this. Jan Harlan revealed that the two directors had previously worked together on the project. After searching Stanley's offices, Jan and Christian provided Steven with notes, notebooks, and over 1,000 drawings. Spielberg re-wrote the script, following Stanley's basic structure. The result is *AI – Artificial Intelligence*, which has already broken box office records.

Chapter Nine –

THERE'S ONLY ONE THING BETTER THAN A GOOD FIGHT

If you can meet with Triumph and Disaster
And treat those two impostors just the same…

If we talk about triumphs and disasters, sometimes you wonder what a triumph and what a disaster is. For instance, I was driving along William Street one day, which is just behind Broad Street. I forget which car it was – probably something you'd give about 20 quid for, knowing me. Out pulls a taxi, without looking what he was doing and 'crunch!' – I hit him.

So we both pulled over and the taxi driver was terribly upset and I said: "Don't worry about it." "Oh," he said, "what am I going to do?" This and that and the other – insurance, and time. I said: "Well your vehicle's still driveable, isn't it?" He said: "Yes." I said: "Well follow me."

So he followed me down to the yard, whereupon I sold him a bonnet, a bumper, a radiator, a grille and two headlights. So I turned a disaster into a triumph – immediately! I drew £240 quid off him; about half past nine that morning I'd got my day in. What a triumph that was! We were shooting Gangsters at the time, for BBC Television.

This chapter is about Pat's film career, together with some of the fight sequences, stunts, techniques used and lessons learned. The films in question exclude those involving Stanley Kubrick, Bond, Indiana Jones and those made for television, which have chapters of their own. Further details about the films covered can be found in the Film Chart at the end of this chapter. To cover all of the films listed would take a second book, so we have selected a few of the most memorable.

Initially, Pat regarded acting simply as a new challenge. He doesn't view the undoubted physical discomfort he's endured, as being solely related to his chosen career: "That's not part of acting – it's part of life." In time, he grew to enjoy all aspects of creating a character, including the use of disguise, but adds the proviso: "Any sort of make-up's uncomfortable."

95

Bear in mind that I've done my share of the three-and-a-half to five-and-a-half-hour make-up session and eight other people to work you. Wouldn't it be easier to walk on stage, having just changed your trousers, shirt and socks? Portraying a character in this way would be much more demanding upon me. I would prefer to do it unaided: nothing technical – no 'high-fallutin' data. Timmy Spall uses a phrase: 'grown-up acting'. He doesn't talk about it much now, because he does all 'grown-up acting'. But many years ago he didn't. It's where you get up on the stage and you have to be really serious for 90 minutes.

Taking each of the films shown on the Film Chart, in alphabetical order, Pat found *Clash of the Titans* a particularly interesting film to make, not least because of the distinguished cast. Ursula Andress, Lord Olivier, Maggie Smith, Jack Gwillim – a great Shakespearean actor who went to America – were all in it. Claire Bloom played Hera, Zeus' wife. Burgess Meredith took the role of Ammon, a poet and playwright of Joppa. Although he didn't like to tell him so, Burgess was one of Pat's favourite actors. *Clash of the Titans* was made in 1981 at Pinewood film studios.

Ursula Andress was cast as Aphrodite and Maggie Smith as the mother of cruel Calibos, mischief-making Thetis, who pitted her wits against Zeus – Laurence Olivier – throughout most of the film. Flora Robson played one of three Stygian Witches who shared a single eye. Sian Phillips was vain Queen Cassiopeia, with Judi Bowker as her daughter, Andromeda. Susan Fleetwood played the role of Athena. Pat was cast as the skilled blacksmith god, Hephaestus: "As the character was immortal, I didn't get killed." Quite a relief considering the number of times, and variety of methods by which he's come to a sticky end, in other roles!

I made the magic clockwork owl that Zeus' son, Perseus, took with him. They showed the blacksmith making the owl. I was one of the gods, but I didn't have a major part in it. The young actor who played Perseus was Harry Hamlin.

Harry starred in *LA Law* afterwards. Lord Snowden took a photograph of Pat and Ursula together. Pat explained, "His assistant set it up."

In *Conan the Destroyer*, described in our *Foreword*, by Arnold Schwarzenegger, Pat played the evil wizard, who inhabited the Crystal Palace. One particular photograph shows red-cloaked Pat in this grotesque role, one eye obscured and a sword sticking out of him; the angled close-up reveals how the sword effect was achieved. As Arnold explained, Pat also played two other roles: Goran, the half-apeman, one of the wizard's other guises, and Dagoth, the horned monster in the temple.

Conan II, as it was otherwise known, was made in 1983, in a studio in Mexico City. It included a rather dramatic episode where Pat flew across a lake at night to abduct the heroine, while her companions slept. According to Pat, "I've got a photograph somewhere – they sent me along a wire." Vic Armstrong elaborated: "It was a body harness and flying wire. Pat had to act as if he had no wire and was really flying, which is the secret of selling it to the audience." When Arnie entered the hall of mirrors, the wizard transformed himself into Goran.

> *There was a complete circle of mirrors and in the centre of the room were six guys working cameras – and you couldn't see them. The guy who shot it was Jack Cardiff. The funny thing was that at the time I'd got the script for 'The Last Place On Earth' with me, in which I was playing Evans. I'd got the tape with me, where John Mills played Scott and James Robertson Justice played my part.*
>
> *I was looking at the script and wanting to be looking at the tape, but couldn't play it over there. Trying to get as much information as I could about the original film. I left there and found five minutes to think about looking at it, only to discover that the person who shot the film was Jack Cardiff – the same guy who was shooting Conan. And I didn't know – otherwise – we used to lunch together in the same restaurant, and I could have been asking him all the relevant questions.*

In a conversation between Vic Armstrong, Pat and myself, at Pinewood Studios, they described some of the difficulties they'd experienced during the making of the film, particularly in relation to stunts and fight sequences, an area in which both men excel. Vic and Pat have a long history of making films together.

> *Then of course there was Gracie Jones – with the spear. There was a square patch on the back of the monster. Vic told her what to do. Without going into too much detail, she was a bit erratic. She picked the spear up the wrong way: instead of picking it up like you would – in the middle where you've got control – she picked it up at the end.*
>
> *So because of the lack of control, she just about caught the patch at the edge and went straight through the monster's costume. Then Arnie grabbed the sword and I'm inside again. As he said, he almost severed my head. I thought, bugger this – another near miss!*

Vic described a sparring incident between himself and Pat, while they were making the film. "Pat and I used to spar every day, on *Conan*, down in Mexico." I was reluctant to ask who came off best!

"I got a little graze under my eye that turned black: a real shiner! Just caught it lightly. Got back in the office. They were saying: "Oh dear me!" All these girls falling over me. 'Oh dear me!'" Later, Pat elaborated on this:

As you know from the 'Foreword', Arnie, Vic, Dolph Lundgren, Grace Jones and myself, all used to train together. Of course Arnie was hell-bent on his weights. Dolph used to do a bit of both – so did I. Vic wanted to learn a bit about boxing. I'd already taught him stuff about wrestling for 'Indiana Jones 2 – Temple of Doom' – because he actually did a 'drop kick' when we did that movie. Credit to him, he really got into that, very, very early. We did this sparring: I taught him how to hit a bag, a glove, and then how to hit with a right-hand. I used to make him do 'left-hands' with his right hand behind his back, and then 'right-hands' with his left hand behind his back – and to duck. I taught him all sorts of things.

Anyway, this one particular day, we were exchanging punches and I knicked him and caught him: gave him a little black eye. The next day on the set, all the girls were buzzing around him and I'm stood there, and this most beautiful girl – about six foot two or three – saw Vic's eye and went up to him. She made such a big thing about it – making a pass at Vic – and Vic wasn't having any of it anyway.

We later learned that she's an ex-model who's bought property and moved to Acapulco – now she's a very wealthy girl. The funny thing was that as she showed Vic all this attention, I stood there and said: "Hey, it was me who gave him the black eye!" (Repeats this) – like a big spoilt child who wants all the attention. I should be getting all the attention, because I'm the one who did it! But, credit to Vic, anything I showed him – about boxing, judo or wrestling – he used to take to it 'like a duck to water'.

It seemed strange to hear Pat talk about training Vic; he's such an accomplished stunt coordinator, that one tends to forget that there *was* a time when he had to acquire various techniques from other experts.

One of the nicest moments while we were there, was when Vic heard that he'd got the job of doing the first of a series of Stallone movies – the Vietnam guy Rambo: the character who takes over a whole town and goes into the jungle. I said: "Come on, I'm taking you into town to celebrate." This was in Mexico City. Like – 'big deal' – you know?

It wasn't a hamburger then!

No. We sat down and had this lovely dinner, and we had a waiter in a one-to-one situation. He did salads and our sweets – crepes.

Flambé?

Yes, and I made such a big deal about buying him dinner – and it came to six quid! I felt such a dope! Of course Vic knew how cheap it was – but I didn't!

I should think Vic would see the funny side of it though, wouldn't he?

> *I thought it was going to come to about an hundred quid – instead it was six! I remember going there at night and eating lobster until it came out of our ears; the bill came to about thirty quid; as many lobsters as you wanted to eat – unbelievable!*

Vic was also stunt coordinator for the fantasy adventure, *Red Sonja*, released by MGM in 1985, starring Brigitte Nielsen in the title role and Arnold Schwarzenegger as the male lead. Pat played Brytag – Keeper of the Key to the Gate. Although it was normally a pleasure for Vic and Pat to combine their talents, this particular film could so easily have ended in disaster!

"We did *Red Sonja*, that night sequence, when Arnold fights everybody." Turning to Pat, Vic elaborated: "And you were the toll-keeper. He'd got this big coat on and bearskin, on a huge bed and he was like the King of Bavaria. Arnold and the gang had to pay a toll to go through there. Well Arnie had a couple of his mates there: Sven – and the other guy – Eric: real lovely guy – but not too smart! So we'd got this fight scene and all Pat had to do is sit on the bed and sit up and roar a couple of times. So he'd got to be there for continuity – a bit boring for him to be lying there, waiting, waiting."

"So Eric can't get his sword fight right. And I'm saying: 'Go blob, blob, blob, and then a big one: use your arms!' He said: 'What d'you mean? Like this?' And went 'whop' into the bed where Pat was lying, spread-eagled on the bed – right between the legs, with this huge broadsword! All you saw was this broadsword go 'whop' and Pat goes: "Aagh!" (Roars)

"He thought it was just a bearskin on the bed – absolutely incredible! Poor old Pat was doubled up. We couldn't stop laughing! It was a horrible moment – he nearly cut you in half, didn't he?" The two men laughed, as they recalled the incident, although it could hardly have been funny at the time. During later discussion, Pat revealed that the *precise* details were even more hair-raising!

> *Vic got that wrong. What had happened was that Red Sonja had already dispatched me – she'd killed me. So I'd collapsed on the bed like that – (mimes) – and I'm dead.*

So you'd got to lie absolutely still!

> *Yes – dead. We had this terrible sword fight and she dispatched me. I had some genuine chain mail on -- it was a good job I did!*

So he actually hit you. I thought from Vic's description that he'd fortunately just missed you!

No, he hit me with his effing broadsword!

Red Sonja was also interesting from a technical point of view. One of the scenes was shot in some famous caves, just outside Rome, a location that had been used in several other films. It was only by using a tremendous amount of lighting power that they were able to shoot the day sequence. According to the film credits, the company supplying the lighting was *Arco*.

> *Because of the movement of the sun, the shadows would have been moving all day. So they started shooting at midnight – and lit it to daylight. The shadows never moved because the sun didn't move, did it? The amazing thing was, it was the blackest part of the night, where it couldn't get any blacker, so that the light wouldn't change. Quite an experience.*

"Is it a bird? Is it a 'plane? No, it's Super Roach!" Cinema audiences of 1983, watching *Superman III*, could be forgiven for thinking that they were seeing the real thing, in the shape of Christopher Reeve. But it was Pat at his versatile best, playing the anti-hero side of Clark Kent. But to do it, he had to embark on a crash diet.

> *'Superman' was very interesting because I played the baddie Superman and the baddie Clark Kent, which I've got photographs of, of course. What happened was I'd got the club in Town at the time. When I went down for the 'try-out', they put me into his clothes and I couldn't get into them. I couldn't do the boots up or anything.*
>
> *So I got back to Birmingham, trained very hard and lost all this weight to the extent that the girls that worked for me used to mop up the rubber mat while I was training, because there was so much sweat.*
>
> *When I went back for the actual film, I found out that they'd tested me in Superman I's clothes. After that first film he trained and got bigger and bigger. So I'd lost all that weight for nothing! He was bigger in the second and third films – and that much heavier.*

Although Pat doesn't have a favourite film role from those mentioned in this chapter – "The truth is – I don't know, because they're all different roles" – he makes special mention of the star of *Superman*: "I have very fond memories of Christopher Reeve. I wore all his clothes: I know what a big fine man he was."

One of Pat's most recent films, *The Big Man*, was made in 1990 and starred Liam Neeson and Joanne Whalley-Kilmer, who played Neeson's long-suffering Scottish wife. Ian Bannen and Billy Connolly also played key roles. Pat and Joanne had already appeared together in the film, *Willow*.

The central theme of *The Big Man*, set in working-class Glasgow, is the hero's struggle to restore his dignity and sense of purpose; unfortunately he chooses the barbaric sport of bare knuckle, or bare fist fighting, to achieve his objective. Pat had first-hand experience of this sport as a young man, on the boxing booths, and subsequently in the *Barry Lyndon* fight scene between himself and Ryan O' Neal.

Pat appears near the beginning of the film, as one of three characters who arrive one night in a Bentley, outside the local pub. He plays the role of Billy, Bannen's henchman, who helps to provoke Leeson into fighting mood, by insulting one of his friends in the pub. In keeping with the role, Pat is required to use very coarse and explicit language – Rabbie Burns it ain't! Scottish actor, George Rossi, the chauffeur who drives the Bentley enjoys a much higher profile these days as D.C. Duncan Lennox, in *The Bill*.

The main fight towards the end of the film is particularly harrowing – definitely not for those of a nervous disposition. Pat explained that when it was staged for the crew's family and other guests, it was so gruesomely realistic that several people were unable to stand it at close quarters and walked out.

To return to a lighter and more fanciful setting, *The Spaceman & King Arthur* was a Walt Disney film, made in 1978/9. It was a multi-million pound movie, made in the early stages of his film career, shortly after the two Kubrick films. True to his usual screen image, Pat played the court torturer, which was a non-dialogue part. Sheila White recalls that he was required to use various noises, such as grunts, instead. As with the other films included in this chapter, it is an experience that holds very special memories for him.

It was lovely for me, because that's when I met Sheila White. We became pals and still are – and I stayed at her house. At the time she was going out with a Swiss photographer fella, Yvon Dorval, who enlarged the photograph downstairs – the big one of 'The Clash of the Titans' – and we all became very friendly. We used to go to the Newcastle Races together, because we were all living in a place called Wideopen in Newcastle. We stayed in the Holiday Inn. That's where we were making the film.

For years afterwards I used to go and stay at their place and I'd help him with his car and different things. I remember at the particular time teaching him silly little things about the English language, and we came across the word 'deal'. I tried to explain to him that you can have a deal, miss something a great deal, there was a wood called deal and how to deal a pack of cards. I was trying to explain the different ways you can use the same word, and how complicated the English language was.

We were very friendly; he was a lovely man. They parted company after a while. At one time he used to run Sheila from London to Yorkshire, almost every day – or something ridiculous. He had a Jaguar. Sheila's got a family – two or three children. Married a lovely man in London – an impresario – Richard Mills. They own theatres.

Part of the film was made at Alnwick Castle in Northumbria. Pat worked alongside Kenneth More, who played King Arthur, Ron Moody as Merlin and Disney favourite Jim Dale. Chapter 12 focuses in more detail on film personalities who Pat met during the course of his career, and those who became particular friends. They include some of the cast of this particular film.

In 1980, Pat excelled in the horror stakes – forgive the pun – by playing a vampire uncle. The film was *The Monster Club*, starring those doyens of the blood-curdling tale, Peter Cushing, Donald Pleasance, Christopher Lee and Britt Ekland.

During the 1980s and 90s, he played four different kinds of role in a variety of Robin Hood films. The first was in the *Zany Adventures of Robin Hood*. George Segal played Robin to Pat's Little John. It was filmed at Shepperton Studios. A long time afterwards he played a good-natured Lithuanian giant, by the name of Jarn Saxa, in *The New Adventures of Robin Hood*. His character's name was a play on words: it had originally been intended that John Saxon should play the part! In 1991 Pat charged into battle as the Celtic Chief in *Robin Hood – Prince of Thieves*.

In a more recent version of the film, he played the amiable giant's highly unpleasant twin brother, Archaos, aptly named, as he left a chaotic trail wherever he went! Appearance-wise the change in character was tremendously subtle: the obnoxious giant had his hair parted on the opposite side! The original, elaborately constructed model village had been retained, and was once again put to good use.

At one time, seven different versions of *Robin Hood* were being produced – and Pat had parts in three of them: Little John, the Celtic Chief – then Little John again. If anyone sees him strolling around *Brum*, dressed in a rough tunic and sandals – and carrying a hefty-looking stick – please let us know!

In February 1988, an article in the Birmingham press announced that he had a key role in a Hollywood movie entitled *Willow*. It was described as 'an excellent film' and Pat was referred to as 'a Hollywood heavyweight'. George Lucas was the producer and the director was Ron Howard – Richie in *Happy Days*. It cost £30 million to produce.

Unsurprisingly, Pat played arch-villain, General Kael – pronounced Kale – the sordid queen's right-hand man. The role gave Pat an ideal opportunity to display his considerable range of combat skills. In a major battle scene, towards the end of the film, he seems almost unstoppable!

Assistant Producer Nigel Wooll said: "It is a fantasy picture set in no particular time and no particular place." It was scheduled for UK release in the first week of December 1988. Leading actors in the movie were Val Kilmer from *Top Gun*, as Madmartigan, and Joanne Whalley, in the role of Sorsha, the evil queen's daughter. Joanne played Carlotta in *The Singing Detective*.

The film featured a castle, which had to be built three times, because of the complexities of filming in New Zealand, Wales and London. The story of the making of *Willow* continues in Chapter 12, and involves some very precarious moments! Security and safety precautions on the film were particularly tight.

In New Zealand, because it was under snow, for safety and insurance purposes, none of the premier artists were allowed to travel anywhere, unless they were in a 'four-by-four' car. We went everywhere by helicopter. 'Willow' had its Royal Premiere in London; by then, Joanne Whalley had married Val Kilmer. We had a party at the Waldorf Hotel in London.

Pat first met stuntman Roy Alon on a film called *Gangsters*, filmed alongside the Birmingham canals. The BBC called Pat in to handle some stunts.

I had no idea – it was very early days for me. I wasn't a stunt co-ordinator at all. I met Roy again on other films. One in particular was the 'Willow' film, where he played one of my soldiers: one of my immediate band of thugs. We did a scene where he had to climb a gate. He ran to a moat gate, dived onto it and it lifted him about 12 or 14 feet into the air. Just before it closed, he had to drop off and fall correctly into the moat, then do a complete turn in a very small distance – very good.

Which all goes to prove, as the title of our chapter suggests, there is only one thing better than a good fight, and that's a good fight – or stunt – sequence!

FILM CHART – EXCLUDES KUBRICK, BOND, INDY & TELEVISION:
(with the exception of 'New Adventures of Robin Hood – Andy Armstrong) which was filmed for television.

In alphabetical order

Title	Director	Producer	Role	Date	Studio
Clash of the Titans	Desmond Davis	Charles H. Schneer	Hephaestus blacksmith god	1981	Pinewood
Conan The Destroyer	Richard Fleischer	Dino de Laurentiis	Dagoth, the half-apeman – Goran, & the Evil Wizard	1983/4	Mexico
Kull The Conqueror	John Nicolella	Raffaella de Laurentiis	Zuleki	1997	Universal
Red Sonja	Richard Fleischer	Christian Ferry	Brytag, Keeper of the key to the gate	1985	Rome
Superman III	Richard Lester	Pierre Spengler	'bad' versions of Superman & Clarke Kent	1982/3	Pinewood
The Big Man	David Leland	Stephen Woolley	Billy	1990	Scotland
The Monster Club	Roy Ward Baker	Milton Subotsky	Vampire uncle Uriah	1980	ITC/Chips
The Portrait Of A Lady	Jane Campion	Monty Montgomery & Steve Golin	Circus Strongman	1996	Polygram Propaganda
The Return Of The Musketeers	Richard Lester	Pierre Spengler	Org the Executioner	1989	GB/France /Spain
Robin Hood – Zany Adventures Of	Ray Austin	*	Little John	1984	Shepperton
Robin Hood – New Adventures of	Andy Armstrong	Fred Weintraub	Jarn Saxa Lithuanian	much later	Lithuania
Robin Hood – Prince Of Thieves	Watson, Densham, Lewis	Kevin Reynolds	Celtic Chief	Morgan Creek 1991 Production	
Robin Hood – New Adventures of	*	*	Archaos – wicked twin of Lithuanian giant	2000	Lithuania
The Spaceman & King Arthur	Russ Mayberry	Russ Mayberry	Court Torturer Oaf	1978/9	Disney GB
Willow	Ron Howard	George Lucas Nigel Wooll	General Kael	1988	England, Wales, New Zealand
Wings of Fame (starring Peter O'Toole)	Otakar Votocek	Laurens Geels Dick Maas	German spy	1989/ 90	Netherlands

Note: Where the studio location is unknown, the name of the distributor is given.
Dual dates: made/released. * = Information unavailable.

Chapter Ten –

BONDAGE IN PINEWOOD

If you can bear to hear the truth you've spoken
Twisted by knaves to make a trap for fools...

What truth did we ever see in a James Bond movie? Most of the fight scenes are not true to life, because a normal person wouldn't, for example, recover almost instantly from being thrown six feet across a room, then come back for more, the way that Bond always does.

Bond films work to their own unique formula. Cubby Broccoli and other members of his production team used the term 'Bondian', meaning 'in the spirit of James Bond'. The characteristics of the genre have followed a predetermined pattern, which began to take shape with the making of the first Bond movie, *Doctor No.*

There are, of course, exceptions to these Bondian rules, but generally speaking, the main characters tend to be played by the same actors and the leading lady is often a relatively unknown actress. Audiences expect an array of 'high-tech' gadgets, but no great acting. Dialogue contains frequent pockets of innuendo and even the most evil characters possess a potent brand of sexual charisma or twisted charm. Things that would normally seem ludicrous in other pictures receive a sympathetic laugh in Bond films. The plots and characters are often wildly outlandish, breaking every cinema convention that ever existed – but still, the crowds of cinema-goers keep coming back for more.

In a similar vein, *Never Say Never Again* had a feeling of *déjà vu* about it, right from the opening shots. Irvin Kershner, the director of *Never Say Never*, was the first American ever to direct a Bond movie. He had previously worked with Sean in *A Fine Madness.* Pat met him again when he walked onto the set of *Temple of Doom*, during a particularly tricky situation between Harrison, Pat and a very famous female star; readers will have to wait until Chapter 13, to discover exactly what happened next!

Pinewood Film Studios have been the home of the Bond movie for many years, from 1962 to the present day. In June 1999, Pat arranged a visit to the studios, where we had a working lunch with his friend and colleague of thirty years, Vic Armstrong. Vic is one of the foremost stunt coordinators to have worked on the Bond and other movies, including a more recent Connery film, *Entrapment*, with leading lady, Catherine Zeta-Jones.

A later part of this chapter explores the personal and professional relationship that Pat and Vic have built together over the years. Then in the next chapter, Vic reveals more about his career. He and two of his production staff also describe their collective involvement in the making of the latest Bond film, *The World Is Not Enough*, which they were working on during our visit.

Pinewood studios are among the most famous in the world. Situated 20 miles west of London, they occupy a 96-acre site at Iver in Buckinghamshire, originally a large area of parkland belonging to a country house called Heatherden Hall, later known as Iver Hall. A photograph taken by the writer, shows the elegant gatehouse entrance, now occupied by a security guard, rather than a sentry, who checks visitors as they drive in. Entry is strictly by prior arrangement. Unlike some of the studios in the States, Pinewood is not open to the general public: Pat and myself were Vic's guests for the day. He kindly allowed us to see some early 'rushes' of Pierce Brosnan's motor boat chase through London's dockland area.

The filming of this boat chase, together with ski sequences in Chamonix, was later covered in a series of three documentaries, televised on consecutive days by *Carlton*, during Christmas 2000. Vic, together with other members of the production staff, and Pierce Brosnan, featured prominently. They included some of Vic's comments, on location, while the film was actually taking shape.

The 007 stage is just one of 18 stages, producing feature films, commercials and television shows. It also houses the largest outside water tank in Western Europe, used in earlier Bond movies and very recently in *The World Is Not Enough*, for an action scene on a Caspian Sea walkway.

In Rachael Low's book, *Film Making in 1930s Britain*, the author traces Pinewood's colourful history. It was first registered in August 1935, as a £150,000 company, in the name of *General Film Distributors*.

British Cinema History, published in 1983, contains a series of chapters, written by experts on various aspects of the subject, edited by James Curran and Vincent Porter. In Chapter 12, *The James Bond Films: Conditions of Production*, Janet Woollacott takes a rather cynical view of production of the first Bond film, *Dr. No*, 1962, describing it as 'an example of the increasing exploitation of cheap film-making facilities in Britain by Americans, attracted by the conditions of the Eady Levy and favourable exchange rates.' She highlights a problem that, almost 20 years on, has only marginally changed – the British Film Industry's lack of a sufficiently large home market to support stable and permanent film-making. This pattern of large-scale investment by American production companies continues to the present day.

Pinewood films rejuvenated by the Bond cult included the 1976 version of *The Avengers*, recently remade, Stanley Donen's *Arabesque*, with Gregory Peck and Sophia Loren, *Kaleidoscope*, *The Quiller Memorandum*, *When Eight Bells Toll* and *The Mackintosh Man*. Vic Armstrong was involved with two of these: *Arabesque* was the very first film that he worked on; the re-make of *The Avengers* is one of his more recent projects.

Vic explained: "I wanted to be a jockey – my dad trained racehorses. I started racing then – when I was in Hampshire. I was 14. Then we moved here and there was a stuntman called Jimmy Lodge. Funnily enough his daughter, Janine, is a production co-ordinator on this now. A little four-year-old thing she was when I first met her.

"He used to ride exercise for us. At the same time, I knew the people who were supplying horses for the film: Johnny Rocks – he's dead and gone; it's his grandsons who are doing it now; they've got a truck out here today – still painted the same old maroon colour. I used to drive horses for him to the sets – just as a groom.

"But the other connection was Richard Todd, who my dad used to train horses for, and I used to ride them in races for him. I'd go and watch his movies when I was a little kid. So I was always interested in the movies, and always fancied being a stuntman, for some reason or other.

"Anyway, it all flipped around and one day this stuntman who was riding with us borrowed one of my horses, to do a jumping sequence for a film called *Arabesque* in '65, with Stanley Donen and Gregory Peck. They had trouble riding it. So I went down the next day – and that's all I've done from then on. That's 34 years ago. It was a cottage industry when I started, but has grown to equal anything that America can offer."

Canadian, Harry Saltzman and the American, Cubby Broccoli, very shrewdly acquired the film rights to the Bond novels, the only exception being *Casino Royale*. At the same time they persuaded *United Artists* to back the enterprise. The Bond films, representing just a handful of major international films made at Pinewood during the 'sixties, continued to have a British base until 1980. Most of the locations, for *Moonraker*, for example, were in the USA and elsewhere; only the special effects were produced at Pinewood.

The continued success of the series, combined with the facility for a permanent base at Pinewood, produced a team of highly skilled experts. This team has continued, with a few changes, to work on the films for several years.

Pat and Vic first met in Arundel, in Sussex, by the River Arun, about 30 years ago. "I well remember it because we used to live down there originally. I was living in Farnham Common in those days. I never lived in London." Pat recalls giving him a lift back home.

They actually met when Pat was working on a Ridley Scott commercial. "Gabby Howard was my agent at the time – she got me the job. I had to go down to Sussex, which was fine, 'cause I used to live down there.

"They were doing this commercial for whisky – for Japan. It was a buy-out wasn't it? So I met Pat and we got talking. He was dressed as a big Scotsman, tossing his caber. It turned out they wanted him to throw me!

"So we were practising this, you know, crossing my ankles and lifting me up, and throwing me into a stack of hay and all that stuff, which we re-created many times since: *Never Say Never Again, Temple of Doom* – into the trolley."

One of the most memorable fight sequences of Pat's career was in *Never Say Never Again*. It was also one of his longest, lasting about six minutes. Connery was 51 years old when the film was made, but still fit enough to give Pat a 'run for his money'. The old charm didn't fail him either. The general opinion at the time was that maturity had enhanced his appeal: women found him more attractive than ever.

There are several similarities between Sean and Pat's respective backgrounds. Despite the fact that they were playing fictitious characters, and leaving aside Pat's obvious height advantage, in certain ways they were well matched.

Both grew up in very deprived areas of major cities, becoming street-wise, almost from birth, and learning to live by their wits. In addition, both left school at an early age in order to earn a living, became boxers in their teenage years, sought to improve their physique with body building, and delved into the world of nightclubs, or dance halls, as they used to be called.

Being accustomed to mixing with entrepreneurs, albeit on a fairly small scale, each of them eventually became an astute businessman in his own right, with an acute sense of the value of money; how to make it, but above all, keep it! The circumstances of their background produced two individuals with a steely determination to make a name for themselves, combined with a talent for self-preservation. Both men are known to be very hard working and, where necessary, very single-minded.

Two recent biographies about Connery were published within a year of each other. Both share the star's name as their title. The first, by John Parker, was published in 1993, the second is by Michael Freedland – 1994. Taken in tandem, the two books provide a very detailed picture of the life and times of an individual who, in 1990, was dubbed: 'the sexiest man alive'.

Sean's big break came in 1962, when he created the original Bond role on screen, in *Doctor No*, the first of seven portrayals of the character, spanning 21 years. Eventually, as Freedland explains: 'it became a monster

Pat with Miss World 1967/8 (Miss Peru), at the 'Silver Blades', Pershore Street, Birmingham.
Pat was her bodyguard: "I got locked out during the 'there's a big wrestler' episode."
PHOTOGRAPHER THOMAS SUMMERTON, EDGBASTON. BY PERMISSION OF RANK GAMING DIVISION.

Pat, throwing an opponent. Does anyone recognise Wayne Bridges in this picture?
PHOTOGRAPH BY JACK BANNISTER.

Mitzi Mueller, the 'Queen of the Ring', with fellow wrestler, Tina Starr.
BY PERMISSION OF BRIAN DIXON, 'ALL STAR PROMOTIONS', BIRKENHEAD.

Pat prepares to execute the final stage of his famous 'Brummagem Bump'.
PHOTOGRAPHER UNKNOWN.

Pat used 'mind over matter' techniques to insert pins into his face. The beard is real. Definitely not for the squeamish!

Judo expert Jim White and Professor Frank Ryder, seated in Pat's Piccadilly Arcade gymnasium, during its heyday, in the 1980s.

Jim White and Howard Green, curator of the Avery Historical Museum, in Foundry Lane, Smethwick. They are standing in front of Murdock's cottage. PHOTOGRAPH BY SHIRLEY THOMPSON.

Pat with 'Killer Kowalski'. Johnny had witnessed his friend's stabbing two days earlier. Pat's hand is covering the wound, which gave him problems later that evening.

Pat and 'Killer Kowalski', aka John Hayles, arrive at Bombay Airport.
BY PERMISSION OF JOHN HAYLES.

Pat holds Randhawa Singh, Dara's brother, in an arm lock at the Vala Bhai Patel Stadium,
Bombay. BY PERMISSION OF DARA AND RANDHAWA SINGH.

Pat takes a second row seat, having taken the precaution of reserving the first two rows!
PHOTOGRAPH PETER WILLIAM.

Pat winning the World Heavyweight Wrestling Tournament, Hanover, 1976. Pat describes his opponent, Axle Dieter, as, "The finest example of a professional you would find anywhere in the world." PHOTOGRAPH PETER WILLIAM.

Pat in wrestling mode - Nechells Community Centre in the 1970s. He was working on Gangsters at the time. BY PERMISSION OF NORMAN FLETCHER, VICTORIA STUDIO, BIRMINGHAM.

Dara Singh of India, as a young wrestler. During a recent London interview he recalled having wrestled Pat on four occasions: "In Bombay, Guhati, Canada and Birmingham." BY PERMISSION OF DARA SINGH.

Dara Singh and Shirley Thompson, during a recent London interview.
PHOTOGRAPHER PAUL MANN SINGH, BY PERMISSION OF DARA SINGH.

A recent photograph of Dara Singh.
BY PERMISSION OF DARA SINGH.

Looking for a fight! - From Barry Lyndon
By permission of Jan Harlan/Kubrick Estate, Ryan O'Neal and Norman Mitchell's agent, as Norman, is now, sadly, deceased.

Found One! - From Barry Lyndon

Pat discards the bullying image of Toole for a few minutes, to practise a judo balancing exercise with the director's daughter, Vivian Kubrick - to help her with her dancing. By permission of Jan Harlan/Kubrick Estate.

A Clockwork Orange: Pat, dressed in white, poses as a bouncer; in the Korova Milk Bar. Seated on the far left is a young Warren Clarke (Dalziel and Pascoe). Malcolm McDowell has his feet up. BY PERMISSION OF JAN HARLAN/KUBRICK ESTATE.

Doreen and Pat on the set of Red Sonja, 1985. Pat is dressed in full regalia for his role as Brytag, the Keeper of the Gate. PHOTOGRAPH BY MARK ROACH.

"I see no ships!" Pat as the evil wizard, one of his three roles in Conan the Destroyer.

Pat, with Vic Armstrong on familiar ground: the Bond studio lot at Pinewood. PHOTOGRAPH BY SHIRLEY THOMPSON.

The elegant gatehouse entrance to world-famous Pinewood Studios. Shirley and Pat were Vic Armstrong's guests for the day, as he put the final touches to the stunts, for The World Is Not Enough. PHOTOGRAPH BY SHIRLEY THOMPSON.

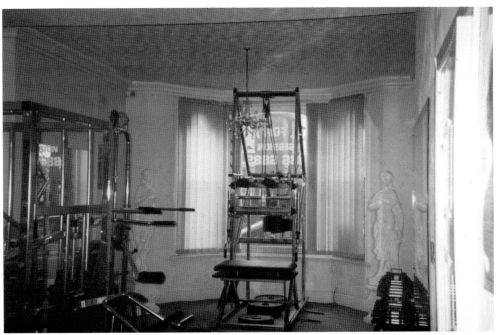

The Bond machine, on which Count Lippe attempted to crush Bond in 'Never Say Never Again'. Pat purchased it for his gymnasium, replacing the bench with a black leather, multi-function exercise pad. PHOTOGRAPH BY SHIRLEY THOMPSON.

Vic Armstrong, Doreen and Pat in the Kendo Gym in Rome, during the making of Red Sonja, 1985. They are holding Sheini sticks, which Pat and Vic used to practise their sword fighting. PHOTOGRAPH BY MARK ROACH.

Doreen and Wilt Chamberlain on the studio lot of Conan the Destroyer, in Mexico, 1983. Wilt is over 7 foot tall and was the first basketball player ever to earn over a million dollars a year. According to Pat: "He was the most well known guy I've ever walked shoulder-to-shoulder with. Everyone in Mexico knew him." PHOTOGRAPH BY MARK ROACH.

Pat met Sheila White while filming The Spaceman And King Arthur, in 1978. Their friendship lasts to this day. BY PERMISSION OF SHEILA WHITE. PHOTOGRAPHER YVON DORAN.

'Happy Days'. BY PERMISSION OF SHEILA WHITE. PHOTOGRAPHER YVON DORAN.

Pat with his family, in Dressing Room 6, at the Birmingham Hippodrome, following a performance as Little John in Babes in the Wood. From left to right are Dolly, Freda and Pat's step-brother, Pete Meakin.

Looking suitably uneasy, in the Sheriff of Nottingham's chair, used more recently in the Lily Savage Show.
BY PERMISSION OF IAN SANDY.

"Is it a bird? Is it a plane? No, it's Super Roach!" Pat plays the anti-hero side of Clarke Kent, Superman III, 1982.

'Raiders' Stuntmen – Group Photograph. Standing from left to right are Paul Weston, Billy Horrigan, Rocky Taylor and Sergio Mioni. Seated from left to right: Terry Leonard, and stunt arranger Glen Randall (Junior) – both from the USA. Peter Diamond is kneeling.
PHOTOGRAPH BY ALBERT CLARKE.

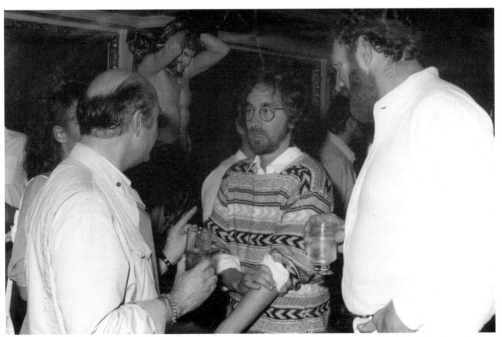

Steven Spielberg, Pat, and his agent Peter Charlesworth enjoy a quiet drink at the Camden Palace, London. BY PERMISSION OF STEVEN SPIELBERG AND PETER CHARLESWORTH.

Raiders Of The Lost Ark: a typical stuntman – hiding his face! By permission of Billy Horrigan, who saved Pat's life in the blazing bar scene.

Billy Horrigan, relaxing between takes, on Last Crusade. He also worked with Vic and Pat on The Spaceman And King Arthur.
BY PERMISSION OF BILLY HORRIGAN.

Pat, wearing his Indiana Jones jacket. To the best of our knowledge, only three were ever awarded. PHOTOGRAPH BY SHIRLEY THOMPSON.

that threatened to consume him. Connery spent the next decade trying to release himself from Bondage. In the 1970s it seemed that Connery would never emerge from the wilderness – but he staged a spectacular recovery unique in the annals of showbusiness, to become, in his sixties, more bankable than ever.' He won an Oscar for his role in *The Untouchables* and has probably played a wider range of roles than any of his contemporaries. On the 5 July 2000, Sean received a much-deserved knighthood from the Queen, at Holyrood House, for services to British Drama, having made a total of 69 films.

Parker makes the point that the Bond role inscribed on film history 'a film character who, more than any other, has influenced the modern male personality.' Pat is unequivocal in his praise of the 'man behind the screen image'; not only through playing Count Lippe, in 1983, in *Never Say Never Again*, but from other experiences. He and Sean spent approximately three weeks filming the fight scene, together with friend and colleague Vic Armstrong, Connery's stunt man, who was also stunt co-ordinator on the movie.

> *Although I've been in four different films with Connery, I haven't worked with him four different times, but I've spent time in his presence. I spent a lot of time with him, obviously, on the Bond film. Despite what little I've heard about him in a derogatory sense, I found him very much a man's man – a straight-talking person.*

Designer Ken Adam confirms Pat's view, adding, "They liked the fact that there were no frills about him." He also found that Sean would fight the corner of any member of the cast or crew, if he thought they were in the right.

At one stage the producer just cleared off to the Bahamas, so Sean had to take control, but did his best to hide the problems from the rest of the cast and crew. Pat explained: "We all knew that some crap was flying. It didn't affect his performance – obviously."

Parker reveals Connery's behind-the-scenes view on all of this: "Quite frankly, I could just have taken an enormous amount of money and walked away from the whole thing and the picture would never have been finished. I could have let it bury itself but once I was in there, I found myself in the middle of every decision. Myself and the assistant director produced that picture."

A *Time* magazine reporter had the task of tracking down the two competing Bonds. Perhaps rather naively, he asked Roger Moore how he used his acting talents to produce the subtle changes of character demanded of James Bond. With typical panache, Moore replied, 'Sometimes I wear a white dinner jacket and sometimes a black one.'

Originally, Sean proposed that the title of the film should be *Warhead*. He began working on the script himself, but others took over. Lorenzo Semple provided the screenplay, but it lacked some of the vital nuances. Sean therefore commissioned Dick Clement and Ian La Frenais, to add extra touches of humour. The suggestion by Connery's second wife Micheline, about the eventual title, was also 'tongue-in-cheek': a comment on her husband's attitude to making another Bond movie. Sean was so pleased with her idea that he requested she should be given credit for it. However, no such on-screen acknowledgement was ever made. Further disappointment followed, when the Writers Guild of America ruled that the input from La Frenais and Clement would not be recorded.

Although the film was a high-tec remake of *Thunderball*, most people would have been unable to detect any similarities. According to Parker, 'what it most closely resembled was the Bond genre. In fact, it could have been interchanged with *Octopussy* which, starring Roger Moore and produced by Albert R. Broccoli, just happened to open at the same time.'

The director of *Auf Wiedersehen Pet*, Roger Bamford, who Pat describes as 'a darling man', willingly gave Pat time off to work on the Bond movie, as he had for *Indiana Jones 2*.

> *Good as gold, Roger Bamford was: I have so much to thank him for. If it comes to that, so have all the other boys in 'Auf Wiedersehen Pet'. Anyway, dear Roger let me off, and off I went to get the first day in. I could then go back at a later date for the continuity shots. Arriving on the scene, feeling very pleased with myself, having sneaked off the 'Auf Wiedersehen Pet' set, although having got permission, who do I walk straight into, but Ian La Frenais? – who was writing stuff for the Bond movie. So I felt such a fool. But there we are – Ian understood. He and Sean are very good friends.*

The South of France, the casino at Monte Carlo, northern Africa and Nassau, were all Connery Bond locations. Final completion was at Elstree Studios in London. Pat's fight scene was originally shot at Luton Ho, but before it could be finished, they realised that the Queen was due to attend an important dance the following day, in the very hall where the fight scene was being filmed.

> *So we had to clear, and only had a certain amount of time. In actual fact we didn't get what we needed in the shots, because the end of the fight scene is where Bond gets lifted high above the head of Count Lippe, who I play, and thrown through some shelves, which have all sorts of samples on them: a sort of Science Room or laboratory.*
>
> *We shot that scene many times on the day. We had to be out of the hall for the ball – it had to be vacated. They actually re-built that set at Elstree Studios, it cost*

a fortune – and shot it again and again and again. Although it was shot many, many times, would-you-believe, in the end, they used the first take – the one we did in the hall!

In this laboratory scene, a very similar sequence to the one in *Indy* was employed, where Bond put his ankles together, and Pat threw him into the mine car.

I throw him into the sample shelves and he crashes down on top of them. During the crash, things fall down on top of him, so he finishes up underneath them. Bond's lying there in the corner. He looks up and Lippe's walking towards him, for the final kill. Bond sees his own urine sample and throws it into Lippe's face. Of course, the ammonia in it stings Lippe's eyes. The rumour was that James Bond had got the 'clap': from the way that Count Lippe reacted, I think they were probably right!

That was probably the extra ingredient that actually shocked Lippe into falling backwards onto all the long-stemmed glass syringes and the receptacles that people used to pee in. And of course, that's what killed him. So that's what didn't do Lippe any good. Now that scene was shot that day, something like 15 or 16 times – I can't remember the exact number. The complete sequence took between two to three weeks to rehearse.

Pat invented a belt, made out of what in those days would be described as three-quarter-inch copper pipe – a bending bar. It fitted around his waist like a belt. But the invention had some very severe drawbacks!

We put a buckle on it and when I just hit this belt buckle, it released a catch and out sprang into my hand this 44 inches of lethal steel; a very heavy pipe that was a bending pipe. Now to anyone who would know what I was talking about, you've got almost solid steel that in fact, would bend in places.

The way that you wielded this piece of solid steel would determine whether it kept straight or not: if you wielded it in circles it would keep straight. It cut right through an aluminium tray – it actually sliced through; it could cut a table in half. I think they were frightened that it might catch on amongst the young kids, so they cut it down a lot. Such a lethal weapon – God!

I got involved with the design of the machine as well – putting a counterweight balance on it. The set designer was largely responsible, but a couple of my ideas went into it. The reason I threw those in was because I intended to buy the machine afterwards, which I did.

A photograph taken by the writer shows the Bond machine, on which Lippe tries to crush Bond.

111

Sean Connery spent 14 hours a day on the film, from 6.30 am. Pat, working alongside Sean, was "… aware that he worked particularly hard on the film." It was clear to Pat that Connery had the strongest of motivations.

According to Freedland, the people at Pinewood who had been making *Octopussy* were told to react as though the Connery version didn't exist. Were any similar instructions issued to people on the Connery set?

There were no politics with us at all. Connery, I think, rose above all that stuff.

Ken Adam agrees; in Michael Freedland's book he's quoted as saying: 'He never played studio politics'. The fight was technically very good – with touches of humour added for good measure!

The lovely piece where I kick Connery in the head – just as England score a goal.

You're knocking seven bells out of him, and the people watching the match don't appear to notice the two of you fighting.

No, they all cheered at the goal. As I kicked him, they all cheered! England had just score: it coincided – the two moves together – which was very good. The old lady in the scene just turned round and nodded as if to say: "That was a good goal." And I said: "Yes." She was talking about one thing, and I was talking about another – kicking Connery's head!

From there, we went to the scene where I fell down the stairs. Then we went into the kitchen. The big fat cook was there. They gave me six pairs of brown trousers to do it – because of the soup being spilt. I finished up afterwards buying one pair for a nominal amount. I didn't really want the other five, as they were the same colour, so the wardrobe guy gave them to me. I went down to 'High and Mighty' on the Edgware Road and swapped five pairs for all the colours of the rainbow – and I've still got them today!

Vic did the stunt coordination and planning for it, didn't he? When I asked him how he planned fights and shots, he said that normally it's visual. He plans the basic moves on paper beforehand, to make sure that he doesn't miss any of the components. But for the shots themselves he uses his visual memory. So when he was planning the fight with you did he show you any notes – a list of moves – or was it just a verbal explanation?

Well no. Vic's very much a seasoned professional when it comes to that sort of thing. When it comes to fight scenes, I'm a bit good at it as well!

I just wondered how you did it. I was trying to visualise the process.

I've worked with Vic before, so it comes across dead easy.

So did you work it out between the two of you?

Well no. Vic was the governor but if I'd got anything to say, he'd always listen to it – let's put it that way. Vic is just so very good at what he does. I can only speak about him from what I've found. If Vic has got something for me to do, he outlines what it is. What makes him such a good professional is that in my particular case, he gave me a lot of leeway. So he put things to me that were very easy to meet and interpret. His professionalism came out very easily. He allowed me all this flexibility and interpretation of what he wanted. It all dropped in so easily, because he's so good at what he does. That's why he's the top man, to direct. Vic pioneered the way for stunt guys.

Would you say that 1984 was one of the high points in your career, because *Never Say Never Again* went to number one in the British Film Charts and was the second most successful picture of the year, behind *Indiana Jones & The Temple of Doom*? You were in both films – so was that year a particularly high point for you?

The high point was 'Auf Wiedersehen Pet'.

Yes, but from a film career point of view?

Yes, at one point in time, the Bristol Cinema was showing four of my films at its three cinemas.

That would be Bond, *Temple of Doom* and two others. Which films did you make at Pinewood?

Clash of the Titans, The Spaceman & King Arthur – also with Vic, Robin Hood, Superman III and Space Precinct.

It was just like old times, too, in the cinemas. Although American business was less for *Never Say Never* than that recorded for *Octopussy*, worldwide it was attracting huge attention. The movie broke records in the Far East, opening in London's West End in seven cinemas. Pat attended the premier.

As we began the new millenium, Pinewood entered a new phase in its history. Vic advises me that the studios have recently been purchased by Deluxe Film Laboratories. According to newspaper reports, former owners *Rank* plan to focus on holidays and Hard Rock Cafes.

Meanwhile, we return for a moment to June 1999. We spent some time, admiring from a distance the enormous building, like an aircraft hangar, that houses the 007 set, with letters a mile high! Then we approached the entrance: a powerful, shiny black motorbike was parked conveniently outside – just the sort of thing that Pierce Brosnan *might* be tempted to ride – I wonder ...?

Once inside, we walked swiftly through a labyrinth of echoing corridors. For what seemed an eternity, the acoustics accentuated the clattering of my hopelessly impractical high heels, alongside Pat's heavy strides: it was obvious that I'd never visited a film studio in my life before! Just as I was beginning to *really* wish that I'd taken a leaf out of the book of our trainer-clad escort, Vic's assistant, Emily, my embarrassment ended: we had finally reached the set. What followed, is the subject of our next chapter.

Chapter Eleven –

TWENTY-FOUR HOURS IS NOT ENOUGH

Or watch the things you gave your life to, broken;
And stoop and build 'em up with worn-out tools…

*I went to see a guy – didn't audition really. I didn't have to read. We chatted for
a while. He said: "Look, can you do these dates?" I said: "Yes I can." He said:
"Well would you mind wearing contact lenses?" I said that would be all right –
really positive, positive, positive. Shook my hand and said: "See you again." And
then you don't get the job. It's a funny old business – and then you get another
person writing an episode – specially for you!*

Pat has described the often quite alarming physical dangers of his acting
career, in conjunction with the vital role that his colleague the stunt director
plays, in damage limitation. Additional frustrations of these closely-related
professions include physical hardship in general, remaining intensely
focused on a project, within the strict time limits of a demanding schedule,
and the possibilities of being 'cubby-holed', or occasionally even priced out
of the market. The lifestyles of both Vic and Pat can be described in one
word – 'hectic'.

Earlier that morning, we had entered the *007* film set very quietly, through
a side door and cautioned by Pat, who's an 'old hand' at this game, watched
discreetly from a distance; Vic and a member of his crew were checking some
shots on a small television monitor. At an opportune moment, we approached
them and had a quick chat, prior to lunch.

On another part of the set there was a scenic, exquisitely painted
backdrop for a typically continental-type lake, reminiscent of Lake Garda, in
northern Italy. A machine spewed out trails of mist, which had already
begun to shroud the watery surface in thick drifts, providing a setting that
was both picturesque and mysterious.

The morning's tasks completed – as usual they had begun at an early hour – Vic walked us across the studio lot. Such is the size of the Bond crew, an entire restaurant had been set aside for their exclusive use.

The three of us ate a working lunch, kindly provided by Vic, and chatted informally about the two men's long association, with stunt work in general, and about the latest Bond film in particular. Understandably proud of his friend – they have performed many a hair-raising stunt together – Pat explained: "He's really paved the way: stunt guys have got far more respect now."

Vic described how dangerous stunt work had been when he first started, because of insufficient knowledge about the various pitfalls. "There was very little equipment. They've invented a lot over the years – no airbags, and so on. It's an hundred percent different now. We have airbags – for descenders, nitrogen rams, pipe ramps: they all make the stunt man's life better and safer. It was 'dodgy' in those days – you just did it. If you had to fall, you just jumped off a horse! You know?" Initially the two of them shared a room on a temporary basis, on the commercial in Arundel in the 60s. Nowadays, it is first class travel and hotel suites.

I wondered if Vic prefers action movies, as he's directed so many successfully? "No, they always come to me, unfortunately. *Young Indiana Jones*, that I directed, had no action it – hardly at all – which was lovely of George Lucas to give it to me. But people 'cubby-hole' you in this business: it drives me mad. They say: 'Let him do the easy bit – the action bit.' But it's the hardest thing in the movie – the action." Pat interjected: "It's difficult to move on to other things."

"Oh yes," Vic continued, "they won't let you get out of your box! They're too used to you in the situation you're in. They won't let you advance." He enjoys films where he can become more involved with the characters themselves.

"I was talking to someone the other day about a *Greenpeace* movie – and whaling and all that: a conservation thing, you know? It's a bit too expensive for me to direct – about 35 million – but it would have been nice." The idea of conservation appeals to him: "I like the idea of it; especially when I saw some videos of this real-life character." Pat and Vic have had similar experiences in this respect:

In a way, it's what happened to me, as a sort of Action Actor. Parts are worth so much money, do you know what I mean? If you've got a part the Production Manager will say, well the budget for this part is 2,000 quid, or 10,000 quid, or whatever. Then what happens is if you're fortunate and you're OK, like I was, obviously your money goes up. But all of a sudden you get out of reach, because your agent's trying to get you that money.

> *There are lots of people around who are capable of doing the job, but cost less. So suddenly, one day you're in work and in demand, and the next day you're a better person – you've got more experience and a bit more money – and you can't get a job! Like you just said, 35 million is too much for you. Why should it be?*

"And yet they get the green light for the film, because I'm going to direct the action." So, would it really have been too expensive for Vic to direct the film? "It's not – they say that, but they often get the green light on the film if I agree to do the Second Unit, because they know it won't go over budget and it will be the best they can get."

We collected our dessert and were joined by Mara Bryant and Sharon Lark, two members of Vic's production team. I asked Vic about the different locations for the latest Bond film, *The World Is Not Enough*, which also stars Sophie Marceau.

"Eight or nine: the chase, the Thames: four or five docks; Chatham – in Kent, France." Of particular interest, later in the year, was the chase through London's Dockland area, with Brosnan at the wheel of the jet-black spearhead-shaped boat, which was jet-propelled. Pat and I had been fortunate to see a video preview of this, during our day at Pinewood. It was interesting to see, at a later stage, how the complete sequence was eventually put together.

"The skiing sequence was shot in Chamonix – right where all the avalanches were on," explained Vic. "They've had it rough down there, haven't they?" He also revealed that since filming took place, there has been a fire in the Mont Blanc Tunnel and further avalanches. "I think they just don't publicise it. Although they took it rather stoically, apparently it's a regular thing." Mara elaborated: "You get there and there's the village and there's almost a vertical mountain on either side, and of *course* there are going to be avalanches." Among the film's other locations were Spain, Turkey, Algeria and the Bahamas.

Sharon joined the conversation, describing their post-production work. "All the bits that we've shot – like all the shots that Vic's done – for instance, the 'headwire' scene, we put all those things together – electronically." Computers have revolutionised this type of work. According to Mara, "I don't think anyone uses other methods these days. Before, they were always done on blue screens and optical printers, but nowadays it's all done digitally." She has always used this method, having only been in films for approximately the last nine years.

Pat worked with an excellent film crew in New Zealand, during the making of *Willow*. Sharon and Mara are also from New Zealand, but met through mutual friends, in London. Mara entered the business after experience with a video graphics company, doing commercials, graphics for television, title sequences and animations. Sharon also came from that background. Mara was doing the film work digitally. When the machinery became available for doing it that way, she was astute enough to see its potential and changed to doing film instead of video, gradually entering the more risky world of the freelance. They are both listed in the film credits, and a prominent place is given to the information: 'Second Unit directed by Vic Armstrong.'

Skills required by Sharon and Mara in order to assist Vic, include the ability to think of things that exist as separate elements, and being able to "visualise and have an imagination for how things are going to look when they're put together – and plenty of stamina." Good organisational skills are also a prerequisite, "because you're bringing together different units." An essential fourth requirement is "an understanding of the way things go together, so you've got to keep reasonably au fait with what's going on in the industry – what you can or can't do."

This is Mara's first Bond, although she's worked on other films in between, and Sharon's second. Mara was quite adamant that increased familiarity with the genre and wider experience don't make the job any easier. "Because you always try and set yourself greater challenges every time; you're more ambitious and so is everybody else. The shots for this film are much more complicated than on either *Tomorrow Never Dies* or on *Golden Eye*."

Working with Vic has proved a valuable experience for both of them. Mara also made the point that, "… on a film like this where you've got so much skill in terms of stunts and special effects, they'll always find a real fit if it doesn't work."

An experienced crew of Bondian experts has developed over the years. Mara confirmed that, as a result, there are still out-takes from the film, but fewer than there would have been with a less experienced crew. She defined their respective jobs more precisely. "My title is *Visual Effects Supervisor*. Sharon is *Visual Effects Producer*." Sharon is more on the technical side. Mara has seniority, as Head of Department.

"Our responsibility is to make sure that all the elements that have to go together to make one composite shot, are shot correctly, understood by everybody who needs to use them – the cutting room and those sort of people. Then finally, that they go together in the way that they are supposed to."

Visual effects have played a key role in creating illusions and disguises, for the wide range of characters that Pat has played. Mara elaborated on this process: "It starts in Pre-Production – working with people like Vic and the Director, to design the way the shots can be achieved, then deciding how they're going to be shot." After shooting, a full time cut with the Editor, ensures that he knows how to use them to the shot. The final film is completed in Post-Production.

Vic and the production team had a tough time in Chamonix. Mara explained: "It was phenomenally cold and the weather was just horrific. There were a few days when we stood on a mountain, in an avalanche zone. It was safe, but it was absolutely freezing!" Sharon confirmed this – the memory still fresh in their minds. A later chapter reveals that Pat had to endure even harsher arctic conditions close to the North Pole, during the filming of *The Last Place On Earth*.

As with many of the location-based films that both Vic and Pat have made, no long-term plans could be made, and creating the right conditions can be a nightmare. Even using a long-range weather forecast, doesn't guarantee success.

"Absolutely", Mara confirmed, "we've done a lot of waiting for weather on this film; it's sunny one moment, raining the next – so it's very difficult." It's less frustrating when artificial conditions can be created: like Vic and Pat's experience while making *Red Sonja*, where the lighting company *Arco*, was required to light a film to daylight, but shooting began at midnight!

The two women explained that "locations are not as glamorous as you might think they are." A prime example of this can be found later in the book, when Pat recalls making the three 'Indy' films.

Sharon emphasised the infinite amount of patience that filming often calls for: "It's jolly hard work! Crews learn how to work in very short bursts, to get things really set up," she explained. "Then there's lots of sitting around and waiting."

Pat has found during the course of his film career, that being on 'stand-by' can be stressful for cast and crew alike. Mara explained that they couldn't play cards or have other recreational activities, in case someone suddenly decided conditions were suitable to start shooting again.

Twenty-four hours is certainly not enough for Vic Armstrong. As Pat and I accompanied him back, towards the *007* film set, where we were to part company, I asked him to describe a typical schedule, in the hope that I could discover exactly when he took his holidays! "Before this one, I finished *Entrapment* on a Friday and started on this one on the Monday. Prior to *Entrapment* I was in the States, doing a Patrick Swayze movie, called *Black Dog*. I finished that and started *Entrapment* the next day.

"Before that, I was going to take seven or eight weeks off, at Christmas, after I did a sequence on *The Avengers*. But I only had seven days off. Then I took the 'plane the next morning. I'm away most of the time – I've been in the States. I only came back for *Tomorrow Never Dies*. I was away for several years before that. I have a home in the States."

He finds all films challenging, but rates *Legend* as particularly tough. "I had to train all these horses to run without any bridles or saddles, or any contact of any sort. Ridley Scott shoots over and over again. By the time they'd finished rehearsing, the horses had got fed up with it. That was a big challenge. There have been others – you know?"

119

Pat suggested that a particular challenge must have been when he first directed. "That was a helluva a leap wasn't it?" "I found it easier though. Second Units are harder than First Units," explained Vic. "I've directed First Units, yes. I did *The Young Indiana Jones* for George Lucas.

"The first film that I directed Second Units for was *Watcher in the Woods* – for Disney – Betty Davis. 74, 75 – something like that. They just asked me to do it. Doing a stunt co-ordinator's job you break down incidents, fights, or whatever the action happens to be. You break it into segments of the story-board for the Director. So you get an in-built knowledge of how it all goes together."

Pat explained that it has to be put together on the day and Vic elaborated: "Oh yes, things change all the way through – even this movie – the Bond film. You set off with one thing in mind. I do a rough synopsis of the chase: the boat chase, ski chase, the night sequence. But that's only just to keep me on the straight and narrow – so I know I haven't missed any incidents. But the actual angles and how I shoot it – how I go about it – is all in my head.

"On this Bond film, I work six days a week in the studio on a film, then on the seventh day I come in and edit, with the editor: quite wearying." Sounds a bit like the familiar bible quotation – but without the Sunday off! How much of a break does he get in between films? "Nothing." No break at all? "Not in the last few years." You just go from one film to the other? Well, I had asked the question – I was definitely getting the picture... and so, a few months later, did we.

The World Is Not Enough was released in the closing weeks of 1999. It is the most expensive Bond movie to date and has been described as 'a $100 million blockbuster.' By early December, it had reached number one in the UK Cinema's Top Ten films, for the second week running.

Two years into the new millennium, the Bond genre remains as popular as ever. Pierce Brosnan, according to a television interview, feels very much at ease with the role. Now able to 'smell the roses', he is about to make another Bond movie. In the closing scene of *The World Is Not Enough*, he delivers a string of innuendo-laden lines that come with the territory, including: "I always wanted to have Christmas in Turkey."

Shortly after our Pinewood visit, Vic Armstrong was on location in the States. He returned home briefly on the 1st of June. Then, just four short days later, he was off on his travels again. In a letter dated 10 July 2000 he wrote: 'I have just finished filming *Charlie's Angels* in Los Angeles for seven months. I then flew to Greece to shoot a sequence on *Captain Correli's Mandolin* with Nicholas Cage. I flew from there to Rome to meet with Martin Scorsese and look at locations for *Gangs of New York*. I then flew to Dublin for meetings with Daniel Day Lewis'. In January 2002 he was in Alaska, investigating locations for the next Bond movie. I wonder if he'll eventually take that holiday ... and where, for heaven's sake, will he go?

Chapter Twelve –

A SHEEPDOG AT THE COURT OF KING ARTHUR

If you can make a heap of all your winnings
And risk it on one turn of pitch-and-toss...

Despite my good fortune, and the variety of opportunities that have come my way, at the end of the day life is still a gamble. There's always that strong element of risk that something unexpected might happen. I've certainly had more than my fair share of near-misses – like the one we had the day we finished filming in New Zealand...

In Chapter 3, Pat 'opened the bidding' by telling us about an entertaining dinner party, where stories were exchanged, mainly about showbusiness personalities, between Kubrick and his celebrity guests, while they were making *Barry Lyndon*. The same party was also mentioned in the chapter about Kubrick.

We continue this theme with additional true-life tales about celebrities and situations, encountered by the 'Gentle Giant' in the worlds of film and pantomime.

This time, we're taking the films in chronological, as opposed to alphabetical order. We'll begin by taking a closer look at some of the cast of *The Spaceman and King Arthur*, made in 1978 and released in '79. Pat has very positive memories of Kenneth More; like the writer, readers may recall his suave performance in earlier years, as the romantic lead in *The Admirable Crichton*, starring opposite Diane Cilento; his engaging personality and subtle charm were irresistible – even to a child of tender years – as I was then. Pat confirmed that, in reality, Kenny More was as intelligent and well educated as the screen image he projected.

Kenny More was a lovely man. He and John Le Mesurier enjoyed a little bet, and they used to discuss the betting across the lunch table every day. They were very funny. John Le Mesurier had a very dry sense of humour.

Kenny told me how difficult it was to play Bader – how it was very demanding – physically. Of course, they all knew me from the wrestling. They used to come to me for advice about training. Kenny More and John Le Mesurier used to ask me about exercises; I used to give them light exercises. As people get a little older, they suddenly realise that they should loosen up. They both wanted to talk about that – and doing bits of training.

Pat played the role of Oaf, the court torturor. Ron Moody was Merlin. Pat's experience of him as a friend lies in direct contradiction to the negative way in which the media often portrayed him, 'moody by name and moody by nature'.

He wasn't – Ronnie was a darling. It was just that when he was doing a film, he was so into the character he did. He got involved in the design of Merlin's cloaks; he got involved in everything. He was writing as well – something separate. He was a very misunderstood person: a very intense person. We 'palled up' and we used to go out together.

Following an established routine, Pat trained each morning outside one of the hotel windows at the *Holiday Inn*, where the cast of *Spaceman* was staying. Unfortunately, he was totally unaware that he was treating the lady occupant of the room, who was trying to sleep, to the sound of his grunts, groans and expletives!

Although I didn't realise it at the time, I used to train outside Sheila's window, when she was trying to have 'a little sleep'. I had a bench and a set of weights, which I kept in my old Bentley at the time. I kept them awake, although I didn't know. I used to put this bench on the grass and do flying exercises. What used to happen was that suddenly I'd be hitting my elbows, all over the place – on the ground and all sorts of things.

As I warmed up and put heavier and heavier weights on, the bench used to sink into the ground; you know, the four legs would sink. For these flying exercise you do that (mimes) and your arms go down. I'd hit my elbow and go, "Oh…!" Sheila used to say: "I can hear you 'effing and blinding' under my window!"

Despite this shaky start, he and actress Sheila White became very good friends and remain so to this day. She married an entrepreneur, had a family, but still works now and again.

Moving on to 1981, and *Clash of the Titans*, Pat has further recollections about some of the stars involved in the production:

Ursula and I had a standing joke, where we raced each other to the cream cake trolley. But in the end we had an agreement where she wouldn't eat any cream cakes and I'd make sure that she didn't.

In his early twenties, according to Jim White, Pat made the transition from a rather heavy diet to a much more health conscious one. Since then he is careful about physical fitness and eating the correct foods, so it can be surprising when he sometimes appears to break the habit:

> *I listen to my body, and if it craves for something, a cream cake or a bar of chocolate, I let it have it. But I do penance afterwards. I always work that little bit harder at training and I am particularly careful about my diet. Just Quaker Oats for breakfast, to which I add protein powder.*
>
> *Ursula was a lovely lady. She used to wear blouses with hearts on, all the time – anything with hearts on, and every day she used to put a heart in her forehead there like that, to stop her frowning. If it came off, it meant she was frowning. I'm not able to tell you much – extremes.*

The contrast between two of the toga-clad gods was particularly marked; the less robust Olivier, who, despite playing Zeus, was of average height, had all 19-stone, six-foot four and a half inches of Pat's Hephaestus, towering above him.

> *Olivier was a wonderful man – so easy to get on with. He used to lean up against me and say: "Come and let me draw my strength from you, dear boy." He believed, as the pagans believed, that if you stood against an oak tree, you could draw strength from it, and you could draw strength out of a strong person. We talked a lot about physical fitness. I used to feed him Vitamin Es every day.*
>
> *Burgess Meredith was lovely. He played Ammon, a poet who befriended Harry Hamlin's character Perseus, when they found the magic armour – sword and shield. I don't know whether it's known, but Burgess and Lauren Bacall were very close friends. I used to sit and talk to him about the old actors. He used to tell me stories about Spencer Tracey and Hepburn.*

Burgess told Pat that despite the fact that Howard Hughes had a reputation for being a recluse, he actually knew the millionaire quite well. This favourite actor of Pat's told him all kinds of fascinating stories.

> *I used to love to listen to him – rather like Jack Warden, when we did 'Three Wishes for Jamie'. We spent hours and hours together, chatting, during the breaks; it was in the summer, in the Cotswolds – in a lovely park. He told us stories about Gable and Robert Mitchum – oh, great stories.*
>
> *Another of my favourite actors is Pat Higgins, the hanging judge in 'Hang Them High', or 'For A Few Dollars More' – a Clint Eastwood movie. When I was in Mexico City, making 'Conan', I'd have my cup of coffee about 5.30 in the morning, after I'd finished training. Sometimes I'd have coffee with Pat Higgins – and he never knew that he was one of my favourite actors.*

Pat made *Red Sonja* in 1985; Richard Fleischer was the director. Despite the film's success, Pat recalls that it was not always plain sailing for the cast.

I played in Red Sonja, with Brigitte Nielsen. I was with Brigitte the day she and her husband split up.

Willow, made in 1988, is next in our chronology of memorable film personalities and events. In Chapter 9, Pat explained that he first met stuntman Roy Alon, one of Kael's soldiers in *Willow,* when he worked on the *Gangsters* series, based in Birmingham. Here he elaborates on his association with Roy.

I was chairman of Equity at the time – for about eight years. They called Roy in to do a high fall. The second time I met him I helped with a fight scene which, although I'm not a stunt co-ordinator, I do know rather a lot about fights – obviously.
    I was at the Nottingham Playhouse, helping out there, to put a fight scene together, for the 'Nottingham Lambs', which were a gang of hoodlums in Nottingham. I did the first scene. Then they wanted to do something a little later and I was working on something else. I rang Roy up and got him the job and he went up and did the second part of it. Nowadays, of course, I wouldn't have thought they could afford to hire him to work on a play.

Roy has worked on some major films. One of his most recent is *The Tenth Kingdom,* a mythical series, shot in modern-day vernacular. At the time of writing it's about to be premiered on *Sky Television.* I met him in 1999, during our visit to the Pinewood Studios, when he knocked on the door of Vic's trailer, to say hello to Pat. The seven weeks spent on location in New Zealand, for *Willow* were eventful – to say the least.

Lots of things happened. When we were in New Zealand, we were down in Queenstown, which is all snow. While I was there they asked me if I would judge the Sheepdog and Shepherds Contest, and take part in the Raft Race, which I said I would. You must remember that 'Auf Wiedersehen Pet' was very big in New Zealand and Australia and nearly got me into trouble over the news people speaking to me.

The contestants were mainly men from Queenstown. There were six or seven rafts with teams of three or four men on each raft. Pat's team won and as they approached the shore, everyone was cheering and shouting.

I was waving to everybody at the side, at a time when we could just afford to do it – for that split second. Everybody else knew what was coming and I was stood there boldly at the front. All of a sudden, I was splattered with about ten eggs. It was so funny!

124

Problems occurred during the last day of shooting *Willow*. They were high up on a mountain, and had to stop shooting due to aircraft noise: hardly surprising in itself in a country like New Zealand, because of the distances. It's a flying country; many people have aeroplanes. Unfortunately the noise from the aeroplane would have brought the film straight into the 20th century, destroying the illusion.

> *So we can hear this aeroplane and we're all thinking where the bloody hell is it? Finally, one of the assistant directors said: "Look, phone the base and tell them to get that bloody aircraft out of here!" So they phoned, but nothing happened.*
> *Then all of a sudden someone said: "There he is!" "Where?" "There!" "Where?" (Repeats this to-and-fro'- type dialogue several times). Then we looked at the fella and realised that the 'plane was below us!*

Below you? That's amazing! The mountain must have been totally enclosed by clouds.

> *Yes, because we were so high up – and that particular day was our last day of shooting. They said: "Right – off you go!" I said: "Hang on a minute, you've finished shooting – right?" They said: "Yes." I said: "I'm not going in that helicopter again, I'm going by car." It was about a four-hour drive by car.*

You don't like flying, do you?"

> *Well, I don't like helicopters, no. About four hours.*

Like South Africa?

> *Yes – that was a single aircraft again, wasn't it? Anyway, the helicopter I should have gone in that day plummeted. It hit an air pocket and dropped by God-knows-how-far. But I would have died on the spot. (Repeats this). All my dressers were in there, all my make-up people, my personal assistant. When I heard about it afterwards, I nearly threw up!*

Were the yoga and wrestling shows a totally different time?

> *Yes, 'Willow' was my second visit to New Zealand, wrestling Johnny da Silva was the first. At one stage, the coach was going up one of the mountains and the wheel went over the edge of the mountain. The bus nearly went over – can you imagine? It was terribly hazardous. But the funny thing was I was at the top of the mountain, which took ages to walk up. I'm in a T-shirt and I'm perspiring like hell: steam coming off me – surrounded by snow and ice! It's a different coldness – a dry*

coldness; there's a lot of stone. Unlike Britain where it's cold and wet; there, you just get cold.

In 1990, Pat and Billy Connolly were working together on *The Big Man*. However, as you've gathered by now, Pat's life has been packed to the hilt with surprises of one sort or another, and this occasion was no exception!

I've had eight Royal Premieres – worked with Liam Neeson and the Big Yinn – Billy Connolly. Billy and I were filming – doing 'The Big Man' and I said to the P.A. "I've got to go early tonight." Then he said: "Would you mind sharing a car with Mr Connolly?" So Billy and I drove to the hotel together and I said, "See you tomorrow Bill."

I showered quickly, jumped on the shuttle to London, to attend the premier of 'The Four Musketeers'. Peter got killed – one of the stars – the chubby guy. So there I was, in the line-up of this Royal Premiere and Fergie came by and said hello to me, with the Duke of York. Then I saw Billy Connolly leaning his head out of the line, looking at me. We didn't realise that we were both in the same movie together! And as we're looking at each other we're going, "You!" Fergie said: "Aye, aye you two. What are you up to?"

Pat has spent thirty years as an active participant in the world of films. During the course of his career he has rubbed shoulders with the rich and famous, the eccentric and the kind-hearted. The experiences that we are sharing with him constitute only the tip of an enormous iceberg; we could fill several books with those which remain.

Being of a gregarious disposition, he has formed many friendships with scriptwriters, actors, producers, directors, and other members of the production team; the closest of these have survived to the present day. Such experiences have enriched his life in a way that most of us can only imagine. Never, in his wildest dreams, could that little tousle-haired, 'raggy-arsed' boy, growing up in the back streets of Birmingham, have imagined that his adult life would take such a dramatic turn.

When portraying more lusty, down-to-earth characters, Pat takes a Dustin Hoffman-type approach: the more 'natural' the performance, the more believable the character. *The White Angel* provides an excellent example of this technique.

Dustin Hoffman arrives on the scene, sweating and out of breath and does a little scene. There was about four miles around this lake. They're about ready to shoot. "Oh hang on a minute," he said, "let's get it right!" Off he went and ran it. Twenty-five minutes later he turned up – all out of breath. This is notorious now – everybody knows about it: it's a big joke! Dustin Hoffman did this and that and Olivier

126

said: "Well, you could have just acted dear boy!" It's a very famous quote now. Dustin Hoffman wanted to do this Method Acting and Olivier said: "Why didn't you just act?" It's a matter of what you want to do.

In much the same way, Pat decided that if a stick fight was required of his character, Little John, in the pantomime *Babes in the Wood*, starring *Cannon and Ball*, that was *exactly* what the audience would get! Ian Sandy, now a seasoned actor/manager, was the poor unfortunate on the receiving end – as Friar Tuck. Originally from the West Midlands, he trained at Birmingham Theatre School, and has been involved in professional entertainment from an early age. He takes up the story:

"We rehearsed in London with a very prominent West End director, who's unfortunately dead now, a guy called Peter Walker. It was my first big 'pro' job and Pat's first panto as well. They said, 'You've got to do a fight scene where you meet back-to-back.' They were a bit of a 'luvvie' company: 'Ooh luv, you hit him once then he hits you!' But that wasn't good enough for Pat. So he went into battle, and I seriously remember thinking: bloody hell, what's he doing?!

"The funny thing is, that inspires you, because acting is about confidence, and Pat very skillfully planned the moves. I credit him with that totally. We rehearsed it and rehearsed it, then went for it – and by golly – it was good! It worked: it was very credible. Pat's absolutely right – I have to say."

Ian still remembers the first entrance that he and Pat made together. "I went on first. And we sort of went on backwards, and he came on and there was a roar – they loved him – straight away. Which is quite funny for another actor, because you think, oh hello! This is going to be good!

"And when we engaged in combat – which we did – he's right: he beat the hell out of me, and I thought, oh sod you mate! I'm going to bash you back! A true story – the stick *did* break. We kept going through it, and the ASM was a guy called Tony Heard. He said: "You're far too rough." Pat wouldn't respond to that at all, and I just found it quite amusing.

"Well, I'm sure it was a matinee, and they were proper wooden staffs – and they went with such a crack – I am talking a *crack*. And the funny thing is that you *know* something has happened. The staff cracked in two, and just hung on the end – and of course, it's very funny – and the audience howled! And I thought. What am I going to do with this? We can't carry on fighting. So I tried to carry on with it, but it was all over by then; a bit of it flew into the orchestra pit.

"Bear in mind, the year after that I go off and do Southampton panto, which Pat's not doing, and there's no stick fight. The year after that I do another *Babes in the Wood* – no stick fight. Three years on I'm back with

Cannon & Ball in Darlington, and the director is Peter Purvis, from *Blue Peter*. Peter says: 'We want you to do a fight.' I said: 'Oh fab!' Now the actor who was playing Little John was 'as camp as sticks' – OK? 6 foot 6 and as camp as sticks! We were at this hotel in Darlington, and he said, 'I've never done a fight. How are we going to do this?' Well, me being a bit confident, I said, 'I'll show you. Pat Roach taught me how to do this,' and I choreographed the fight.

"I said to this lad: 'Look, we're going to do this very slowly, 1,2,3,4,' and we did it about twenty times. When we got to the rehearsal stage, Peter Purvis said: 'Let's run it now.' I said to this actor: 'O.K, we're going to do it. I'm going to hit you now – and I'm going to mean it.' He said: 'Are you sure?' I said: 'Yes, so for goodness sake be ready!'

"We were back-to-back, turn round, spin around, look at him: 'Who are you?' 'I'm Friar Tuck', whatever it was that we used to say. 'Oh are you mighty friar?' and we started the fight. Well I gave the first move *such* a crack, a la Pat Roach style. This guy dropped the stick and the six foot six nanny went: 'Ooh, you're ever so rough!' and ran out of the rehearsal room. Absolutely true! And much to everyone's amusement, he couldn't cope with it. But Pat's absolutely right: you have to make it look realistic. But it's like everything, if it's choreographed well and if everybody knows what they're doing – that's when it works. I can still remember it. I've 'nixed' the Pat Roach Stick Fight, and used it when I've played Friar Tuck – for quite a few years.

"Pat was at his mightiest then, I would say. Obviously, with all the credit from television, the moment he walked on the stage he got a cheer. The moment he came on; the audience warmed to him immediately. When I walked on they thought, who the hell is that? The problem was, it's like anything, the more you do it, the giggle factor sets in."

Pat's sense of humour is well known among his friends and fellow professionals, and the pantomime was no exception. "He's a bugger for it! We used to look at each other. I must tell you one of my Pat Roach stories I've never ever got out. We'd just come to the dress rehearsal and he's in his dressing room – Room 6, nearest the stage."

As Pat was unsure what to do about stage makeup, Ian purchased it, then attempted to explain how to use it. But Pat wanted to try it out himself. "And I learnt something: you always look at an actor just before you go on stage. Because the first time Pat was on stage, he actually came on and he was like – bright red! I took one look at him and went." (Laughs). "Then he started to laugh. It was just before we were about to do the fight – and it's not good – when you've got to beat the hell out of somebody! He's a great learner. I was no expert, but he adjusted very well – you know what I mean – to that circumstance?

"Tommy and Bobby were great characters and they treated him as 'Big Pat'. I'd met him when I was fourteen and always got on well with him. When I got my Junior Equity Card, he was the Chairman of the Birmingham branch of Equity." Pat held that position for eight years. "It was quite funny that a well-known wrestler was chairman of an actor's thing. The meetings were held once a month in Broad Street, in the Ex-Servicemen's Club, directly opposite Bingley Hall. I used to go there and it was a grotty building: on the present site of the Hyatt Hotel."

Ian recognised several of the actors because, ironically, they had been 'extras' when he played the lead in children's television. "Pat, I always remember, came over and said: 'Hello Ian, welcome.' He was just terribly nice – and you never forget things like that – *ever*. It's like when I got the part of Friar Tuck – and you've got to bear in mind, this was Birmingham's biggest panto. It ran forever, December 14th 1989 to February 28th 1990: the last of the biggest long runs." Pat recalls that there were 138 performances.

At the time, *Cannon & Ball* were at the top of the comedy tree. It was a particularly prestigious show, for a newcomer. The duo preferred to include jobbing actors – not just celebrities. "We were the plot people," continued Ian. "There was myself and a wonderful actor called Tom Hardy, who played about eleven parts, and Maurice Thorogood, as the Sheriff of Nottingham. Then there were the 'celebs': Bernadette Nolan, as Maid Marianne, and of course, Pat.

"I remember walking into the rehearsal room and meeting Pat. He came straight up and said: 'Hello kid, how are you?' You know what he's like. He said: 'Great to see you!' And we were saying we're both the 'new boys' on this. We got to lunchtime and we were both staying at the YMCA in London, which is now a hotel – round the corner from Tottenham Court Road.

"I didn't know where to stay, but Pat said: 'You're going to stay here – it's brilliant!' It was fab. He used to give me his breakfast tickets – he'd got some deal or other – I never know. I always got breakfast for free. I think on about the third night we finished rehearsals and he said: 'What are you doing?' I said: 'Not a lot, to be honest with you Pat.' He said: 'Well let's go for a walk.' "

They walked the length of Oxford Street. Pat was stopped at regular intervals. " 'You're Bomber aren't you?' 'Hello Bomber.' They called him 'Bomber' – always. He responded very nicely, which was funny, because as a wrestler he never did respond: it was so different to his response as a television celebrity. I remember going to see him wrestle as a boy, and he was the 'baddie': he was Big Bad Pat Roach."

As they reached the end of Oxford Street and turned left, Pat did a temporary disappearing act. "He said: 'I'll just pop in to get something – something you'll enjoy.' And I lost him – which is difficult with Pat! Then he appeared three minutes later and put this bag in my hand. He said: 'You and me are going to walk down the road and enjoy these.' They were chocolates – it was a really kind thing to do. We just got on so well through the whole thing."

Back in Birmingham, he disappeared again! "He was out in his costume talking to the builders working on Birmingham Royal Ballet – because Pat is one of the people. Which he really shouldn't have been doing, because of theatre discipline; but that's Pat. I'll never forget: 'Where's Pat gone?' The wardrobe master threw a wobbly-and-three quarters, because it's a cardinal sin. As my career's progressed I've become a company production manager, so obviously I see that side of it more than anything, and the thought of an actor going out in his costume, you know what I mean? I'd curl up at the thought! And lo and behold, Pat did.

"I think it's those things that are very special about somebody. He's human – terribly normal. We went through this long run, and he was just lovely through all of it. But he was a big star – he had the common touch – he was on the telly every week, and because of that he was very identifiable."

Taking the train back from London rehearsals, to Birmingham, Ian wondered if his return journey would be a solitary one. "I'm pretty sure Pat had a first-class ticket and I had a normal jobbing actor's second-class ticket. We went through the barriers together, and he just came and sat with me. On the way back, obviously people walked through and they're all going, 'Hallo Bomber. How are you Bomber?' And he was just lovely with them.

"Subsequently I've met Pat, he's come to pantos and I've seen shows with him. He's one of those people who's had the persona of being a bit of a rough diamond – it's almost from the wrestling side – isn't it – that he's Big Bad Pat Roach? And the man is such a pussycat – and such a sweet kind man – and I will argue with anybody – that's what Pat Roach is."

Conversely, as we mention elsewhere in the book, Pat doesn't 'suffer fools gladly'. He and Ian were having a meal, when somebody interrupted them to request his autograph. Ian recalls: "He didn't exactly snap at them, but he said: 'Do you mind? I'm eating my meal. When I've finished my meal you may come and ask for it.'

"I looked after Frank Bruno for two years on panto, for *Goldilocks*, in Birmingham and Southampton. Frank was a big guy – Pat is a big guy – and for many reasons, that's why they were suited to the roles they did. There has to be something in his upbringing – he's quite old-fashioned in his values – does that make sense – what I'm saying? In the sense that he likes to be treated well, and if he is, then he treats other people well. When you're a celeb the public can be horrible: 'Sign this, do this!' It's very much the case. And you see, Pat won't respond to that. He *never* would respond to that – and I don't blame him!"

Tommy and Bobby went to Pat's Health Club, but Ian decided against it. He recalls: "Tommy and Bobby at that stage were very big stars; they're still stars, but they were massive. I think they were going through their own, do-you-know-what-I-mean times. It must be very difficult for an act like that. But everyone got on with Pat – that was the *interesting* thing."

Ian is the first to acknowledge that the acting profession is tough. "You have to accept that, from 100 actors in the field, 93 of them are 6 foot 3, dark-haired and good looking. If you are a definitive character, you've got something different to offer. Pat's got one because he's a big guy. It's a distinct advantage, because you're a character, before you even open your mouth." Bomber was typical of the genre, but despite people's preconceptions of this type of role, Pat stuck to his guns, and deliberately understated the character, making him quietly spoken. Ian agreed: "That's often the perception. You see if you're a big actor you're either a 'heavy', thick, or mental, you know what I mean? That's the classification for it!

"Pat's played 'heavies', and all character parts, and that's a good thing to be. I mean, I'm happy to be type cast. He falls under that classification of modern day hero, doesn't he? There's Pat the wrestler, Pat the actor, Pat the scrap merchant – the dealer, or whatever else he does. He seems to do everything and combine them all very well. But the interesting thing is that I can honestly say that in fifteen years, he never changed.

"I saw him in a U.K. Gold repeat of *Casualty*, playing a lorry driver. I was in the same series block, when Megan the nurse and Robson Green were in it. I was an awkward patient, in Episode Three – *Victim of Circumstance*. Tim Healy was in it. He played a carpenter who worked with his son. Tim's character had a heart attack, but they couldn't get an ambulance because there was this fool, me, wasting hospital time. Then about four episodes later, there was a story about a lorry driver, and it was Pat. So actually, we worked on the same series together, in 1984."

Ian's comments about Pat seem very perceptive; one observation in particular is almost uncanny, as Pat hasn't told Ian about his grandmother Amelia's background: "I go back to the first time I met him," observes Ian. "He's always got this aura around him – it's almost a mystery. It's a bit gypsy isn't it? Almost a bit Romany: I can see him in that guise." His admiration and regard for Pat are completely sincere. The entrance hall in his house is lined with showbiz photographs, ranging from classical actors to Lily Savage. But who's the first person that you see on the wall as you walk in? Pat Roach!

Having played such a range of outlandish, often manic characters, Pat is the first to acknowledge the importance of keeping a firm grip on reality. Human nature and the human psyche are fragile things; it could therefore be reasonably argued that the more bizarre or barbaric the character that an actor is required to play, over what is usually a period of several weeks, the greater his need to return to normality afterwards.

In my very first interview with him, for a previous biography entitled *There's More Out Than In (Ellen's Story)*, I asked: "What are the special highlights of your career so far? If somebody said to you, what have you done that you're *really* proud of?" The reply, at a time before I knew him better, was totally unexpected.

> *The number one thing I've done in my career is, having done individually separately, all these things, I resorted back to no boots on my feet and my arse hanging out – and fish and chips. I'd just come back to normal each time. I was invited to go and live in Hollywood and never went. And the biggest thing to me – the most impressive thing about my career, is to always come back from London or abroad and just go straight back into grubby old Birmingham, and go down and have a bacon sandwich at my favourite café, the A1, in Wainwright Street.*

Chapter Thirteen –

HANGING ON TO HARRISON

And lose, and start again at your beginnings
And never breathe a word about your loss...

I suppose you can associate my characters in all three 'Indiana Jones' films as 'losers',
but each time, I started again at a new beginning, because I was a new character.
What was great was that people never ever knew that all those four characters were
me: no one ever knew unless we told them. That's what was lovely; although the
characters lost each time, they started again at completely new beginnings.

Before filming began on the first *Indiana Jones* movie, Lucas and Spielberg
made a pact to produce a trilogy, which required some of the crew to sign a
contract for all three films, before they began the first. Work began in 1980,
with *Raiders of the Lost Ark.*

I was sat in my office at the Health Club one day when the telephone rang and my
agent told me that we'd got this job in 'Raiders of the Lost Ark', which was all
rather lovely. But I didn't realise at the time how the films would grow on me.
When I saw Spielberg for the part of the Sherpa first, which was a non-dialogued
part, he said to David Tomblin: "This guy could play the German too." Whereupon
they asked me if I'd shave my head and beard, and I said: "Well, what is it for?"

Pat had refused to shave his beard earlier, while working for Kubrick, but once
Spielberg explained that he'd also like Pat to play the German, he revised
his plans. His mother, Dolly, was quite surprised by Pat's decision, but it's
one of those memories that come particularly to mind, when she talks about
Pat's career.

"You've got a cutting in that lot where he's normal," she explained, referring
to a collection that she'd kindly lent me. "You see him sitting in the barber's
chair. It says: 'Pat Roach shows a few wrestling scars on his head.' Then you
see him when it's all off, and his beard. I said to him: 'It's a wonder, 'cause
you think so much of your beard.' He said: 'Mother – it's money, isn't it?'"

The fact that I would be playing two parts was even more attractive – so I agreed to do it – and off came the hair! Peter Carter, who runs a local health and tanning salon still to this day, cut it off for me, and did it in great style. The press came down and did the photograph.

I actually kept the cutting in my passport, because I'd given it no thought that there I was – travelling under a passport with lots of hair, then later passing through customs, looking like a billiard ball! I'd never get through – would I? So I carried the newspaper cutting. A Chief Inspector of the police at the time, who I was friendly with – and hopefully still am – named Dave Speake – also wrote me a few words saying that he would verify that I was one and the same person.

Pat set off for Tunisia, meeting Vic on set quite late, because his friend had been working on a Ryan O'Neal film. Vic explained: "Dave Tomblin, our mutual friend, kept trying to get me to do this film, 'cause he reckoned I looked like the actor – Harrison Ford." Stuntman Billy Horrigan – a man Pat is never likely to forget, as he saved his life during the filming of *Raiders* – was then a member of Vic's stunt team, *Stunts Inc.* Billy was present when Spielberg realised just how accurate Dave's assessment of Vic's potential was.

"They were shooting close up on the Ark, and we were on the set, in the truck behind, because we followed through – machine-gunning things when they start the chase," explains Billy. "Vic came over and he said, 'Well they're not going to get to us before lunch. Let's wander across and get there first before the crowds.' So as we're walking across, someone is shouting out: 'Harrison!' We carried on walking. The next thing, Vic swings round, because Spielberg has grabbed him by the arm and said, 'Wow! You're *not* Harrison!'

"Well anyway, he shouted out for his First Assistant, which was Dave Tomblin. He said: 'Dave, come and have a look at this!' Dave said: 'I've been *telling* you – he's a blinding double!' From then on, he became Harrison's double."

Vic recalls: "I finished working on *Green Ice* in Mexico, flew out to Tunisia and met the stunt co-ordinator who was doing the show at the time – Peter Diamond. He gave me the storyboard about the fight under a revolving wing. So I talked to him about it and was asked to co-ordinate the fight." Peter is featured in a group photograph of stuntmen who worked on *Raiders*.

"I turned up on the set and lo and behold the big shaven-headed German doing the part with Harrison was Pat. So we started talking – 'chin-wagging' – and I still hadn't met Spielberg. They do a couple of shots and Pat gets kicked in the balls. Then he threw a punch and I heard Spielberg say 'OK that's good.' I didn't like to be pushy, but I'm watching behind a camera and making sure the hit is OK. 'Excuse me,' I said, 'that was a miss.' Spielberg said, 'I saw it. It was a hit.' I said, 'OK, but I promise you, they've missed!' Spielberg said, 'OK, we'll do it again.'

"When he found out I was the co-ordinator, because nobody had introduced us properly, it was fine.   Five days later we're sitting there watching 'dailies' and lo and behold this shot that I'd said was a miss – he'd printed it. So it came up on film and you could see that it was quite a miss – the punch. He turned to me and said: 'Good call!' So from then on I was all right – you know?"

Pat never asks whether he's come into a film early or late, or about the stars of the film and locations, until he has the contract.

If they're exotic locations and you're working with terribly popular people – film stars so-to-speak, you build your hopes up about being in the Seychelles with Julia Roberts – or whoever – and you finish up not getting the job anyway. You can feel awfully sick about that. So I don't do it – I don't ask. I finished up in Tunisia, looking like a billiard ball!

Travelling without a hat, he must have felt conspicuous – especially in view of his normal appearance. But that was nothing compared to what awaited him!

We had the situation arise on Raiders where everyone got the inevitable stomach trouble. One morning they said to me: "Would you mind travelling with Karen Allen?" I said: "Of course not!" Obviously, she was the star of the film, but they asked me purely out of courtesy. I was fortunate to have travelled with her. There we were, in this great Mercedes limousine. It must have been about 25 feet long: the biggest thing you ever saw! Karen and I sat in the back. We were driving along and we were actually on the edge of the Sahara Desert.

I suddenly got this awful feeling in my stomach – that I was about to fill my pants! I thought God, what am I going to do? I can't do anything about it, so I'll just have to sit on it for a bit longer. So I did that – and the more I thought about it, the worse it got!

Bear in mind – there was nothing: there wasn't a tree, a rock – not even a camel I could go and stoop behind! It got so bad, I said, "Oh Karen, I'm going to have to get the guy to stop in a second. I might have to go and stoop behind the wheel on my side." She looked at me and I felt so embarrassed. She said: "If you do, I'll go on the other side!" It was so funny: she'd got the same trouble! Everyone on the set had it.

According to Minty Clinch's biography of Harrison Ford, the star of the film had it too – for at least five weeks! Spielberg, however, managed to escape the dreaded affliction by eating canned food; each time someone visited the set, they bought cans for him, so he didn't eat the same food as everybody else. According to Harrison's biography, Spielberg ate a wide range of English canned foods, while making the film; Pat recalls him eating countless tins of beans. But Pat's troubles didn't end with the limousine ride!

> *It was actually in the air, you know. Anyway, we get onto the set and I'd got this beautiful Winnebago. As I arrived, there I was, in a hurry, doing these very short steps that you do. I don't know whether you or the readers have ever experienced it. If you need to go to the toilet, although you're in a hurry, you're doing short steps: you're frightened to stride out!*
>
> *The Italian guy who was there looked up at me. And there I was, this great German powerful character that he knew he was looking after, doing these little short steps. He looked at me and I don't know what he must have thought about me!*
>
> *He was doing something with some water at the time, and rattled off something in Italian at me. I said: "Good Morning!" Got myself up the steps – somehow – I don't know how I did it. I think I sort of pulled myself up. I don't think that I parted my legs! I got into my van and Karen was whisked off into her Winnebago – her mobile home. They'd bought them all from Italy for some reason..*

Luckily, Pat had his own accommodation, but the Italian was still following him, muttering something about 'aqua' or 'agua'.

> *But I didn't know what it meant. So I headed for this toilet, thinking – thank God – what a relief! Only to find – no water. I was in a terrible panic. Of course, we were in the middle of the desert. All I had on was a T-shirt, a pair of trunks and some flip-flops. So I didn't have any old bills in my pocket.*

They hadn't so much as a loo roll – Pat was in a terrible state! Reluctantly, he ventured outside, to be confronted again by the Italian guy, who'd walked to the bottom of the Winnebago in disgust, thinking that Pat had ignored him.

> *So I said to him: "I need some water." And he said: "Yeah, yeah – aqua!" I thought, oh my God; now I know what he means!" Amongst all the flow of the Italian, I hadn't understood him. He went to shove past me. I said: "No, you give me the water – I'll do it!" He said what I assumed was "No." This shoving backwards and forwards was going on and he succeeded in shoving his way past me into the door and went: "Oh, oh, oh!" He came racing past me, again with a bottle of blue whatever-it-was.*

As realisation dawned, the Italian ran back, got the top off the bottle, and though he meant to put it down the toilet, sprayed Pat for good measure, on the way past.

Then it went all over the Winnebago and he was going, "Oh!" – holding his nose! It was the funniest thing out. I was so embarrassed. When I walked back on the set, it was the scene where Indy's looking for the hiding place where they've rolled the stone back and left it there. He puts down the eye; the sun shines through and points to the spot where it is.

Of course, there were literally thousands of people when I arrived on set. I swear every one of them must have known about me – and the toilet! By now they were all talking about me in Arabic; they were all laughing and looking at me. It was the funniest thing out!

In true 'Indy' fashion, both of Pat's characters meet an unpleasant end. In his role as the German lieutenant, he is chopped to pieces when he runs into an aeroplane propeller, during his fight with the hero. Billy Horrigan recalls the scene: "I remember the fight in the desert with Vic and Pat, when Vic was doubling for Harrison. I tell you, that was very 'hairy', 'cause those blades were going around; it was a terrific fight."

The propeller fight scene is probably one of the best fight scenes ever filmed. It took them a very long time to do it, because of the shadows: obviously, they could only film when all the shadows were right overhead, otherwise everything would have been a mess – afoot; trying to marry/match all the shadows would have looked terrible. It was so successful in fact, that everybody knows about it, but very few people, to this day, know it was me who did it. They still re-enact this same evergreen fight scene, that won it's way into cinematographical history, at the MGM film studios – albeit with different actors.

The writer recently witnessed the reconstructed scene, accompanied by appropriate soundtrack, during a visit to these same studios in Florida, and purchased a postcard of the hero and heroine fleeing the burning aircraft.

Earlier, in the mine, Indy was in there and Otto the Sherpa comes crashing onto the scene. I remember I sort of got hold of him, bashed him against the wall, bashed him against another wall and proceeded to punch him on the nose, and one thing and another. Spielberg said: "Just a minute. When you bang him against the wall, we need some dust to come off." So they used on the set – what was it they used now?

Fuller's Earth?

Yes, of course. So they put it on the walls.

I've used it in Amateur Dramatic productions – it's useful for making hair grey too.

137

Yes. We did the shot again; although Harrison was very physical – very good – we didn't get this cloud of dust that we thought we were going to get – in the mine. Someone suggested that Harrison should, as he hit it, just blow – to make the dust rise. So he did it again – and it still didn't work. And I said: "How on earth did you get the leading role – if that's the best blow job you can do?"

The fight scene with Otto the Sherpa continued into the bar area. They were trying out a new gel just in from Australia – for the first time: the fire burned well but didn't give off a lot of heat too quickly, because of the gel.

Billy Horrigan helped prepare me for the scene where my arm went into the fire and set on fire – which was the beginning of the end for that character. Harrison hits him with a table, which knocks him out, and he proceeds to burn away happily – to a cinder – I suppose. What happened was we blocked it out, so-to-speak – walked it through, then ran it through without the fire, in the early stages. But the whole set needed to be alight for lighting purposes; obviously, we had to get the correct light for shooting the whole scene. So in actual fact, I had to be alight!

They rehearsed the whole sequence a couple of times, Pat rolled into the fire without the arm igniting. As they continued, Harrison hit Pat with a table that broke. The scene ended with Pat falling into the corner. Harrison is quoted as saying that it's not the really complicated stunts that you have to watch out for – it's the ones that you *think* are well planned. Billy agrees: "You get kind of blasé with simple little things: like falling off a chair – you could damage an arm, or twist your back; silly little stunts like running into a room or banging a door open. It's those that take a while to set up where you've got more chance of getting away with it." What followed in the bar scene was a classic example of how a relatively simple part of a scene can prove to be its undoing.

The fire crew was standing by with quite a complement of firemen. They proceeded to put the set out with the small fire extinguishers. They had the larger machine outside. The first run through was one scene with one or two things to put right. Then the guy ran on and put the set out. We ran it again and they lit everything again – and we just about got it right.

Went through the fight; Harrison hit me with the table a first time, then a second time. So this time it's going to be a take and everything's lit up. We do the fight; I run Harrison to the bar, he looks at Karen and says, "Whisky!" She says, "What?" He says, "Whisky!" She thinks he must be mad; I've got him bent over the bar – killing him – and he's asking for a whisky!

Indy actually wants a whisky bottle, which Karen hands him, whereupon he hits Pat on the head with it, causing him to fall backwards into the fire. We're now towards the end of the scene as the fire lights. Pat attempts to hit Harrison with the lit arm. Ford ducks a couple of times, then hits him with the table. Although they were using balsa wood furniture, Billy confirms from personal experience: "… you can still have nasty accidents."

This time, the table didn't break!

Oh my God!

But during the kerfuful it doesn't really matter.

But didn't it knock you out?!

Yes it did. I go down, and I'm out.

Were you supposed to stay down?

Yes. But I'm supposed to shout when I'm burnt enough – because I'm on fire!

So you can't warn them?

By now, I'm igniting all over. But I'm unconscious. And they're waiting – as long as they can – we're only talking seconds – because they're shooting over Harrison's shoulder now and they've still got me behind there, burning away merrily! I'm supposed to shout to Billy Horrigan: "OK – I've had enough!" – as soon as this gel starts to get hot. But I was unconscious, and I would have burnt away. Billy noticed that I was unconscious and he ran in front of the cameras and put me out.

So he probably saved your life.

Yes, he probably did.

It doesn't bear thinking about!

But credit to him – he 'took it on his own bat'.

Were you injured at all?

No, I was OK. But the thing was, I would have carried on burning and then I would have been injured, because I couldn't say: "I've had enough."

When they prepared Pat for the shot, he was padded with fireproof material, but eventually, with the gel burning, it would burn through.

It's a flame – you know – like calor gas doesn't burn so hot as ordinary gas; well, this stuff doesn't burn so hot. It was on that long, because the shot was obviously a good shot, that when they tried to put the fire out they'd lost it, they couldn't put it out with a small extinguisher. So they opened the doors, which of course fanned the flames, and they had to get the big equipment in, to put it out.

Pat has no idea how long it took to extinguish the fire: he was unconscious at the time! Luckily, as Billy explains, he was standing by. "Having rigged jobs and set them up over the years, you know by instinct when he's had enough. You think, right, he's not getting up, he's not reacting – so it's time to get in quick!

"As far as I'm concerned, he could have been unconscious, or he could have just been sort of waiting. They'll carry on filming until the last minute. I mean, the cameraman wasn't aware that he was knocked out, because I wasn't. Once you see the fire starting to spread, you get in quick, knowing full well that it shouldn't have been anywhere else but on his arm."

Vic and Pat recalled a second out-of-control fire on *Raiders,* during our Pinewood visit. Wendy Leech, who eventually became Vic's wife, doubled for Karen Allen, and the other leading ladies in all three *Indiana Jones* movies. Vic explained recently: "This is something of a record. She also doubled for Michelle Yeogh, on the motor cycle, in *Tomorrow Never Dies.*"

We set the 'plane on fire in Raiders and Vic and Wendy ran from the plane – in the long shot. There was a big explosion. Then the fire brigade, with all their beautiful, bright shiny helmets arrived, unrolled all their hoses, stood there, switched on the water – and nothing happened! It was like in a movie! Nothing came out of the engine. It all came out of the pipe, because it was punctured all the way up.

George Lucas directed some Second Unit filming on location in Tunisia for *Raiders,* but Pat recollects that his own shots were all First Unit – with Spielberg. They used the so-called *Star Wars Canyon* in Tunisia. Pat remembers filming in a large canyon but didn't know the name of it. He filmed *Raiders* in Tunisia and at Elstree studios.

One of the shots we filmed in Tunisia included a scene where Indy was inside a mock-up cave. The crew tricked Spielberg into going inside the cave where Indy found the eye, by pretending they needed his approval for something. Then they rolled the rock across and locked him in for a few minutes. I don't think Steven minded too much, because he'd probably got his tin of beans with him!

Vic was Harrison's stunt man in *Blade Runner* and all three Indy films, as well as stunt coordinator. In Minty's book, Ford pays tribute to him. "Guys like Vic never get any credit, they are invisible." Vic describes Harrison's attitude towards stunts as 'very game'. Pat has no doubt about this: the two men worked very closely together, in situations where trust was paramount.

Harrison did just about all the fight scenes; the number of times Harrison and I punched each other on the nose is countless. We just threw many, many thousands of punches. He never minded; he never complained once.

One of the days I came on to the 'Indy 2' set. My wardrobe and make-up took absolutely ages, because I was really blacked, all over, to the satisfaction of Spielberg, who was a demanding director: he likes things to a standard of perfection.

So I get onto the set and I'm absolutely blacked down and looking like my blue-eyed Afghani, only to find that, walking past one of the guys, his eye was blacked – and the second, third and fourth guy. I quickly realised that everyone had got a painted left black eye – everyone on the set. Then I soon realised why – "What's going on?" They pointed out that one of the guys on the set had got a genuine black eye, so what everyone else did was to black their eyes up for him, so that he didn't feel embarrassed – or out of it! The only person on the set who didn't have a black left eye was me: I had two black eyes!

The truck chase was directed by Mickey Moore – described by Pat as "a great Second Unit director. Mickey wanted me to go to America and thought that I had a great future, but I didn't go." *Raiders* became undisputed box-office champion of 1981, grossing $363 million world-wide; Spielberg was nominated for his second Oscar as director. In the event, the film received five Oscars, all in technical categories. Pat talked about his experience of Spielberg, as a director:

I found him nothing short of great. I think that one of his secrets is that he's got the knack of watching what he himself is filming, from a punter's point of view – he's never ashamed of remembering what excited him as a punter himself. He once admitted to me, on and about the time I was wrestling at the Olympic Auditorium, on 15th and Grand in Hollywood, that he actually stood at the stage door, collecting autographs – having already directed his first film. I respect him very much for that.

He is an altruistic director, who would say things like: "Why spoil the shot for the sake of a million dollars? Instead of the film making 300 million, it will make 299."

A prime example of this is when the director raised Pat about three inches trying to obtain the right angle for shots of Pat whipping Short Round, bringing filming to a halt to do so. David Tomblin was also on set.

Spielberg said: "You know, when I shot 'Jaws' I had a chair built in the water, so I could sit there and see Jaws coming along: my eyes were at water level, but I just dipped my head slightly." David Tomblin said, with his usual dry sort of humour, "Steven, I thought you could walk on water." Steven retaliated: "After they saw the receipts, they thought I could!"

Harrison modestly described himself as 'a bag of bones', not keen on workouts, but according to Pat he became keen. Pat set up a gym, at Elstree for Indy 2 – *Temple of Doom.*

It wasn't the best gym in the world, it sufficed and they had their personal trainer – Jake. He had his own TV programme afterwards in America, 'Train with Jake'. He's in the credits for 'Indiana Jones'. Harrison's former wife was there, Melissa: she trained with him, and Spielberg trained as well. Steven also had some equipment at the Saint James hotel where he was staying.
    Harrison was never an exercise freak, but he became interested. He needed to be very fit: the schedule was quite heavy. You must remember that the fight scenes that he and I did were quite demanding – hell, they were demanding! I'd done this all my life and I found it demanding – so he had to.

He'd got lots of stamina?

Oh yes. It was natural for me to throw punches, duck punches, take bumps; it never bothered me. But it was very demanding for him; he was very game.

Billy Horrigan, who particularly enjoyed working on *Raiders*, recalls Ron Lacey, who played the Gestapo villain, Toht, but sadly died later of cancer. "A friend of mine used to run the Film School in Bournemouth. Ron Lacey used to come down – they'd sometimes invite actors down to help out with the students. He was a great patron of the Bournemouth Film School."
    Despite Ron's screen image, Billy describes him as: "a lovely man." Toht was dressed in black during filming. "He must have been absolutely roasting in those temperatures," comments Billy. Malcolm Weaver, Billy's friend and fellow stuntman, played one of Toht's Nepalese bodyguards.
    An interesting comparison can be made between the demands of *Indy*, and Harrison's latest film – *Six Days and Seven Nights*, with Anne Hersche, filmed on location in Hawaii – again, very demanding physically. Despite the fact that he's now older, he seems to have met the challenge admirably.
    They originally offered the role of Indiana to Tom Selleck, but he was tied up contract-wise. He was understandably disappointed, particularly in view of the eventual success of the *Indy* trilogy. Minty Clinch illustrates this with a quote from Selleck: "That should have been my role."

*Like Glenda Jackson said: "It's parts that make great actors." If the part's right you can be a great actor – but without the right part, you can't be a great actor. If Selleck had done Indy he would have been very good, within his own interpretation; I'm not saying that he would have been better. It's like Moore playing Bond. You couldn't say that you liked Moore better than Connery's Bond, because they're just different. He was wise enough to do it **differently**, you see. There's lots of other stuff we can talk about in connection with Raiders, but we can possibly keep that for another time.*

In *Indiana Jones and the Temple of Doom*, otherwise known as *Raiders II*, Pat had a fairly substantial part as the Chief Guard. Attempting to confiscate his whip was hardly a task for the faint-hearted, but one famous actress, with a good sense of timing, managed to do just that!

It was a lot of fun. During filming I met Barbara Streisand, which was a nice thing to do. I was quite busy at the time – whipping Harrison Ford! She sneaked up behind me, clad all in black leather, snatched the whip out of my hand and took over; shoved me out of the way and proceeded to whip him! There were two guys holding Harrison, with chains, and he couldn't get away. They weren't stunt men actually; they were just two guys that they were using. Harrison wasn't very pleased about how hard they were pulling on the chains.

In the end they changed them to stunt guys, as the others didn't have the knack of making it look genuine, without really doing it. But at the time, the guys were pulling the chains too hard, I was busy whipping him and suddenly Streisand walks up and says: "Give me the whip!"

Harrison's previous films provided her with a lot of scope; fortunately the two stars are friends.

She whacked him half-a-dozen times and said: "That was for making that lousy film Hanover Street." Then she whacked him again: "That was for making all that money in Star Wars!" Irvin Kershner had just walked on the set in front of her. They shot it to use in the Christmas Movie stuff – they do faux pas and all that sort of thing. So 'Kersh' walked on the set and laughed. We broke.

This is the moment, mentioned in an earlier chapter, when Kershner, Pat and Spielberg then went over to the editing rooms to view the six-minute fight scene between Connery and Pat from *Never Say Never Again*. It was all the inspiration Spielberg needed: not to be out-done, he was determined to do a fight scene of longer duration!

That conveyor belt scene between Harrison and myself, you've never seen such a cheat in all your life! It was only as long as this room. We were on it six minutes! They kept cheating us back – checking us back – to make it last longer. I distinctly remember I'd had an Indian meal the night before and my breath stank of garlic. I said: "Harrison, I had an Indian meal last night." He said: "I know!"

The conveyor belt eventually draws the fight sequence towards its conclusion, culminating in the death of Pat's character, in a gigantic stone-crushing machine.

What happened was, we're in the mine and Harrison gets into it. I pick up Short Round, the little Korean boy and sling him to the side with one hand.

At the time Spielberg said: "What can we do that's different?" I said: "Just look at this; just 'sell' this Harrison." And I gave him a right-hander – right under the heart. And Harrison's mouth dropped open. I'd copied the fight from an incident when my father killed a lumberjack in Canada.

Harrison's mouth just dropped open and you'd have thought he was screaming, but he wasn't – no sound came from his mouth. It was this powerful punch to the heart. Spielberg said: "Oh yes – marvellous!" But I think they cut it.

A later check of the British version of the videotape revealed that the shot had been cut. There were a lot of complaints about the film's violence afterwards. According to Joseph McBride, in his biography about the director, 'Spielberg said that the more violent episodes in *Raiders* were more to Lucas' taste than his own – scores of people violently eliminated.'

Pat explained that they showed the more grisly version in America – where an Asian villain pulled the first victim's heart out. Minty Clinch's biography of Harrison reveals that the slow burning of a victim was retained in the American version, but like the heart sequence, this was also cut by the British film censors. Nevertheless, *Temple of Doom* could still be described as quite horrific in places, even with the cuts – enough to make your flesh creep!

So originally, Harrison and Pat filmed the punch to the heart, just after Pat had thrown Short Round to one side. Then he picked Indiana up above his head, and dumped him into the truck: very similar to the Pat/Vic sequence in *Never Say Never* sequence, where Bond is thrown from a great height and comes crashing down into the shelves. This was followed by a highly dangerous incident, which Pat and Vic recalled later, at Pinewood:

We nearly got killed on that, if you remember. We were in a big steel truck and Vic and I were doing the fighting. There's a scene where we have to move as we're fighting. We go up the slipway and we can only move one way really, which is down. What we did, we contributed weight to the bottom end. This thing must have weighed about three-ton, mustn't it?

Well, half way up it turned over and Vic and I had to jump, and below us were all the picks in the ground. They were obviously set for the best camera angle. In other words, they were sticking prominently out of the ground, so that you could see them. We very quickly decided to jump different ways – he went one way and I went the other – and we had to land between these big picks in the ground. Of course the steel end was sticking up, wasn't it? We both jumped and both landed in between – luckily enough!

This chase through a mountain in a mine train was an idea originally intended for *Raiders*. They finally reach the top, and are tipped out onto the conveyor belt. Harrison and Pat continue to fight along the length of it.

At the time, Kate Capshaw, who became Spielberg's wife, is throwing stones at us – she's lovely – Kate. So she's throwing stones at me and I think, at one stage, my character throws one back at her. I think I may have hit her. I can't remember now – it's so long ago.

There are at least two shots of Kate throwing stones at Pat, but there didn't seem to be one where he throws a stone and hits her – it was probably cut! She also hands something to Indy, that looks like a large metal box and he hits Pat with it.

The fight continues until they reach the lethal crusher. I wondered how far away the two men were from the crusher when filming was taking place. They appeared to be so close – and how had they controlled it?

Harrison was just unbelievable! It wasn't controlled. I'm surprised that he did it.

I thought it must have been Vic – that's amazing!

No, it was Harrison. At one stage, he was leaning backwards with his head and this thing was touching his hat – you couldn't believe it. It frightened the life out of me! I went close when I went down – when the thing round my waist got caught.

Did they control that – to make sure that you weren't pulled into the machine?

They didn't: it was a risk factor. It kept rolling, and we were there!

Audiences saw a wide red band of blood smeared across the roller – and that was the end of you– at the close of that sequence – but there had to be some controlling mechanism at that stage. Couldn't they just suddenly switch the entire machine off?

It's difficult to remember. I think what happened was that they shot the camera at an angle where they could see the edge of the thing going round; the camera's shooting from there, so you can see how close it is. Then as they drop the camera down like that, they could move the wheel away, couldn't they?

So it's a case of synchronisation?

Yes, it's like which finger is nearer to you there? Now you can tell from that distance, but from another ten feet back, you wouldn't be able to tell which was closer – if they were strips of paper, for example. So they widened the gap, and you went down in the gap?

It was *very* dangerous though.

Absolutely dangerous – yes. Just before we actually did it and dropped through, everything had to be just in place.

Weren't you scared?

Oh yes – very aware, and Harrison too. We just trusted each other; I held him.

What was Vic doing at that point?

Well, he'd probably got his hands over his eyes: probably terrified in case anything happened – because it would have been his fault. Vic wouldn't just come as a stunt double – he was a bit further along the line than that by that time. He was stunt coordinator. So I imagine they were all hiding their eyes behind their hands at the time.

So it really was just you and Harrison at that stage of the sequence?

It was absolute trust. Harrison trusted me to hang on to him and vice versa. Just complete trust. Harrison's head was down there. Unbelievable really!

Film number three also starred Sean Connery – *Indiana Jones and the Last Crusade*. By then there was a joke on set, between Spielberg, Dave Tomblin, Harrison and Pat – about Pat being their lucky mascot.

In the third one, there were about three very small parts that Spielberg put all together – and made one character, which I played; that became the Adolph Hitler type person with the moustache – on the photograph outside this room. He had the short German haircut because he was Gestapo. I appeared on the airship and did a whole speech in German, but it was cut out.

Just a few seconds of me, walking into the airship: ardent fans spotted me; it was very disappointing – unbelievable! There was a great fight scene. At one point they jump into the airship and they go straight through the bottom and get killed; they killed me in two different ways – and couldn't use either one.

Pat is one of only three actors to have been involved with all three *Indiana Jones* movies: like Billy Horrigan and Vic Armstrong, he has the jacket to prove it. The three of them also worked on *The Spaceman and King Arthur.* Billy is now retired: "I'm too old for it. I must admit that I miss it, but the thing is, I have my own injuries, and because so many of my age group are … well … they're dead!" Of Pat as a person, he says: "He's a great character and performer – a kind bloke. He's also highly professional, so very few retakes are needed."

Chapter Fourteen –

AUF WIEDERSEHEN PAT

If you can force your heart and nerve and sinew
To serve your turn long after they are gone …

We always used to film on Friday evening, which, if you can imagine, was the time when everyone was about to commute back from London. When we were in the hut all that we could hear were trains and aeroplanes. If ever you had to force your heart and your nerves – and dare I say – your sinews – not to scream! Because you were doing your lines, and thinking to yourself: it's my turn to do my dialogue now. Have all those trains gone, or should I hold off against the next one? But then, if nothing comes, it's a waste of time. So you have to have the will to go on.

You'd be saying, "I phoned home this morning and spoke to Beth," – and you'd hear this chug-chug-chug of the train. You'd continue: "Beth was quite upset"… and your eyes are gone. You wait for the director to say: "Sound interference – cut!" So while you're doing it, you've stopped believing in what you're talking about. Then all of a sudden, an aircraft's taking off – when you're trying to deliver the same lines!

Paddington residents out walking their dogs, early-morning joggers circumnavigating the lake, or those strolling leisurely through Strauss Park, Little Venice, would have been taken totally unawares by the spectacle of a giant-of-a-man attempting innumerable free squats. Then he'd head for the church in Warwick Avenue, in a triangle between the Harrow Road and Maida Vale, just a stone's throw from the tube station. Once under the tap, he'd enjoy a re-invigorating wash. But this wasn't some unusually tall vicar or churchwarden; it was

Pat, preparing for the morning's rehearsal for the first series of *Auf Wiedersehen Pet*, spruced up and clean before the others arrived. Saint Peter's Hall in central London, and Elstree, were venues hired for rehearsals. Meanwhile, other cast members were on their way, from different parts of London. Ten o'clock seemed a reasonable starting time, in view of the traffic situation.

149

Timothy Spall had been filming *Metal God* for Warner Brothers, in Hollywood, when we contacted him. He played Black Country Barry Taylor in *Auf Wiedersehen*. He explained that working on the series involved two types of schedule, the most demanding being rehearsal sessions, which sometimes lasted twelve hours, in blocks of three weeks. "We'd usually 'turn over' at eight o'clock, so we had to be there sevenish – seven-thirty." Filming, however, occupied the bulk of the time and involved more sociable hours. "We used to start at 10 am. and finish quite early at lunchtime sometimes. Not because people were actually falling over, but we did like to have a drink. So shooting was often from 10 am. to 2.30pm."

As Tim is a Londoner, born and bred in the Clapham Junction area of Battersea, I wondered how he'd created such a convincing Black Country accent. Family connections helped: "When we first got together, my wife was living in Bilbrook, near Codsall, which is Wolverhampton really, her father is from Walsall. I think Barry's whole persona was informed by the way he spoke; I always find that with characters anyway."

Scriptwriters Ian La Frenais and Dick Clement created an hilarious character for him – described in Birmingham newspapers as 'an educated Brummie'. "When I got the scripts I read them very carefully and Barry didn't really come until the end of the first episode. He's kind of sketched into it, for the first three or four. It concentrated mainly on the Geordie characters. I didn't want him to be a minor character, you know? Because I could see that it was very interesting writing and that they were doing a very nice job of making it an ensemble piece. But of course it concentrated mainly on Oz, Dennis and Neville, because it took them from Newcastle to Germany. At the end of the first episode Barry turns up on his motorbike.

"What was really interesting about the character to me," explained Tim, "wasn't the fact that he was from Birmingham in particular, or that he was a motorbike enthusiast, although the two things were immediately striking. It was more the fact that everyone called him 'Boring Barry'. He was actually a person from a slightly different class from the rest of them. More of a lower middle class character, in a sense. But he's not really; he's just one of those odd boys – chaps – young gents – from a world that he considered not to be superior, but his interests were more of a kind of pastoral nature, you know?

"He was more of a *Blue Peter* character, one of the original quintessential 'anoraks' – in a sense – although he had a leather coat! There was a kind of innocence and sensitivity to him that I think was possibly always there." Viewers may recall one particularly memorable episode when he decided to go brass rubbing, while all the others went for a pint – a lovely touch!

Kevin Whately began filming the final episode of *Inspector Morse* in spring 2000, the grand finale to a series of Morse repeats on *ITV* that summer. He first appeared as Sergeant Lewis in 1987: this and other roles are discussed in more detail in the next chapter. When the first series of *Auf Wiedersehen Pet* was being cast in the early 1980s, he had already made considerable headway with his career. He and Tim Healy were the first of a group of actors to become associated with the programme.

Rights to the series, about the fortunes of a group of building workers, recently reverted to their original creator, Franc Roddam. The third series will probably be broadcast in March or April 2002, and will comprise six one-hour episodes. All six surviving actors will resume their original roles.

Recalling the first series, Kevin explained that the 'Geordie Mafia' had heard about it. Having previously been heavily influenced by the *Likely Lads*, a triumph for the same scriptwriters, Ian La Frenais and Dick Clement, they were desperate to get in. Approximately two hundred Geordie actors expressed an interest. Preliminary interviews were held with the London Geordies, including Kevin, then afterwards in Newcastle. Ironically, Jimmy Nail was the last of this second group to audition. Meanwhile, Kevin was off to Greenland to film the *Shackleton* series for the BBC. Initially, Pat had some misgivings about the series.

> When Roger Bamford cast me I thought: do I want to work for someone who is such a bad judge of an actor, as to cast me in this part? I even made a mess of the audition: I didn't read the lines well. I wasn't an actor – I'd never done it. I even had my doubts about Roger because he'd picked me! Why's he picked me? This can't be any good!

Did you think: what are the others going to be like if I'm in it?

> Yes, that's true, that is. But from a mercenary point of view it was fine.

In the event, casting for the series proved particularly astute. Just as each character was very much an individual, the actors themselves possessed a wide range of talents. Tim Healy was originally a stand-up comedian, and Pat was from the sporting, television and film world, eventually even trying pantomime. Tim Spall and Christopher Fairbank, who plays Moxey, the Liverpudlian 'ex-con', are both classical actors with RADA training. Kevin had a range of acting experience.

The opportunity to play Moxey was ideal timing for Chris, who'd just had a disillusioning experience with the *Royal Shakespeare Company*: "I desperately needed to work, in order to prove to myself that I was still employable." Initially, Chris and Tim Spall shared a similar problem: in four completed scripts out of an eventual thirteen, Moxey had even less dialogue than Barry, because the character had been created for a musician friend of Ian's, who lacked acting experience.

Chris trained at RADA for two years, although unlike Tim Spall, he didn't graduate, preferring to get some acting experience behind him. He readily admits to having "a low boredom threshold." He describes Moxey as "the sort of bloke who's wonderfully out of touch with mainstream life. I had a few wild years and met the person I base Moxey on in a police cell. I was just in overnight for 'drunk and incapable'. This guy was in because his ex-wife had called the police, saying that he'd tried to burn the house down." It transpired that she'd locked him out of the house, and he'd simply set fire to a dustbin to keep warm!

Pat's character, Bomber, is someone who's 'done it all before' and is about ten years older than the 'boys'.

Bomber was the strong, physical leader of the group. Whereas Dennis was the boss, in charge of the money, Bomber was a leader in his own right. They followed him because he knew what it was all about – and where it was all happening. When the others arrived in Germany, he was already there. Thinking that he was German, they asked: "Do you speak English?" He replied, in a West Country accent: " 'Tis my mother tongue!"

Kevin revealed that Tim Healy was short-listed for the part of Oz, before they discovered Jimmy. Kevin's character, Neville, has been described in various ways: a fresh-faced, homesick 'brickie', naïve, an idealist. He had two people from his past in mind when he played the part. Although Kevin prefers not to make judgements about his roles, he commented: "He had more depth to him, and was more sensitive than most of the other characters."

Tim Healy recently played the Geordie lead in a second series of John Sullivan's hilarious comedy, *Heartburn Hotel,* which is centered in Birmingham, and took part in a foot-balling film called *Purely Belter.* He rented a London flat during the filming of *Auf Wiedersehen Pet.* Commenting on his role in the series as the group's elected leader Dennis, he said: "They would put him forward: 'Oh Dennis, go and see the boss. Dennis, what are we going to do?' " He continued in an even broader Geordie accent: "He'd say, 'What's it got to do with me? What are you asking me for?' That's the sort of character he was really." By the second series he'd become the foreman.

Tim remembers his first meeting with Pat: "We all arrived at Elstree in this room and there he was. He was a monster of a guy, you know – a great big tall guy. The first thing they made us do was go down and have our costumes – get kitted out, you know? So we all went down into this costume department. There was a little gay guy running it – that we'd never met. A tiny little fella he was called Sean – Irish. He came out with a load of clothes on his arms."

Sean wasn't aware that the cast were already waiting and walked straight into Pat's chest, hitting him just above the waist with his head. "All he said was 'Halloo!'" continued Tim, in a comic Irish accent. "Pat said: 'Hello there!' Sean stared up at this monster guy, you know?"

"It was funny when Pat first started," Tim continued, "he thought he was the only one of the gang who wasn't an actor because he hadn't had the experience that I and some of the others had, like. He asked for advice when we first started. He used to say: 'Oh you're a proper actor and you've been working for ten years. Help us out a bit.' But of course, he was brilliant in the role. That feeling disappeared eventually. But at first he was a bit worried about that."

> *I was a very fortunate fellow. I was thrown in with these six brilliant actors. I didn't know sugar from salt. I was terrible. Everybody knew it: I knew it, the director knew it! Tim Healy and Kevin were friends from way back. Jimmy didn't know them because he was a builder in those days – not an actor.*

Tim Spall remembers Pat's early attempts at the part: "The wonderful thing I shall never forget was actually the first 'read-through', because I could see that Pat was nervous. I knew he was going to be playing a Bristol character and I'd met him earlier that day. I knew he wasn't thought of as being an actor."

Although the second series was filmed more than fifteen years ago, its principal actors retain vivid memories of the experience. The two series involved a total of twenty-six episodes. "As history tells you, you couldn't have got a more diverse bunch of people together," recalled Timothy Spall, "although there was a common denominator in that everybody was all right: there was nobody trying to play ego games. Because Jimmy had come from nowhere really. Pat had come from his world, which was obviously wrestling and stunting – that area. Kevin had come out of doing theatre a bit and Tim from comedy."

The Birmingham press reported that one of the things Tim Spall most enjoyed about the series was the absence of pretentious or 'actorish' behaviour. Was this purely luck, or could it have been inspired casting? "I think it's both. I think it was clever casting, but you can never cast personalities – you never know quite *what's* going to go on." Following the second series, broadcast in Spring 1986, Tim commented that they all 'exhausted by the pressures of the show – and from Gary Holton's untimely death.' Was it totally unexpected, or were there signs beforehand that something might happen to him?

"Well, one sensed that he wasn't very happy," Tim explained. "His relationship had broken up and he was surrounded by a group of people that nobody really knew: an entourage of people who really weren't doing him much good. I never say anything about what other people do, because it's up to them. But Gary had a history of using drugs – and so on. We all thought he'd got over it. But one did get a general sense of him being more *lost* than really in trouble."

Chris Fairbank recalls: "There were lots of scenes which should have been with all seven of us, which were turned into two or three handers, to try not to make his absence more notable, by having the rest of us in the scene – and not him."

After interviewing his mother, Joan, Gary's death seems even more tragic. According to the press, it was from a drug overdose, although the inquest recorded an open verdict. Gary had already established a substantial career for himself before the series. One would have expected, following his successful role as cheeky cockney, Wayne, that life couldn't have been better.

"Before he went to Grammar, we used to go ballroom dancing," recalls Joan. "We used to travel all round; he won lots of trophies for ballroom dancing – Latin American – he won the trophies for everything. Then when he went to grammar school, he had a music teacher there – Peter something. He liked Gary so much, and could see that he was gifted. Talent-spotters came to the school, when he was twelve and picked Gary out for a part in *Quatermass and the Pit.*"

Gary's acting career began at the age of eleven, with the *Sadlers Wells Opera*, followed by the *RSC* and the *Old Vic*. He appeared in *Breaking Glass* and *Quadrophenia*, played Eddie Hairstyle in *The Knowledge* and made guest appearances in *Gentle Touch, Minder, Shoestring* and *Bloody Kids*, a controversial feature film.

As a schoolboy, he was in the chorus line for various shows. "He was also the Milky Bar Kid, but he wore a blond wig and glasses," explained Joan. Then just like Pat, in *Clash of the Titans*, Gary worked alongside Sir Laurence Olivier, in this case, for three seasons, in *Love for Love*. Acting with John Stride, he received four standing ovations as the drunken brother-in-law, in *A Girl In My Soup*.

Joan explained: "When he came out of *Hair*, he started up a group called *Heavy Metal Kids*. Then he went on *Top of the Pops*, to promote one of his records." Gary also played several musical instruments. He joined highly-acclaimed Norwegian singer/songwriter Casino Steel and after signing with *Polydor* achieved three hit albums and singles in Norway.

A photograph of Pat holding Gary above his head provides a graphic illustration of their rapport. John Harwood-Bee, who despite Gary's death remains his manager, was on location in Spain during the filming of Series Two. He commented recently that, whilst not condoning Gary's use of drugs,

Pat seemed to understand the problems that his friend was experiencing in coping with fame; experiences from his own past undoubtedly helped him to understand the pressures involved.

Gary's mother spoke about this friendship recently. "They used to do lots of things: they had fun and games together. Gary looked upon him as a big brother. I don't really know how to explain it – he was so close to him. After they'd finished the first *Auf Wiedersehen Pet*, he said that Pat had a part where they were going to be 'snowmen' – and Gary was offered a film part too." He was referring to Pat's role as Evans in *The Last Place On Earth*.

"He and Pat liked being together all the time. He never spoke about the others as much as he spoke about Pat, let's put it like that. They were all good 'buddy-buddies', but Pat was number one, in his book. They used to get up to little tricks and Gary used to phone me and tell me about them."

Auf Wiedersehen Pet, was first televised on *ITV* in 1983, changing the lives of all the leading actors, by making household names of them almost overnight. Pat's character, 'Bomber' Busbridge, was a married West Country bricklayer, with an older daughter and two sons – in reality, the sons of Ronald Lacey, a fellow actor in *Raiders of the Lost Ark*. One of them, David, is now a television producer in America. Although Pat has had a tremendously varied sports, film and television career, he still regards the series as one of his most significant achievements and is looking forward, with great anticipation, to the third. The media obviously agreed with him, and often referred to the programme in subsequent articles.

I have been in lots of films, but usually in disguise. It was only after 'Auf Wiedersehen Pet' that people started to know my face. I enjoyed filming the series, but found that getting the timing right for comedy is an art, and the schedule was demanding.

Tim Spall, at that time a young man of twenty-four, noticed the change almost immediately. "I went out one day and I was famous – which was very peculiar. Because that is something I never understood would make your life different." Sitting in a Cambridge Circus pub, having a quiet drink, he was suddenly approached by a complete stranger. "I wasn't looking particularly miserable I don't think, but often people tell me to cheer up, when I'm perfectly happy. I said: 'There's no need to be concerned, I'm perfectly happy.' But he said,'Cheer up mate. With the money you should be getting, you *should* be happy!' I thought: my God – that's a bit rude! So I realised – actually that means I'm now famous – you know?" He has come to regard it as an occupational hazard and can joke about it philosophically. "I keep my head down. It's an odd relationship, but it's our fault: we shouldn't go on the telly!"

For Kevin, the popularity of the series also resulted in a loss of privacy. His wife, Madelaine Newton, was already an established actress. But on a positive note he acknowledges, "I've never been out of work since. At the time it was a big shock. Madelaine was already familiar with the situation. She warned me, but I hadn't realised the extent to which we would be affected."

He explained that it was almost like being one of the *Beatles* – although not quite to that extent. When half-jokingly asked: "You weren't actually mobbed were you?" he revealed that he had been! He, Tim Healy and Jimmy Nail went to see a Billy Connolly concert, but couldn't get past the foyer. In the end, Billy sent his stage crew to rescue them. Seats had been booked for them in the main auditorium, as opposed to a special box.

For Tim Healy, instant fame meant that he could no longer look people in the eye, because they saw it as an open invitation to approach him. As an actor, he had naturally been an observer of people. He could no longer do that, and found himself looking in shop windows or down at the ground, which was very disconcerting.

Tim Spall, like most celebrities, shares the same problem. "You can smile at somebody, or nod to them – just in passing. Then all of a sudden you see their expression change, and you're turned into something else. It's difficult to meet a lot of people on a normal level, because they make assumptions and a big wall goes up – not of your making – but because of the assumptions of the people.

"You're not on a one-to-one basis really. You're not meeting people like two ships in the night. There's also a talking point. It will take you twenty minutes to 'talk them down' – from assuming that you're something other than what you really are. Often people will be a little bit offensive – inadvertently."

Tim Healy spoke of the positive aspects of the series. "I got a mortgage for the first time and I got paid properly for the first time." He was on holiday in Spain when the programme was first televised, returning two weeks later. "I think it took something like two weeks for them to get to 10-12 million, then it went up to 15 million within three to four weeks – huge! It gave me the opportunity to do the sort of things that I would never have done. It set my career up. I was offered all sorts of work after it.

"Everybody was talking about it – all the pubs started emptying. Literally, from one day to the next, my life changed. I walked down the street and everybody turned their heads. I was instantly recognisable, which is fantastic … for a fortnight… and then you realise it's a big problem. And every day it happens. The *same* things happen every day, the same comments are made, the same questions are asked, and after a fortnight you think that it's quite boring; this is a bit of pressure on me."

Chris found that he had to be much more pragmatic when planning everyday things, like buying newspapers or cigarettes. 'Where's Oz?' was the most frequent remark. "It made me extremely self-conscious. What goes is your humanity, but believe me, I suffered the least of anybody. Jimmy, I think, caught the full blast of overnight success. People have this idea that those who work on the telly live in some 'Never-Never-Land'." Consequently, the question that came a close second to the 'Oz' version was: 'What are you doing around here?' Shopping became "a nightmare experience."

Life as an entertainer has generally been a very positive, often lucrative experience for Pat. Nevertheless, he has always taken great care to guard his privacy, and his family, from any unwanted attention on the part of the media, the public at large, and from those who presume to know him, simply by virtue of his being a celebrity. As Chris observes: "Fame is a many-splintered thing!"

The success of the series can be attributed to a number of factors; each of the cast has his own theories about this. First and foremost must be the quality of the scriptwriting. Ian La Frenais, one half of the winning team, has worked on many successful series, including *The Likely Lads, Porridge and Spender*. He is godfather to Denise Welch, Tim Healy's wife. In a magazine interview, Denise explained that her family and Ian's had been Geordie neighbours, living at opposite ends of the same road in Whitley Bay, for many years. Her father, Vincent, and Ian had been friends since they were boys. Ian has lived and worked in Los Angeles for many years. Stan Hey also wrote a couple of episodes.

According to Chris, the success of the series wasn't due to any one particular thing. "I think certainly with the first series, which was the most successful out of the two, it was timing – nobody can do anything about that. The 'random floating X factor'. Thatcher was closing all the loopholes that allowed builders to go off to Germany and work for tax-free money. All of this was happening just at the time the series was screened. Up until that point the Harwich to Hook of Holland ferries were crammed to the gunnels with builders going across to the continent tax-free.

"So there was a massive identification with the situation, on top of which, in those days, television was a nationalistic industry: programmes were made for here, whereas nowadays they're made with a view to overseas sales. Because of that, there are certain things that have to occur, in the casting, the way stories are scripted: it's all geared to viewers and overseas sales. Whereas it seemed in the early 80s, that wasn't the case; ratings were always important, but nothing *like* as crucial as they are today. The terms of reference were completely different."

Tim Spall comments: "Dick and Ian are such good writers, about men together, that they got a great deal of comedy out of them. There were seven hugely different personalities, all with their own idiosyncrasies and good and bad points. They just got better as they began to write according to what the actors were doing with their parts." Chris confirms this: "Ian's head was a tape recorder: he listened to what we were all saying, then incorporated it into the characters, which is fantastic really!"

Kevin agrees: "The script was superb. All of the characters were three-dimensional, so each of them displayed a wide range of characteristics throughout the two series. They weren't stereotyped. Ian La Frenais and Dick Clement are particularly good at writing characters with depth."

Pat is unstinting in his praise of director Roger Bamford, identifying him as another major reason for the success of the series.

> *Roger Bamford, God bless him, one of the directors of 'Auf Wiedersehen Pet' – I have so much to thank him for – you must put that in the book. He never dulled anyone's enthusiasm for one moment: he always made it work.*

Other members of the cast made a point of mentioning him. "The way that the director, Roger Bamford, cast the series and then handled the cast was superb," Kevin explained. "It wasn't like a normal programme. We were an odd lot. Jimmy was particularly green, but his energy motored the show. Roger channelled our exuberance: rather than suppress it, he harnessed it, and used it to enhance the programme even further."

As with all well-observed situation comedies, the delight – rather than the devil – is in the detail: Wayne's 'shades' and dangling ear-rings; Oz, fixing a treasured photo of Arthur Scargill in the gap between curling wallpaper, alongside a topless pin-up; filching strawberries from a sweet trolley, and talking about Wayne's need for moderation while loading his thousandth can of lager into a supermarket trolley; casually cleaning his toenails with a trowel, during a conversation with Bomber. Barry's apologetic demeanour, domesticity, philosophical outpourings and mud-splattered van after trout-tickling.

Bomber's solid, reassuring presence, and his favourite saying: "Bomber's away!" when he was ready to go out. Neville's plastic apron with a bottle of beer on the front, when he returns home, and Rupert Bear poster on his kitchen door. Moxey wearing his woolly hat in every conceivable situation and having a permanent cold. The seedy underwear of the 'lads', as they emerge from their sleeping bags, in stark contrast to the affluent Spanish lifestyle of their boss, Ally Fraser. Bill Patterson played this Scottish role with panache, in company with fellow 'shady-dealing' entrepreneur, cockney Kenny Ames, alias James Booth.

Tim Spall explains: "I think the programme appealed to the older generation because it was a classic army situation, you know? Seven guys in an enclosed space, who wouldn't normally be anywhere near each other. I think people recognised that from their National Service days.

"Also, it was about guys who were trying to make a living because things were bad at home. They're missing their loved ones and they're 'out on the razz' a bit, because they're away from home. Another thing was that *some* of the guys weren't used to being among foreigners. Instead of the Germans being foreigners, *they* were the foreigners: they couldn't work that one out!"

Tim Healy made the point: "At the time there were 30,000 Brits working out there in Germany. So it was a statement too: 'How dare you send these people abroad because they haven't any work here?' It had that wonderful truth underneath."

Kevin recalls: "We thought that everyone would want the part of Oz." Perhaps not surprising, as he was the most flamboyant and outspoken of all the characters. Pat remembers taking Jimmy to the gym, but the following day his friend probably wished that he hadn't!

> *He did some 'flyers' on the machine out there. The next day he had planned to take some furniture from Newcastle in a transit van. His wife had to drive, because his muscles were 'locked up' from training the night before.*

Kevin and Pat enjoyed working together and remain good friends to this day. "I'm very fond of him. My kids call him Uncle Pat. He's always been great with children. He knows us really well." When their daughter Kitty, christened Catherine, was born, Pat sent her a letter, enclosing five pounds, with the advice: 'Ask your daddy to buy you a premium bond with it.' We have included a copy of the family's response to the letter, written as though the newborn baby had replied to Pat, together with Pat's original envelope. The Whatelys have kindly allowed us to reproduce it.

Kevin says of his friend: "He's a 'driven' man, with a very strong work ethic. My overall memories of him are that he was always exercising, or doing something. He has more energy than anyone I've ever met. We had totally opposing political views. In the nicest possible way, he looks for people's weak spots and winds them up about them – in a good-natured way. He has a huge laugh; we'd be helpless with giggles for a lot of the time.

"I have memories of him related to wherever we happened to be at the time. For example, he might find an old motorbike or some other machine and he'd say: 'Ere, I could use that kid!' He was very much into 'wheeler-dealing'. He used to get frustrated, because none of us were entrepreneurial. During the first weeks of the series we were in Germany. In the first week, Pat was with Victor Tablian who he knew well because Victor played an Arab in *Indiana Jones*. He played a Turk in *Auf Wiedersehen Pet*. Pat said, 'Look at this,' and burst a whole apple in Vic's face – squeezed it in his hand – that's how strong he was!"

159

Chris remembers Pat as a man with traditional values. "You were brought up, certainly in Pat's day, and mine to a large extent, not to show your feelings – your vulnerability – your pain – and you certainly don't cry! He embodied all of that. He was quite mysterious. Nobody even knew how old he was; what we surmised was that he was a lot older than he would like people to think."

The writer pointed out that despite Chris's recollection of him as a traditionalist, Pat has a youthful, energetic outlook on life. "Absolutely," he agreed, "this is his uniqueness really: he fitted in absolutely perfectly – there was no way that he was on his own within the group – not at all: he was *very* much a part of it. In many ways, off camera, he was as big a catalyst as Jimmy, or anybody else.

"He came out with classic quotes; we were waiting for the 'Pat Roach Quote of the Day'. It usually involved a session with the *Daily Express*. I remember one day, which to my memory was the ultimate remark. We were all sat around waiting to go back to work – kicking a football, having a fag, cup of tea – whatever. Pat was buried in the *Daily Express* and we were joking and mucking around. At which point, Pat put the paper down. What he used to do was pronounce: 'theme for the day fellas.'

"This one was a cracker. He turned to us all and said, (Chris did this in a broad Birmingham accent) 'Now listen fellas. A word of advice: never employ anyone who's unemployed.' We all looked at each other and did 'double-takes'. I think it was Jimmy who said: (Geordie accent) 'Why, pray tell us Pat?' He said: 'Because they can't be trusted. That's why they're unemployed in the first place. If you want staff, nick 'em from other firms!' That summed up the whole health club scenario, and Pat's outlook really – certainly with regard to business."

The night they finally burned down the Dusseldorf hut was a cause for great celebration. Although there had been some shooting in Hamburg and Dusseldorf during the first series, Tim Spall explained that, "most of the hut was built at Elstree, in Borehamwood – on the back-lot of *Central Television* – which is now Albert Square."

According to Tim Healy, "There'd be sand in between your toes and sand in the bed. We said, 'At the end of this series we're going to burn this bastard down' – because we hated it that much. The writers said, 'Oh, shall we put that in the script?' So we had an accident in the last episode."

"Most directors would have filmed the hut scenes in a studio," explained Kevin, "but Roger decided to use the real thing. We were stuck in it. It was full of sand – damp and cold. It really helped to create a realistic situation." Wayne accidentally set fire to Barry's bike, with a discarded cigarette end. "It was quite a celebration – a night shoot."

Tim Spall explained that plans for destroying the hut took a rather dangerous turn during rehearsal. "When they set the device inside the hut to blow it up, it all went wrong. A couple of Special Effects guys and a cameraman had to jump out of the windows! It was very bad: I think Gary was in there." Pat recalls feelings of unease while these preparations were actually being made, for reasons that he still can't explain.

> *It seemed to me at the time that it was highly dangerous, and I said, several times: "We've got to be extra careful here." Sure enough, that went wrong. I'd been in a similar situation a short time before, playing Otto, in 'Raiders', when I could have been burnt to death.*

"Special Effects guys tend to get over-excited," Chris explains, "particularly where explosions are involved, and you had all these guys, sorting out charges and 'Belindas' and God-knows-what-else! What they failed to take into account was the back draught that's caused by the explosion. The door from the hut, leading out to safety, was open at the start of the actual sequence. The hut ignited and did all of that. There was an interior shot going on, of Barry's motorbike, which had caused it – and the lead up to it. The back draught caused the door to be slammed shut, so there was no way out. Roy Simper, who was the cameraman at the time, lost all the hair on his arms, eyebrows, and a bit of the hair on his head, I think. It was a hairy moment!"

Chris explained that when they filmed the first series, "Nobody really knew what we were all up to. We'd troop into the canteen for lunch every day, and we were just looked upon as these 'Herberts' who were pratting about on a pretend building site – or maybe it was real? They didn't really know what was going on! So there was nothing attractive or remotely glamorous about any of it.

"Ninety per cent of what we did, was in that hut. We went to the studio occasionally for non-hut scenes, but by and large we were in the hut for nine months. These days, you don't get things running as long as they did; they took about nine months a-piece, those two series. There just isn't the luxury of that time any more."

Conditions were hardly glamorous during Series 2! "It was a nightmare," Tim Healy explained, "because we had to stay white. All the Spanish episodes were shot, then we had to come back to England, to film the shots that were supposed to have happened before we'd gone! So for six weeks they said: 'Come inside guys, inside, inside!' We all had hats on. There was only one person got it wrong, and that was Gary Holton, because poor Gary was going off the rails a bit by then.

"He just sunbathed. He came back brown. So we had this brown guy – in England! Makeup is very difficult – to make somebody white that's brown. You can make somebody brown, but if you try it the other way you look like a flour grader, you know what I mean? So everybody was looking at the weather, and sitting inside – covered in sun block. We had to swim at night in the pool, as soon as it got dark. As soon as we finished that series, I went straight abroad, because I was so frustrated about it."

Filming in the Peak District was no picnic, as Tim Spall revealed. "Not only did we not have any trailers or dressing room facilities there, the location manager had to bribe an old lady with a tenner so that Jimmy could dry his feet and get changed in her toilet." This was during the filming of the 'trout tickling' episode. "After that was done," continued Tim, "we had to help push the scanner – the vehicle with the electrical equipment in it. So any pictures of it being a glamorous profession, particularly in the second series, when we were all supposedly these household names – not true!"

Tim Healy and Kevin's wife, Madelaine Newton, have been friends since their *Live Theatre* days in Newcastle. She played Tim's girlfriend, Christine, in the second series. Kevin explained that Madelaine had originally been short-listed to play Dennis' wife, but in the end the part was given to Caroline Hutchinson. Sadly, Caroline eventually developed cancer and was unable to continue.

The obvious thing would have been for Madelaine to take over the part, but the script was re-written to include Dennis' sister and also a girlfriend. As things turned out, Kevin explained, "Madelaine only had two day's notice before she took the part of his girlfriend."

He described their experiences working on location, while making the series. "Endless laughs; we all had a different sense of humour. It was very funny all the way through. We had the same crew for both series. Everybody got on so well – the chemistry was good. So often it's the luck of the draw – it's 90% luck." He also explained that it was helped, just a little, by alcohol! "*Scottish and Newcastle* provided bottles of *Beck's* beer on Series 1 and *San Miguel* for Series 2."

The making of *Auf Wiedersehen Pet* coincided with Pat's nine-year abstinence from drink, so when the rest of the cast went to the pub, he pursued his training programme. Tim Healy confirmed, "He did that all the time, after the first series had gone out and he changed his whole image. He used to be a 'baddie' and all of a sudden he was a 'goodie', because he was Bomber. Audiences loved him, because he was a lovable fella in the series, so they changed towards him.

"I went twice to the wrestling, as his 'second'. Once was down in Croydon. I pretended to play the role of Dennis – 'bollocking' him and telling him off, and he acted and pretended to be frightened of me, you know! Which was really funny, and I loved it of course."

Tim and Pat are both car enthusiasts, a fact that brought them to the edge of disaster! "One day he had his Rolls Royce, and initially it was *Pat*

111: a white Rolls Royce Corniche. I'd never been in a Rolls Royce. He said: 'Do you want a lift to Nottingham?' I'll never forget it! He had the roof off: it was a lovely sunny day. And I'm thinking, oh this is fantastic!

"It was brilliant," continued Tim, "can't afford a Ford Cortina – d'you know what I mean? Anyway, we were stopped at these traffic lights, and these two young lads – one had turned round and said: 'You fascist bastard!' to Pat. I'm not kidding you, he leapt out of his car – one of them ran off – and he grabbed this kid by the shirt – right? He picked him off the ground with one arm – like that. He said: 'Tim, do you want to hit him, or shall I hit him?'" Tim's imitation of Pat was particularly funny, because he exaggerated Pat's Birmingham accent – normally there's only a slight trace of it. "His legs were going like that. He put him down on the floor and just kicked him up the arse, and said: 'Bugger off!' I'll never forget that – it was hilarious!"

Tim also revealed that the two of them had been involved in a car accident, albeit not of Pat's making. "He'd bought a Porsche and instead of me getting onto the bus to go to work – the van – the minibus to pick us up, he said: 'Do you want a lift? Do you want to see what me Porsche can do?' I said 'Yeah!' There was a long, private drive leading up to Thornley Manor – in the second series; the house we were supposed to be working on; in the show it was called that."

The Porsche was ill fated – right from the start. As Chris observes: "Pat and cars are not a marriage made in heaven! The first day of rehearsals for Series 2, we got a message saying that Pat was going to be late for rehearsals because his Porsche had caught fire on the Bayswater Road. The day he got it back, within three hours, he'd rammed it up the front end of Mike Edwards' Volvo!"

"There was just a one-way drive to the house," continued Tim. "We were always there first, the actors, in the morning, you know? So when we got there Pat decided: 'I'll just show you what it can do' – because there's never anything coming the other way. So off we went, and he opened his Porsche up, down this drive, and there's a little bit of a hump.

"The next thing we know, we're going over the top of the hump and I wasn't watching where we were going, I was looking at the fields, at the side – looking out of the window. And I heard 'Shit!' There's the designer, coming this way. And the next thing I know there was this terrific bang! He'd wrote the Porsche off – smashed all the front end in. Pat, being so strong, he didn't have his seatbelt on.

"He just held the steering wheel like this. And he pushed the steering column into the other car – otherwise it would have gone like that" – mimes it going forward into Pat's chest. "He just braced himself. Of course, I didn't see this. The windscreen shot out and I hit the dashboard with my chest and moved it five inches out of line. I hit it that hard, I thought I'd broken all me ribs. I nearly passed out." Pat takes up the story:

I dragged Tim out on the floor and he was writhing – and there was a big crowd all around us. What had happened was this was a one-way road and we were going the right way. This other guy had spotted the convoy, which was behind us. I wouldn't speed on the main road, but decided to show him in the private road: one-way traffic, open road – no danger.

Of course, I 'opened it up'. On this particular day they wanted us to do something different. So they said to this guy: "Dash up and stop them coming down, because we want to shoot – up that road." So he's going full speed one way and I'm going full speed the other way – and hit him. I dragged Tim out. He's lying there groaning and incomprehensible. I said to him: "It's all right for you, you so-and-so – I'm down to one Rolls Royce!"

Pat injured his neck and his back. Tim considers himself lucky, "because if the windscreen hadn't come out, me head would have gone through it. But Porsches are designed so that the whole lot jumps out if you have a crash – the windscreen just comes out, and my head followed it, then I came back. But I felt terrible for him. He came to see me every day – he felt terrible like. But there was nothing seriously wrong with me; I was very badly bruised – that's all." Nowadays, Tim drives a Porsche himself.

"I was very friendly with him, probably closer to him than anybody, I would think, out of the whole cast. He's a very generous man, who's had this passion for being young, and staying young and fit. He must be a bit older than me, but it was like having a mate who was the same age."

The public perception of a wrestler or action actor can be that he isn't particularly intelligent, whereas in Pat's case he's very astute, with a broadly based general knowledge. Tim Healy discovered that he also had a great business mind. "He was always looking for deals. He'd come in, in the mornings and he'd have six fur coats. 'D you want a fur coat mate?' you know? He used to come in every day with something."

Tim Spall describes Pat as "a typical Brummie – 'ducker and diver'! We used to film in very odd places. I remember him looking at all this equipment once – these great big diggers. He had a kind of glow in his eyes and he said: 'Oh, I love plant.' I know he's had scrap-yards and he's got all these kind of business deals. And you never quite know – and he'll often try and sell you something. I'll often get a call and he'll ask you if you might know anyone with a name which will match one of his number plates, you know?

"I've always thought of Pat, again it's a cliché – of being a big, gentle man. He's got that kind of street wisdom – that he never foists on you – and you could always rely on him to get you out of trouble. He brought such charm to the character; the lovely thing about Bomber is that he was the quintessential 'Gentle Giant'." To make the role even more convincing, Pat had fake tattoos put on his chest, shoulders and arms and learned the art of bricklaying.

"I remember watching Pat one day when we were filming. He had quite a long speech. I could see earlier that he was nervous – but he'd obviously worked on it. I remember sitting there watching him doing it, and he'd really got a handle on the character. He had a lovely way of delivering it. He reminded me a little bit of Burt Lancaster. I thought, God, this character is really going to work, with Pat playing it! Obviously, getting to know Pat quite well afterwards, I could see that he is, very much, what the character is.

"He had a very sweet, gentle manner about him. Obviously I don't want to make him sound like an angel, because he's not. He's one of the biggest men I've ever worked with. He's got a gentleness, and a sweetness and a shyness, that I think was always going to work with that character."

Pat's role had tremendous audience appeal. "It was really nice to watch him go from being shy and making a few mistakes – because everybody does anyway – and obviously being crucified with embarrassment by it," recalls Tim. "But then to see him triumph in the role was wonderful – and really make that character work."

One of Tim Spall's favourite episodes is when Pat's daughter goes missing, and she comes to stay in the hut. Having watched it again recently, together with other episodes, it certainly gave Pat the scope he needed, to develop the character, when he returns to Bristol to be with his wife. Tim comments: "Bomber is quite discreet, but he does like a little bit of a visit to the 'ladies of the night' now and again.

"The wonderful thing about the character of Bomber, especially in the writing, is that they do give him a kind of nobility. Whenever Bomber was around, the other boys felt safe. Bomber was never a person who went looking for trouble, but he was the one who had to sort it out if they were in a scrape. The same thing went for being with Pat. When we were out and about in Germany, if there was going to be any bother, you always felt safe when he was around. Especially if the location was dodgy." Several of Pat's friends have expressed the same sentiment: "If Pat is your friend, you can rely upon him to 'watch your back' – to look out for you." Tim adds: "When you're that imposing, you don't have to shout about it."

On the subject of Pat and wrestling, he observes that Pat and wrestlers in general "will never talk about it – let you know what's going on. I suppose it's like magicians in the Magic Circle. That's probably one of the reasons wrestling's still so popular. Anyone in the know can see that it's a mixture of improvisation and fumbling. But Pat has got a bit of mystery about him. He's got that kind of 'gypsy' thing that is quite interesting. Although he's a very personable, gentle, amiable man, there is something a bit mysterious about him."

The following chapter deals with the careers of all the actors who have contributed to this chapter, taking us beyond *Auf Wiedersehen Pet*, providing an up-to-dated picture of their families and their latest achievements. Meanwhile, Tim Spall brings our present chapter to its conclusion.

"With comedy, people have an expectation of it. The best comedy is always when it's real. That's another reason why I think *Auf Wiedersehen Pet* was a big success. It was funny – but it was born out of realism – out of the way that people *really* behave, not the way that we *think* they behave when they're being funny."

Chapter Fifteen –

HOWAY THE LADS

And so hold on when there is nothing in you,
Except the Will, which says to them 'Hold on!'

Evans reached this stage when his toe became septic and he began to lose his mind – yet there was still this will within him to hold on. In that episode, he breaks from the main party; it's my feeling that he was allowed to do so, and find his way to his own demise. I can only imagine that within the hardship of trying to walk in the snow – through exhaustion – they glanced over their shoulders and thought: poor Edgar, there really is nothing we can do; we have to save ourselves.

And with his thoughts – his mumbling, rambling thoughts, on the day – or was it the night? We really don't know because it was continuous daylight, he walked along, then crawled – those last few hundred yards. Then, as the film shows, he found a little crevasse – a little niche in the snow – where he curled up and died.

(Whispering) And in that last moment before his demise, he hung on to his precious memories. And he said to himself: "Hold on – hold on to the thought of your wife's cooking – the smell of apple pie." He tried to hold on to the memory of his wife, in the kitchen.

The most effective kind of research is usually to go straight to the heart of the matter. Pat was following this line of reasoning in 1984, when he telephoned Reynoldston police station, on the Gower, not far from Swansea, asking them to recommend someone in their local Amateur Dramatics Society. Then he spoke to his new contact saying, "Look, can I come over and buy you dinner?" The man on the other end of the phone said, "No, but you can come to my house and have dinner." "I did, and took a load of booze with me," explained Pat. "We were sat there and when I heard his accent, I couldn't believe it!"

Sixteen years later, the task was to find the same man: to pick up a trail that had gone cold with the passage of time. The available information was that he lived in one of the fishing villages on the Gower Peninsula – and the

Amateur Dramatics connection. Eventually, we re-discovered farmer-poet John Beynon, giving us an excellent starting point, for our story about the making of *The Last Place On Earth*.

Although it wasn't apparent at that time, Pat was at a mid-point between the eventual filming of two series of *Auf Wiedersehen Pet*. The programme was to collect several accolades, including two major British awards: *Best TV Drama of the Decade*, presented on a highly auspicious occasion at the London Palladium, and also, the Pye Awards.

Evans was originally played by that doyen of British character actors, James Robertson Justice. To the best of our knowledge, Robert Falcon Scott selected Petty Officer Evans as a member of his ill-fated Antarctic expedition, because he was one of his favourites, although according to Oates' letters, he was also a drunk!

> *I'm closer to what my character thought – or didn't think, because I got into him. I went to the village where he was born and lived, on the Gower Peninsula in Wales, which is very interesting. Because they didn't consider themselves Welsh, would-you-believe? They actually had poems talking about the 'dreaded Wellian' and they inter-married with families in Devon, Somerset and Cornwall; it was only a short distance across from Gower – by sea.*
>
> *They ostracised themselves from the Welsh nation – very much like the Cornish people, although the Gower Peninsula is in the middle of Wales. They do not speak with a typically Welsh accent. When I went there, I found that they had a slight lilt to their accent – 'sing-songey' – almost like Bomber.*

John Beynon, farmer and poet of Rhossili on the Gower peninsula, helped Pat with his research into Captain Evans, almost eighteen years ago, as our book goes to print. Pat, seated at the farmer's table, was intent on adopting the Gower accent of Edgar Evans, although somewhat surprised by it. John continues the story:

"We'd built a new house two years previously, in the field next door to the farmhouse. Pat was going to take us out for a meal, but Kaye, my wife, decided that she'd cook a meal here instead; she was feeling a bit rough. After the meal we went to the village, it's only a mile from here and I showed him where Edgar Evans was born – or where we thought he was born. Then we took him to Saint Mary's church to see the plaque on the wall, which was erected by his wife, Lois Beynon." The inscription on the plaque, in memory of Evans' bravery, read: 'To seek to strive, to find and not to yield.'

Pat tape-recorded John's accent, which tends to be most prevalent among the old Gower people. "It's all dying out now," John explained. "The area used to be known as 'Little England Beyond Wales' – that's Pembrokeshire. There are books out in Gower with that title." Researching Evans provided first-hand evidence of the nature of Gower people. John describes them as determined, but also "…kind and generous people – they'd help you out in a minute."

Rosemary Brangwyn, postmistress in the nearby village of Porteynon certainly did, providing the final link in the chain in our search for John, and supplying additional information. Gill Wales, who is church-warden for both villages and works in Rosemary's post office, provided extracts from local newsletters relating to Evans.

The first announced: 'A Civic Ceremony in Honour of Petty Officer Evans (1876-1912) is being held at the Brangwyn Hall Swansea, on Thursday 17 February 1994, at 7.30 pm.' This was to commemorate the 82nd anniversary of his death. A bust of Evans was specially commissioned for the occasion.

A second newsletter from April '98, described an entry for 31 March 1882, in the old logbooks of Rhossili village school: 'Annie, Edgar and Arthur Evans left school this week, gone to Swansea to live'. Edgar, who was born in 1876, later joined the Royal Navy. It also gave details of Scott's expedition.

Lois Beynon was from a different branch of the Beynon family, and therefore not related to John. He described how she and Edgar Evans met. "She used to live in the *Ship Inn*, it's the *Ship Farm* now, in Rhossili – her parents were the landlords. He married her on 13 December 1904. She was his cousin. There are accounts of letters and marriages available from the *Evening Post* in Swansea."

After his visit, Pat practised the typical 'sing-along' type of accent for several weeks, but, as John explained, "when he played the part I was quite surprised that he didn't put on any kind of accent at all!" Pat was equally disappointed, but his director instructed him not to use any particular accent because it was going to be sold to the American market: they wanted clear diction – but no Gower accent! However, according to John, "It was very true to the pictures that you see of Edgar Evans – he looked the part."

"The poem I said to him was written by Cyril Gwynn, who was noted as the local Gower bard. John repeated the poem *The Smart Recruit*, recorded by Pat for practice purposes. "Pat stepped on his tape recorder – big man that he is – and we had to borrow somebody's tape recorder from the village.

"When the children in the village heard that Pat was coming – the man from *Auf Wiedersehen Pet* – and that he was a wrestler – they were excited," John explained. So did any of them actually meet Pat? "No, they were all peeping and hiding! He was a nice chap," elaborated John, "the same height as me when I was standing on a step! I'm about six foot. I see him in *Mr. Blobby* – my daughter has it: Pat was wrestling in the *Noel Edmunds Show*."

We have included a photograph of John with his wife, Kaye, and daughter, Elinor, and a poem from his book of humorous verse, entitled *From Bard to Verse*. This is reproduced with John's permission and relates directly to Evans.

It was inspired by problems that arose, two years after Pat's visit, when the local council, of which John is a member, wanted to place a commemorative plaque on Evans' birthplace. The illustration is by local artist, Gary Sheaf.

Just a few short weeks after visiting the Beynons, Pat retraced the steps of this famous son of Rhossili – back into history and out into a frozen wilderness: in this case the Arctic, not the Antarctic; recreating the heroism of Petty Officer Evans.

WHO KNOWS

Edgar Evans' birthplace was quite precious to his soul
A native of this Parish who perished at the Pole,
The Council tried by census form to find his birthplace
But the actual old cottage was difficult to trace.

He once had lived at Pitton, where he went to school,
And bottled many tadpoles on the way in Watch Pool,
His wife had lived in Pilton in a cottage all alone,
But a cottage next to Fernhill is what we called his Home.

So a plaque's to be erected on the house by the heath,
And added in small writing in brackets underneath,
"This may be Edgar's birthplace, or house of abode,
But if it's not it's the pink house just down the road."

Copyright © John Beynon, (Gower Poems, From Bard to Verse). Illustrated by Gary Sheaf.

'The Last Place on Earth' was a very interesting thing to get involved with. We actually went to Canada to film it. Martin Shaw was the lead artist in the series. It ran for about seven hours and had four different directors. It was such a hard-pressed job that it wasn't until they got to the fourth director, that he lasted until the end.

Martin Shaw, who played Scott, was born in Birmingham, in Erdington funnily enough – where I am right now. We had lots of fun together – speaking across the dinner table with our Brummie accents. We used to go to town on the accents.

"How are you our kid, all right?" (In best Brummie accent).

Of course, in Canada we could speak in that way, and although the Canadians would know that we were speaking English of some kind, they wouldn't know what we were talking about. We used to take great delight in this, and have a little smile to ourselves. Bill Nighe was in the film – an excellent actor. He worked with Jimmy Nail and Timothy Spall, more recently, in 'Still Crazy', the film about a rock band who stage a comeback.

We all toddled off to Canada, and it was somewhere like four hours flight north of Montreal. We went to Frobisher Bay for a while and then we went even further, up to a place within striking distance of the North Pole – just a few miles away.

Didn't you mention something about the light there?

Yes, it was almost daylight all the time. Although it was very, very cold you didn't feel it, because it was a dry cold – I didn't feel the cold at all.

Like New Zealand, in that respect?

Yes, it was a dry cold. I was wearing a fur coat at the time. We used to train. When we arrive at a place I usually look for a gym. The first thing you always find when you get to these places is a Scot. You find the remotest place in the world, you walk round the corner and there's some Scottish guy!

Tom Gerrard was a very wise man – a Scottish actor who worked with Michael Caine – and played a member of the expedition in the Scott film. He lives in Brighton; a blond-haired lad who played supporting roles, for example, the sergeant in 'Zulu' – with a moustache. He used to bring me a glass of rum as I came off set every night, into the 'dis-robing' room, because we dis-robed all our skins. Then we went to 'make-up' afterwards and got all our make-up off. Tom used to say: "I've run you a hot bath!" Everyone was so envious, because we'd got the only bath. We'd go out on the ice with the skidoos – it was so interesting. I've got all the scripts and call sheet.

Accommodation, as they soon discovered, was very basic, but Tom and Pat grabbed a double room containing two comfortable beds. "It was over the heating complex, which meant that it was very warm, of course." Although Tom wasn't particularly big, he was nevertheless determined. Pat recalls: "One particular actor came and tried to claim the room, Tom squared up to him and said he'd better 'p' off – in no uncertain terms! So he did, and we got the place."

It was so cold near the North Pole, that a nurse instructed them: "no 'going' behind an igloo, in case your private parts freeze!" Pat was surprised to discover a gym, located in a former school building.

I actually found one out there, would-you-believe? Tom and I used to work out there. In its day it was quite a comprehensive gym, but most of the machinery had broken down. We got the Special Effects boys to sort it out for us. They did all of the wires, and in the end we got the whole gym working – great it was. We used to go there every night. It was an enormous big building.

The only other people there were the local people, what we would call 'Eskimos', which is actually an Indian word meaning, 'man who eats fish'. The real name is 'inuits'. We'd start to train in the gym and within a very few minutes, all the inuits used to turn up and for some reason, I commented on it one day. I said; "It's funny, the place seems deserted, but as soon as we get here, you all appear from various parts of the building." They said: "Yes, we smell you" – true! Everyone has a special smell, according to what you eat.

But up there, there were no toilets; it was very Spartan to say the least! The Eskimos would leave their seals outside the back door, and sea bass. Where we were was voted a 'dry area'. But of course, Tom and I took a bottle of rum in with us anyway.

The film, based on a book by Roland Huntford, took a controversial look at what was destined to become a glorious failure. It was first televised on ITV, on 18 February 1985, and also starred Susan Wooldridge, as Scott's wife. Its aim was to show the true story of the man behind the myth. Filming took place in London, Scotland, Greenland, Canada and Norway. Scott's team covered 1,500 miles in 1911. The cast had to undergo similar conditions to those endured by the original expedition.

Coincidentally, Harrison Ford's biographer, Minty Clinch was one of a team of scriptwriters working on the film. The script required Martin Shaw to portray the leader in a poor light, as a man who, allegedly, despite being a first-class scientist, had bungled most of the major decisions. There were *two* Evans on the expedition: Pat's character, Petty Officer Evans, and a last-minute addition, Lieutenant Evans. Pat recently presented the huge pair of gloves that he wore for the role, to his co-author: not *exactly* the right size, as our photograph shows!

Cast and crew on the Elstree Studios back-lot 15 September 1982.
BY PERMISSION OF CARLTON TELEVISION AND THE PRINCIPAL ACTORS FEATURED.
PHOTOGRAPHER TONY SMITH.

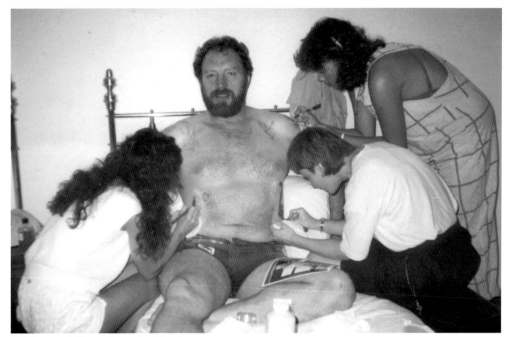

Make-up girls applying Bomber's tatoos.

'Bomber', plus tatoos, taken on a Spanish beach, during the filming of the second series of Auf Wiedersehen Pet, 1988. Doreen is on Pat's right, on his left is Pat's lifelong friend Diane, who is a member of the Harris family. PHOTOGRAPH BY DIANE'S HUSBAND AND PAT'S FRIEND, TIM CLARKE.

'The Best of Friends': a heart-warming illustration of the special rapport and friendship between Gary Holton and Pat. BY PERMISSION OF CARLTON TELEVISION AND GARY'S MOTHER, JOAN PUGH. PHOTOGRAPHER TONY SMITH.

Bomber, with Hamburg prostitutes. BY PERMISSION OF CARLTON TELEVISION. PHOTOGRAPHER TONY SMITH.

Pat and Jimmy in affectionate mood!
BY PERMISSION OF CARLTON TELEVISION AND JIMMY NAIL. PHOTOGRAPHER TONY SMITH.

Gary on location in Marbella, waiting for things to 'hurry up and happen'.
BY PERMISSION OF HIS MOTHER, JOAN PUGH.

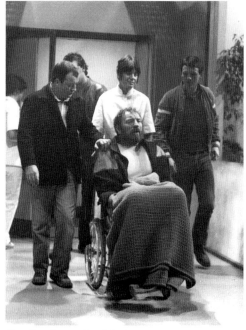

Bomber in a wheelchair.
BY PERMISSION OF CARLTON TELEVISION, JIMMY NAIL, TIM HEALY AND KEVIN WHATELY. PHOTOGRAPHER TONY SMITH.

Gary and Pat on location in Marbella, for the second Auf Wiedersehen series. Gary's mother, Joan, recalls that Gary and Pat were often in close proximity, on these type of shots.
BY PERMISSION OF JOAN PUGH.

Group photograph of the 'boys', outside Thornley Manor, BY PERMISSION OF CARLTON TELEVISION AND ALL OF THE ACTORS FEATURED. PHOTOGRAPHER TONY SMITH.

Signatures belonging to the cast of the Auf Wiedersehen series. BY PERMISSION OF CARLTON TELEVISION AND ALL OF THE ACTORS FEATURED.

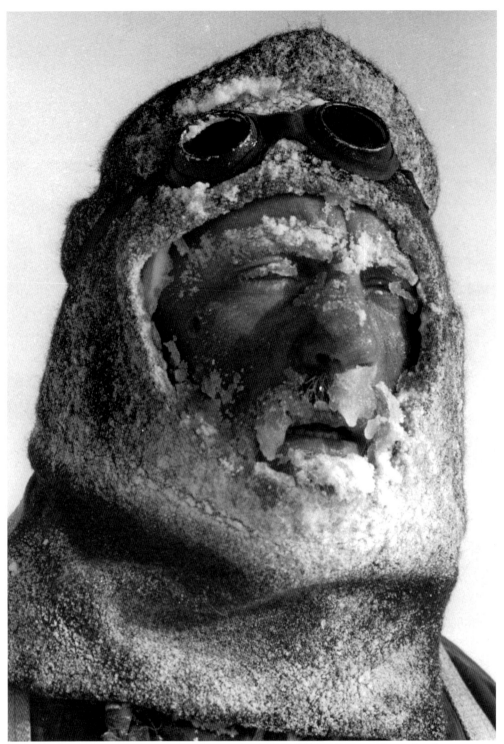

The Last Place On Earth – Pat, as ice-encrusted Petty Officer Evans, after a few hours filming in the Canadian Arctic, at -30°.
BY PERMISSION OF CARLTON TELEVISION. PHOTOGRAPHER NICK LOCKETT.

Martin Shaw and Pat, on location for The Last Place On Earth, 1984. Shaw played Captain Scott and Pat was Petty Officer Evans. BY PERMISSION OF MARTIN SHAW. PHOTOGRAPH BY TOM GERRARD.

Pat recently presented the enormous pair of gloves that he wore for the role of Evans, to his co-author: not exactly the right size, as our photograph shows! PHOTOGRAPHER PAT ROACH.

John Beynon, farmer and poet of Rhossili, on the Gower of Peninsula, helped Pat research Captain Evans, for 'The Last Place On Earth'. *BY PERMISSION OF JOHN BEYNON.*

Tripod and camera ready for action, only miles away from the North Pole. *PHOTOGRAPHER PAT ROACH.*

Pat plays Doulton, Juliet Bravo, 1980. A caption on the back of the photo reads: 'Voted Best Dressed Thug Of The Year!'.

A letter to 'Big Bad Pat Roach' from his smallest fan, Kitty Whately. *BY PERMISSION OF KEVIN WHATELY AND MADELAINE NEWTON, KITTY'S PARENTS.*

Pat dressed for a pantomime, in the TV series Marlene Marlow Investigates. The series was about a female detective. Pat played a villain. PHOTOGRAPHER UNKNOWN.

Jack Warden and Pat in bowler hats, playing gypsy roles in Three Wishes For Jamie. Jack is one of Pat's favourite actors. PHOTOGRAPHER UNKNOWN.

Broad Street, Birmingham: several places relating to the first half of Pat's life are situated nearby. To the left was Stoke Street, one of his first addresses as a married man. Over on the right is Sheepcote Street, where Amelia was born. BY PERMISSION OF BIRMINGHAM LIBRARY SERVICES. PRINTED BY JOHN WHYBROW LTD.

Ladywood 1954, prior to demolition. The urgency for new housing at that time is self-evident. BY PERMISSION OF BIRMINGHAM LIBRARY SERVICES. PRINTED BY JOHN WHYBROW LTD.

The original Chamberlain Clock, at the junction of Warstone Lane and Vyse Street, marked the centre of Pat's Jewellery Quarter world. As a young boy, he lived just a stone's throw away. He and Frank sometimes ate at the Victoria/British Restaurant nearby.
BY PERMISSION OF BIRMINGHAM LIBRARY SERVICES. PRINTED BY JOHN WHYBROW LTD.

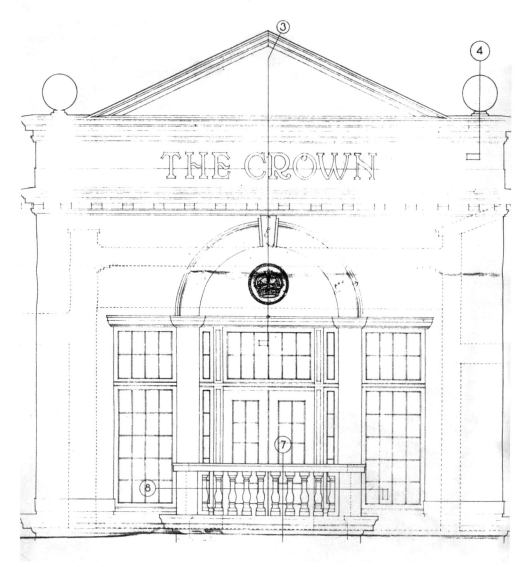

The Crown Public House, Broad Street. Architect Alan Goodwin's drawing of the front elevation, for its re-design in the 1990s. In Edwardian times, Amelia visited her friend, in a house opposite Bingley Hall, close to this same pub. In later years, Dolly and Freda met friends there, for a drink. BY PERMISSION OF ALAN GOODWIN.

One of Pat's original business cards for his Hockley Street club, The Rendezvous.

Snow clearing outside one of Pat's Birmingham night-clubs. Pat is on the far left - minus beard!

The Birmingham family histories of both co-authors overlap in four areas: the Jewellery Quarter, Sheepcote Street, St. Chad's and entrepreneurship. Shirley's grandfather and his two sisters spent their early years in Morville Street, close to Amelia's birthplace, and the canals where she and Grandad Jackson earned a living. BY PERMISSION OF EILEEN WAREING.

Shirley's great-grandfather, William James Wareing was manager of a pen factory in the Jewellery Quarter. Grandfather Harry. Senior is on the left, his sister, Elspeth on the right. With older sister Una, she later owned a tailoring business, like several family members. Other Wareings were Birmingham jewellers and solicitors. BY PERMISSION OF EILEEN WAREING.

Bernard Wareing, shown here as a councillor, had his own business in the Jewellery Quarter from 1877 - 1927. BY PERMISSION OF SUTTON COLDFIELD NEWS & DRAYCOTT GALLERIES.

Saint Chad's Cathedral, Birmingham c. 1925. BY PERMISSION OF HIS GRACE, THE ARCHBISHOP OF BIRMINGHAM.

Jim White identified this old tunnel entrance, on Avery's site, as being similar to the wide tunnel at Pig Hill Farm. His father's tunnel was accessed by climbing down iron steps on the inside of a well. The tunnel led in the direction of Avery's.
BY PERMISSION OF GEC AVERY LTD.

Murdock's home, the 'White House', another name for Sycamore Hill House - c. 1927. The building behind it, left, is Pig Hill Farm - site of the Budokan.
BY PERMISSION OF GEC AVERY LTD.

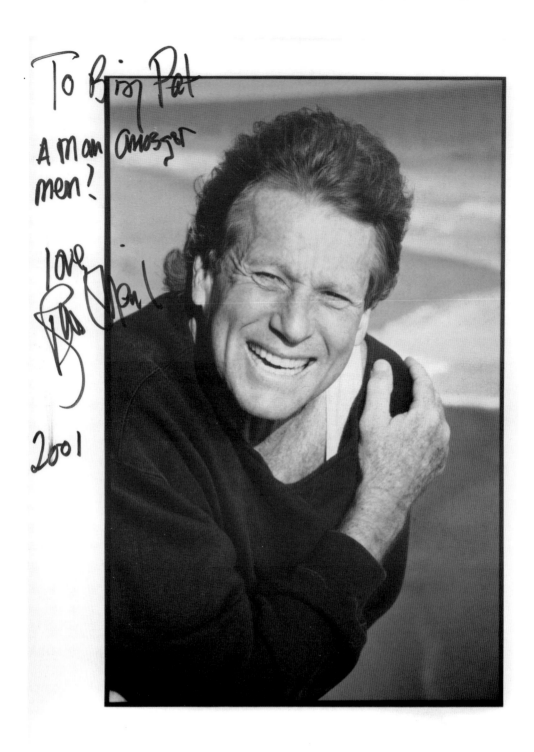

A recent photograph from Ryan O'Neal, - with a special message for Pat.
BY PERMISSION OF RYAN O'NEAL.

We used to come in, in all our very original gear. We wore finneskos, which are boots, made of fur indigenous to that particular area. It's one of the things that Scott insisted on doing. One of the other members of the team didn't wear them because he had the dogs – the sleighs. Amundsen's crowd didn't use them either although the Eskimos sometimes did. Lieutenant Evans was originally going to the Pole and threw his lot in with Scot, when he realised that the other expedition had a higher profile. Scott wasn't too happy about the situation, but capitulated on the basis that the newspapers were unlikely to cover two separate expeditions.

The Norwegians reached the Pole 34 days earlier, and were already on their way home, as Scott reached it on 18 January 1912. Evans was the first to die, a month after they began the terrible return journey.

If we could have turned back the clock, I could have told Scott what a waste of energy it was to use the big man Evans – with the extra weight, sinking into the snow. The others didn't break the crust, but Evans did. He was lifing his legs up into the air and walking at the same time – and dragging his feet. So he was using up tremendous energy, which he had got because he was a big strong man, but it was no good to him – because he was raising his legs and pulling himself along.

When I did Evans' final death scene, the cameraman looked at me and said, "You've got it" – and he was gone. They told me that the man in the cutting room also shed a tear. The director, Ferdy Fairfax, was short of time, because of the conditions, so was forced to rush. Although in reality it probably took longer, during actual filming, Evans died in those few long drawn-out seconds.

Another member of the expedition, Captain L.E.G. Oates, was the 'very gallant gentleman', in the famous painting of that title, by J.C. Dollman. Those involved with the film were, in a way, indebted to him, as the entire project stemmed from his private letters, written to his sister, at the time of the expedition.

Oates's sister swore that she would destroy the letters from him, which is where the story for 'The Last Place On Earth' was taken from. She did destroy them but she'd also copied them. She was asked to destroy them by the British Government, not by Oates. That's where the true story of Scott came from – hence 'The Last Place On Earth'. She kept copies of the letters. They also came to the conclusion that Scott may possibly have committed himself to suicide.

Was this northernmost area of Canada more suitable for filming than the South Pole?

Well yes, it should have been, but they'd miscalculated one or two things: there were no bloody penguins there!

Ship them in!

The other thing was, there was no effing snow there either! They had to use false machines – you can't believe it! They actually used plastic something-or-other, and the entire cast went on strike and refused to work, because of the possibility of the intake of these plastic particles. There were some interesting characters over there, for example, the guy who played the latest 'Doctor Who', Sylvester McCoy. I met him later at the NEC and we had quite a pleasant reunion.

Evans was a bit sub-ordinate at times, but a likeable character: a big man – a strong man. Nowadays, a big man isn't 6 foot 1 inches tall, as Evans was; in those days he would have been. Scott decided to go on and leave certain men out. He included Lieutenant Evans as the leader of the second sledge.

Edgar Evans was a fifth man on Scott's sledge, because of the number of men he decided to take; being a big, strong man, he was supposed to be an additional advantage. It turned out that he wasn't, because being such a big man, he should probably have eaten a little more food, in that temperature – for his body warmth alone. So his body temperature would suffer more than anybody else, because of lack of intake.

Under such adverse conditions, his toe became septic after the slightest injury. Due to a combination of factors – pressure, the poison, frostbite, and concussion following a fall, he lost his powers of reasoning, and was allowed to wander off on his own. They could have fetched him back, but they allowed him to do it. He just carried on walking – into oblivion.

Nick Lockett has kindly allowed us to include his very dramatic photograph of Pat, encrusted with real ice, taken while they were filming at temperatures of more than thirty degrees below!

I depicted his condition as being absolutely freezing cold, certainly out of his equilibrium, not knowing what he was doing. Scott and the crew were not entirely oblivious to the fact that he was wandering off – saying to themselves, 'Well what can we do anyway? We can 'down tools', go and find him, pick him up, bring him back.' He wandered off – delirious.

Oates was the next to die, on 17 March 1912. His final words were, 'I am just going outside and may be some time.' Then, rather than be a burden to his starving friends, he walked out into a howling blizzard. The remaining three, Scott, Dr. Wilson and Lieutenant Bowers, were trapped in their tent by terrible weather conditions. When they finally died, less than a fortnight after Oates, they were only eleven miles from safety.

There were some dangerous situations. I remember something on one of the horses actually froze to the ground, and was unable to move: maybe he'd got some leather on him. It was the scene where the dogs run in to eat the horse. I don't know whether they cut this stuff in the end – they probably did. They got the horse to lie down with its back to us. There was a dog in camera shot. You didn't see this, but meat was thrown in to the horse's belly; the dog went for the meat but you presumed that he went for the horse. The poor horse was terrified though. And we actually got genuinely stuck with the machines that they tried to use!

The very interesting thing about Evans was that he was a fifth man, pulling at a sled that normally only four men would pull. We were pulling sleds that weighed about 200lb; they were pulling sleds that weighed 800lb. We were absolutely exhausted in just a few minutes, so how they did it, we will never know! Bear in mind that you're talking about modern day. I used to do 500 free squats very morning – training, so although the others were just actors, I was a very fit guy.

In May 1985, just after Pat had finished filming *The Last Place On Earth*, the *Auf Wiedersehen* cast were guests of honour at the FA Cup Final, between Liverpool and Everton. They sang *You'll Never Walk Alone*, in the club's hospitality suite, accompanied by singer Gerry Marsden.

In addition to the tremendously varied career already described in this book, Pat has appeared in approximately 24 different television programmes, including *The Bill, Juliet Bravo, Casualty, Heartbeat, The Detectives, Minder, Telly Addicts*, and others too numerous to mention, and taken part in two radio broadcasts. A full list can be found in Appendix D. *Auf Wiedersehen Pet* also provided a successful launching pad for its other leading actors. Jimmy Nail, who took the rebellious role of Oz, is now a well-established actor and musician.

Timothy Spall's career has blossomed since he played Barry. "It's not often you get a chance to do 26 episodes of something – to develop it. It was a great pleasure, but it's also been a yoke that I've worn around my neck for a long time. I've been lucky enough to pursue all areas of the business, you know? My first real love, I think, is film."

His most challenging part to date was playing Margaret Rutherford, in an half hour Arts programmes for BBC 2. Between making the first and second series of *Auf Wiedersehen Pet*, Tim joined the National Theatre, playing the title role of the Dauphine, the king of France, in *Saint Joan*, with Frances de la Tour as Joan.

"I also did a play by Machiavelli, called *La Mandragola*, in which I played a kind of evil fixer called Ligurio. Then the second time I was there I did Bottom the weaver, in *A Midsummer Night's Dream*. I played the lead in *A Bourgeoise Gentilhomme*, which is a play by Moliere." The part in question was that of Monsieur Jourdain. "I did two stints: I was there for a ten-month period and then ten months again.

"My favourite role has got to be Maurice, in *Secrets and Lies*. It was a big thing for me – and a big success film-wise. It's helped me in my career. It's lifted me up to another level as far as getting parts in films is concerned. It was a kind of 'bringing together' – and I did it just before I was ill."

Tim made the film in 1995, and it went to Cannes in early 1996. "So when I was having my treatment and I was in hospital it was going all around the world, winning awards. Although I had a year off, it seemed like I hadn't been away – if you know what I mean?"

That was five years ago, since when he has made a full recovery from leukaemia. "I'm fighting fit now. I'm actually off to Hollywood on Wednesday to do a film." Tim described his role in what was then his latest film, *Metal God*: "...the road manager of an English rock band, who has a great talent for arranging girls, drugs and everything for the band."

He starred in *Topsy Turvy*, which won an Oscar for costumes. "It's about Gilbert and Sullivan. The part I played was Richard Temple, who is *the* lead baritone in the company, and actually plays the Mikado. I sing *The Punishment Fits The Crime*."

During an interview on Michael Parkinson's Sunday morning radio programme, this versatile actor sang a song he performs in Kenneth Brannagh's modern version of *Love's Labours Lost – I Get A Kick Out Of You*. "I play a bizarre Spanish gentleman – Don Armado. Before *Topsy Turvy*, I've just done a film in South America with Richard Dreyfus called *The Old Man Who Read Love Stories*, as a really unpleasant mayor of an unpleasant little town.

"Eventually I'd like to go back to the theatre and do some Shakespeare. I really will have to play Falstaff one of these days. I love characters that make you laugh one minute – then cry the next. I like quirky characters and I love tragic-comedy characters: that's my favourite."

Tim's son, Rafe, now in his late teens, would like to be an actor and has been working with the National Youth Theatre. Tim remembers doing squats with him in Spain – when he was 18 months old. Balancing family life with an acting career is notoriously difficult. "I have been travelling quite a bit," comments Tim. "In the earlier part of last year I did a film in Paris with Gerard Depardieu, Ulma Thurman and Tim Roth."

Secrets and Lies was a turning point for him. "But when you do films, you tend to have more gaps in between them. In a film you might, for instance, be working on it for twelve weeks, but you might have five of those weeks off. You might be abroad – so if it's Paris you can come back." His family visited him in L.A. during Summer 2000. "They paid for Shane to come out – which is nice. My oldest daughter is Pascale – she's 25, then there's Rafe – 19, then Sadie – she's 16. We've also got two cats and a bulldog!"

Still on a rising tide of success, in 2000 he starred in a three-part romantic comedy for *ITV*, *The Thing about Vince*, about a forty-something builder, with a thriving business, and an interesting hobby (tropical fish). Unfortunately, his wife, played by Marion Bailey, threw him out of the house over an innocent encounter with a young woman, during a fish fancier's trip, and he got into various scrapes as a result. This character, written especially for him, bore a strong resemblance to Barry, possibly 20 years on – an ordinary 'bloke', trying to make the best of a potentially grim, but true-to-life situation. A television reviewer described Tim as 'Mike Leigh's favourite leading man', adding that the series reminded him of a frothier version of Leigh's *Secrets and Lies.*

Tim Healy could have used the services of a competent builder – although perhaps not one of Vince's team – to repair his seedy, *Heartburn Hotel.* Like Timothy Spall and Kevin Whately, in 2000 he played the key role in a television series. Having already played such a variety of characters, he's in need of a real challenge.

"I'd like to play someone you'd never expect to cast me as – got me now? Somebody you would just ignore. For example, Edward Woodward played a bin man. I know when I did that series, *Common As Muck*, I said, 'Who's playing Neville?' They said, 'Edward Woodward.' I said, 'Edward Woodward's a bin man! And he was brilliant as a bin man. So I don't know, I'll play somebody – Prince Charles maybe! Or somebody like that.

"I'd like to play a woman – I mean seriously, not as a pantomime dame, a gay person – someone you wouldn't cast me as. But again, I'm not talking about *Are You Being Served* – 'I'm free!' I'm talking about someone who's gay, but looks like me. I'll have to write it myself, I think. I'm not a writer who can sit in the kitchen and dream something up – you know? I could write about being a comedian."

Having two actors in the family can present difficulties, but as Tim explained, "… she's my biggest fan and I'm hers. I think Denise is a brilliant actress. She can play anything: any voice, any accent, any class. It can be difficult, but it works wonderfully – in a way." Denise was living and working in Manchester at the time of my visit, and was therefore able to see their son Matthew, every night.

"When we were doing *The Grand* it was fantastic, because we were both working for *Granada* and coming home every night, which was great. But I tend to work at the *BBC* more than anywhere else, so I'm off to London a lot of the time. But then I do have times when I'm here a lot. We see a lot of each other."

Although Tim was also in Coronation Street, in 1975, he and Denise met over twenty years ago at an actress friend's dinner party, the night after New Year's Eve. "We knew each other, but at the time we never really liked each other. When I was a comedian, I was a very dry comedian, and I think it did affect me for quite a while – in the way I was as a person. She thought that I was grumpy, and I thought she was a flirt.

"We were sat opposite each other at this dinner party and I'd just broken up with my lady. Because *Auf Wiedersehen Pet* really changed my life and the lady I was with at the time *hated* fame. Hated it. She was a very private person, and it wasn't going to work. She wasn't happy with who I'd become, you know? So that fell apart and I wasn't seeing anybody. Denise and I realised that we had a lot in common; all of a sudden she thought, oh I didn't realise that you were like that! – and vice versa. Six months later, we were married."

Matthew may follow in his father's footsteps. "He's grown up with this business – with us both being on the TV," explained Tim. "Until he was about five, he thought everybody's mom and dad were on the telly! Now he's not impressed at all. I mean the *Street* comes on and his mates want to watch it, but he doesn't want to. But he is interested in the theatre.

"I think that's how he survives in school: he makes everybody laugh – he's the funny lad in the class. He's doing all right at school. He's very good at English – got a good imagination; writes great stories. Loves people, language, music. He plays the drums, the saxophone, the piano. He's a very good drummer already; he's been having lessons. I bought him a kit of drums when he was seven."

In view of Matthew's hobby it's probably fortunate that the Healys have recently moved to a farmhouse, surrounded by fields. "He's in the outbuilding now – I've put his drums out there. He's in the school orchestra. I think he'll do something that involves some sort of performance." Denise and Tim now have a new addition to the family, a baby son named Louis.

Kevin Whately appeared on our screens during the latter half of 2000, as the ever-popular Sergeant Lewis, in a re-run of some of the previous *Morse* episodes, followed a few weeks later by the first televised version of Colin Dexter's final Morse book, *The Remorseful Day*, on 15 November. Reading this skilfully crafted book is an entertainment in itself, and represents Dexter at his most playful. Each chapter is introduced by a very apposite quotation: unavoidably excluded in the television adaptation.

Work on the final *Morse* began in Spring 2000. Kevin had stopped doing the series, but it was essential that Sergeant Lewis be in this final episode, in which Morse is killed. As the author explained, in a recent television interview:

"Lewis is very important at the end of Morse's life. We're all glad to see him back, as he plays a pivotal role in the last scene. I think the *real* sadness is the death of Morse, as perceived by Lewis." Dexter concluded by saying that John Thaw and Kevin Whately have always given a hundred per cent to the series: "If anyone deserves the accolade, it's the cast."

Lucy Gannon created the role of Jack Keruish, the doctor in *Peak Practice*, especially for him. He has performed in several of her plays. Kevin explained that because he and Lucy know each other well, and have mutual respect for one another, she's able to write for him. He has no favourite role, but his most challenging part to-date, because it was so out of character, was in one of her plays: a very violent person – the wife beater, in *Trip-Trap*.

Kevin recently took the Henry Fonda role in a stage production of *Twelve Angry Men,* working with the legendary Harold Pinter as producer. "It's a great play and works as well as a play as it does on film. It lasts two hours. The curtain rises on a jury room and the whole play takes place in that room. So there is just one set. The jury is stuck in that one room for the whole duration of the play. All twelve jurors have stories to tell; each tells his story as the play unfolds. In the film, most of the focus was on Fonda. In the play it broadens out into the twelve stories. Harold Pinter is as good a director as he is a writer and an actor."

A performance of *Genesis,* at Worcester Cathedral, involved Madelaine and himself in bible readings. It included other actors, a choir, the Stan Tracey Jazz Band, and a range of other music. A few months ago he finished filming Lucy Gannon's new *ITV* project, *Plain Jane,* which is set in the Edwardian period and concerns a man who comes down to London from Newcastle. This will probably be on our screens some time during 2002.

Mark Herman's foot-balling film, *Purely Belter,* could easily have been like old times, because his good friend, Tim Healy was also in the cast. However, as Kevin explained: "There were no rehearsals and we didn't meet on set!"

Kevin would like to play Angelo, in *Measure for Measure.* The play is essentially about the corruption of power – the way Angelo changes as a result of being put into a position of power. It's one of the most political of Shakespeare's plays.

Madelaine and Kitty appeared with him in the second series of *Auf Wiedersehen Pet.* He met his wife when they both appeared in the stage comedy, *A Nightingale Sang,* and has since worked on a range of productions with her. Just before the first series of *Auf Wiedersehen Pet,* they were in a very successful stage play together by Michael Wilcox called *Accounts.* It was set on a sheep farm. The play won a top award and later transferred to London. Madelaine has also played Morse's girlfriend.

Lucy Gannon's play, *Pure Wickedness,* was another departure for him. He played a character whose personality changes almost totally, as a result of events. Kevin explained that the main difficulty was that the audience should be able to see a *gradual* change in the character, to make it believable.

With regard to balancing family life with acting, he commented: "It's potluck – you muddle along. Two years ago I decided not to do any long-term series. Kitty was doing her GCSE's and I wanted to spend time with the family." He considers himself fortunate to have been involved in long-running series, and is now sufficiently established to a degree that they will "work to your timetable."

Madelaine appeared on television in Catherine Cookson's *Tilly Trotter.* Kevin explained that following this, "She did a theatre show in London called *Turns*, about a Country and Western show that performs in Northern clubs. She played one of the singers who's also the bossy, organising member of the group."

Commenting on the likelihood of their children, Kitty and Kieran, following Madelaine and himself into the acting business he said, "Difficult to say at present. Kitty is 19, Kieran 18. Both are good actors, appear very natural on stage and have taken part in a lot of school performances."

Ironically, despite his cultured accent, Chris Fairbank has spent most of his twenty-eight-year career playing a variety of villains. "It's the old type-casting thing, because of having endured acne as a teenager, and a young adult really, people tend to see you as the bad guy.

"I went through a phase, starting with *Batman,* of playing 'the first guy who gets it', in movies." He and George Roth mug Batman's parents in the opening scene, steal a wallet, and threaten his mother with a gun. "Another 'first-guy-who-gets-it' role was in *Alien 3* – that actually took me out to Hollywood for two weeks." Chris's alien 'dog' character was found, by an American-based computer analysis system, to be a more sympathetic character than the original 'ox' alien, played by John Hurt.

His favourite role, to date, was playing Sid James in a play called *Cleo, Camping, Emanuel and Dick*, which was based upon the love affair between Sid James and Barbara Windsor. "For me it was Hamlet, Lear and everything else, all rolled into one."

The play began life at the National Theatre, with Chris taking over the title role when the original actor was unable to go on tour. "There was a three-week rehearsal period, then on the road for eight weeks. I loved it – it was the best part I've ever had. I could play him any time within the next fifteen years – and would dearly love to."

Chris has recently been filming *Anazapata* in Wales. Set in the 14th century, around the time of the plague, it became a classic case of 'art imitating life'. "We started filming right at the beginning of the foot-and-mouth outbreak, and that event became the film's executive producer. We lost location after location, script and schedules were constantly being rewritten." For insurance reasons, the production had to finish on schedule. "In the end, we needed one extra day, but we got it done." In financial terms, the film role which Chris completed more recently was "a 'five-star liner' compared to the 'dinghy' that was *Anazapata*." But he adds: "… for creative resourcefulness and ingenuity – give me *Anazapata* every time!"

Chris is the only member of his family in showbusiness; the others have different interests. He has a Polish wife named Anna and a seven-year-old son, whose name, Mateus, is not dissimilar to that of Tim Healy's son –

Matthew. Anna prefers to plan well in advance, but an actor's life precludes this. "As I say to her on many an occasion, when a holiday that's been booked in advance suddenly has to get kicked into touch because a job's come up, 'Well, you knew the job was dangerous when you took it on!' There's nothing else I can do; if there was – I'd do it – actually. But there's not, you know? But I've got bills to pay and a boy to put through school and all the rest of it, like everybody else."

When Chris said of the year, 2001, "What a great year it is, with great adventures still to come," he was undoubtedly referring – at least partly – to the gathering of the *Auf Wiedersehen* clan, for the new series; acting, once again, with people who Pat describes as having become "like a family", on the previous two series. This has since taken place, initially in Middlesbrough and the London area, followed by a month's filming in Arizona. The final session of filming was at Bray Studios, Windsor, on Wednesday 19 December 2001. The writer was privileged to be 'on set', during Monday of that final week.

On the darker side, although six of the seven leading actors launched by the series, continue to have successful careers, as they reunite for the new series, their thoughts must surely return to that absent 'seventh man' — a young actor whose early promise was snuffed out – like a candle.

Timothy Spall described how revelations to the press about Gary Holton's private life, only compounded his problems. "That led to his eventual demise, you know? Then his mother read this, was very upset and became ill." John Harwood-Bee, Gary's manager, explained recently that Gary hadn't made these revelations. "A year earlier in late summer of 1984, I discovered from Lou Coulson (Gary's agent) that Gary had a drugs problem. I called Barry Matheson in Oslo and we arranged a meeting with Lou and Gary. We informed Gary that we had discovered his problem and he was very upset.

"For the next year," continued John, "we all worked together to get him straightened out. It was imperative not to publicise the problem. Back then it was treated with much less sympathy than now. Gary did well until certain events in the summer of 1985. *Central* asked me to accompany him to Spain for the shoot and it was whilst we were there that his ex, Susan, sold the drugs story to the *Daily Star*."

The exposé occurred just after Gary returned from Spain. "He was confronted next day by a reporter and a cameraman," explained John, "whilst he was having a quiet drink in a pub where I was to meet him. He was with somebody who took exception to the intrusion and who snatched the camera. The next day the headlines read 'Heroin Hoodlum'. Gary never had the fight."

Kevin recalled the tremendous strain on the rest of the cast, following the tragedy and how, although they initially thought it might be the end of the series, "the sound boys cobbled together bits of his voice." Tim Spall remembers: "We'd had to leave a game of snooker and go back and shoot some more, as if Gary was there. There was a double, in his costume; it was very weird and slightly upsetting. Although Gary had got himself into a bit of a state, it was such an awful shock – because there was a true sense of camaraderie. Obviously, Gary had come from rock n' roll – and we all know what comes with that territory!" Chris comments – in retrospect – "Gary's death defined the difference between shock and surprise: it was a helluva shock – but it was no surprise."

Gary remains very much in the thoughts of his immediate family. The oldest of three brothers, he was born in September 1952. In 1957 Joan's second son, Tony came along, followed by Nigel, in 1961.

Gary was first introduced to Ian La Frenais by his girlfriend at the time, Sue Harrison, with whom he later had a son, named Red. According to Joan, Red lives abroad and is about twenty years old. Sadly, she hasn't seen him since he was a baby.

Joan explained that, like many actors, when Gary came to visit he didn't talk much about showbusiness, preferring to catch up on family news and just relax. Fans of *Auf Wiedersehen* may recall that Gary seemed particularly 'at home' during the pub scenes. All was revealed when I visited Joan – now a widow in her early 70s – at her retirement bungalow. "He loved to curl up in a chair and go to sleep, or 'pootle' about in the garden. 'What time's dinner?' – and that sort of thing.

"We were living in Houndwood at the time, that's up the road from here. I was a pub landlady." In Welshpool she and her first husband, Ernie, Gary's father, were landlords of the *Wellington*. In Minsterley, they ran the *Crown & Sceptre*. Gary was accustomed to socialising with the customers. "Later he served behind the bar. When we were at Welshpool, he had his photo over the bar, when he was eighteen. They all sent him birthday cards. He'd go and sit with the customers and play dominoes. He'd come home and relax there."

Gary and Tony were born Cockneys, in Clapham Common, so he used his normal speaking voice for the role of Wayne. However, unlike Wayne, Gary was a hardworking person, and was also heavily involved with charity work. "He went on charity walks with Jimmy Saville – he had blisters on his feet. He was lovely – he just wanted cuddling," commented Joan. John is quoted as saying: "Gary lived his life at 150%. He believed that for things to happen, you had to make them happen. He was very active for any charity event that asked him." He didn't publicise the fact.

British born actor Noel Clarke, whose parents were originally from Trinidad, plays Wayne's half-caste son, Wyman, in the new series. Speaking at Bray Studios recently, this talented young man described the generosity of the established members of cast, in helping him settle into the new role. Noel also likened the rapport, which quickly developed between Pat and himself, to the relationship between a nephew and a favourite uncle. Life seems to have come full circle: in the early days of *Auf Wiedersehen* the more experienced actors helped Pat.

Noel is happy to play serious roles or comedy. His rise to success has been meteoric, due in no small measure to a previous role as the scriptwriter's son, in the Channel 4 series, *Metrosexuality*, broadcast in February and March 2001. Writer/director Rikki Beadle-Blair who chose him for the part, played one of two gay fathers. Noel has also appeared in two short films, *The Bill*, three current episodes of *Casualty, Waking the Dead* and the 'pilot' of *Judge John Deed.*

A few months before his death, Gary fell into bad company with one particular couple. His death came as a complete shock to Joan. "The night before Gary died he'd phoned to say he was coming home, so I was just expecting to see him." She had been particularly upset that week, by scandalous press articles about him. "He said: 'Mummy, please don't believe what they've said.' A conservative councillor took Seth – my second husband and I to London – to identify the body." When an Open Verdict was recorded at the Coroner's Inquest the same councillor "… phoned up the newspaper and said they had to retract what they'd written. I wanted a written apology, but they wouldn't give it to me. Some time afterwards, Joan became "paralysed for a year."

Following discussion with John Harwood-Bee, Joan re-released one of Gary's single records on 28 July 1986, donating the proceeds to help the fight against heroine addiction – a cause dear to his heart. Since his serious addiction in 1984, he'd fought the habit, aided by *Narcotics Anonymous.* By 1985 he was, once again, working hard on his career, just as he'd bounced back before from *other* traumatic experiences.

As John explains, "He was found dead on Friday morning, 25 October 1985, at the Wembley flat of an acquaintance." There was just one fresh needle mark in his arm. Death was due to alcohol and morphine poisoning. In May 1986, Mat Vosse, journalist for a music magazine and admirer of Gary's wrote: '… from what close friends who saw him that week say, the man who gave so much pleasure, died unhappy and broken. Auf Wiedersehen Gary.' "When he died," explained John, "I had wonderful letters from people who only wanted to remember the kind loving Gary."

A national newspaper, eager for an unusual story angle, interviewed Pat about his friend. Prior to attending Gary's funeral, Pat had put his funeral suit in the back of his Rolls Royce. On trying to open the boot to access the suit, part of the key broke off. He made an off-the-cuff remark: "If Gary's up there, he's probably laughing!"

Unfortunately the journalist fabricated the rest of the article, implying a psychic link between the two of them. Pat was subsequently invited to appear on a programme about the paranormal, but was never given the chance to put things right; he felt badly that the public could be deceived by someone else's account of what he was supposed to have said.

Our chapter concludes on a lighter note, with a true story from Tim Healy, about their *Auf Wiedersehen Pet* days: "Spall is the funniest I've ever met. We were in the hut this day, right? And it rained all day. And you're sitting in the Elstree hut – where they make *Eastenders*. They'll not let you go home, in case the rain stops – you know? So we're cracking gags. And I've been through my whole act. I've pulled every gag I've ever known. Eight hours of gags – and we're sick-to-death of them.

"It got that bad I turned to Tim and I said: "Hey, what do you call a bloke with a seagull on his head?" It's an old joke, the answer's 'Cliff', you know? Tim went: 'Albert Ross!' It was funnier than the original gag! He made his own up. He's the funniest man I've ever met!"

Chapter Sixteen

MENS SANA IN CORPORE SANO – A SOUND MIND IN A SOUND BODY
– (Juvenal, Roman satirist, AD c60 – 130)

If you can talk with crowds and keep your virtue,
Or walk with kings – nor lose the common touch…

"Have you no homes to go to? Have you no respect for the law? Go home to your wives and children!" This is what we used to shout to the crowds of illegal drinkers in our clubs, when we thought it might be time to close.

If there's one adage that Pat must surely believe in, it has to be 'variety is the spice of life'. It would be very difficult to find someone who has led a more varied life, in professional *and* personal terms. So, kings… and the common touch: how's that for a challenge – comment-wise?

I never did walk with a king, but maybe a prince will do? When I was at the European Olympics for Handicapped Kids, in Glasgow, Prince Albert of Monaco introduced himself to me, in the VIP Lounge. It's unusual for me to be up there, because I usually stay with the kids and have a cheese sandwich with them. I've been fortunate enough to have eight Royal Premieres, which – if you recall – included meeting Fergie. Ollie Reed was also in the same film – how common can you get?

Having left school at the age of fifteen to work for his father, it wasn't long before Pat took the plunge and launched out on his own, not just as a general dealer, but in a wide range of different businesses. World-wide travel not only enabled him to deal in spare parts, many of which were eventually for commercial vehicles, but also provided him with a whole range of experiences that would be difficult for anyone to match: we have only covered a *fraction* of these in the book.

As Pat approached the age of 17, he was already involved in 'tatting' – the rag-and-bone trade, and, as earlier chapters revealed, worked for coal merchants down by the canals, at Hockley. It was around this time that he became very friendly with the Harris family.

I used to almost live at their house at the time. Although I was at my Gran's, I never got home to her house until late at night. I'd leave about 8.30 in the morning – because we used to meet at the coffee house.

Harold Harris lived on Hollyhead Road by Hockley Brook – where Hamstead Road goes off to the right. He was father's driver and lived across from where I had the coffee-house years later – 'The Fly-over' at Hockley Brook. Young Billy Harris, his son, came to work for me, and then his mother came to work for him. We had a bust-up over it – a terrible row; we all fell out over it.

Harold Harris had 17 kids; he was from Featherstone in York. He was married to Ethel. Ethel's brother's name was Bill Bradbury. Bill was quite a character. He ate more porridge than the three bears – you can draw your own conclusions from that!

Harold is the oldest – named after his father. Then there was Margaret, Maureen, Rosie, Diane and Billy – so many of them – my God! Diane is my lifelong friend. She was photographed alongside Doreen and myself on a Spanish beach, during the making of 'Auf Wiedersehen Pet'.

During this same period, Pat met Eddie Fewtrell, who later became a successful nightclub entrepreneur. Eddie was a car dealer, in partnership with his brother Frankie.

They had a car pitch in Washwood Heath. Frankie's dead and buried now. I suppose I sold the odd car for them and got myself a tenner for a drink – I don't know. I was always buzzing about and going into the club business – we had three nightclubs. I suppose that was a whole new area. I'm jumping on a few years – to about the age of 25.

Pat's friendship with Jim White was now firmly established. He was also helping Jim to run the *Budokan* school of Judo, combined with nationwide judo exhibitions and competitions: "Jimmy and I spent years together doing judo all over the country. Kevin Murphy – Jimmy's cousin from Scarborough – asked me to be a national coach, but I didn't have time." George Cullen was another of Pat's friends and business associates.

George and myself had some illegal-drinking clubs, in the sense that we didn't have a license to run them. We had the 'Oyster Bar', in George's mother's house, on the Stratford Road – we won't mention the number. Just 100 yards below Seamus Donleavy's club, 'The Talk of the Town'. Seamus is a great character!

We had the 'Rendezvous', in the Jewellery Quarter. Paddy White was the doorman. It was a vegetable shop that Tommy Richardson owned, and we bought off him; his son Paul ran 'City Waste' until recently, with an 11 million pound a year turnover. I remember seeing Paul when Tommy was on one of his out-of-town absences in Wisbech, and Paul was a baby-in-arms; Peter was small too.

The *Pieces of Eight* was in Smethwick, he pronounces it *Smerrick*, whereas the *Oyster Bar* was on the Stratford Road. The *Rendezvous* was above a downstairs greengrocery shop – difficult to imagine in these more sophisticated times. George and Pat used to meet people on the step.

There was a Fighting Room. They used to come in drunk, and say something incoherent. We'd say: "Are you gonna go home or do you want a fight?" Very often they'd say: "F*** – we'll have a fight." We'd say: "Come in!"
We used to have a sign over the door that said 'Fighting Room'. They'd go through there – we'd knock them out. We'd give them a bottle of beer when they came round, send them home and say: "See you tomorrow." They're true stories these!

Despite the name of the room and the nature of his business, Pat never actually *had* a fight there and has never been a doorman. He remembers one particularly bizarre occasion at the *Oyster Bar*, when the place was full, everyone was drunk as usual, and two customers decided to invent an unusual competitive sport.

Two fellas jumped up and started to fight and I said: "Hey-hey-hey!" They looked at me and I pointed to the sign 'No Fighting Allowed' – that was so that they wouldn't start fighting me – obviously! They looked at the sign, and at each other, then at me again, and sat down. They were in a hellish quandary and the one had got a pack of cigarettes, and stubbed it out onto the other fella's face – like that (mimes). The other fella did the same to him (acts out the scene). The other fella – the original first fella – lit his second cigarette, which is the third stage of the 'Burning Tournament', and he went to do the second guy for the second time. But he just got up and walked out, and that was the end of the event.
We built a machine into the wall; it was put in a corner: a one-armed bandit. You know the industrial wire that they used to use for automatic capstans? When they pull them down they're about a quarter of an inch thick? We built it into the wall, so that they could just get one finger through and put the money in, then get the other finger through and pull the handle. They tore the wall down (laughs) and got in the back!

Why did they pull the wall down?

Oh, they were terrible people! Did I tell you about the crates against the wall – that we used to get down – one at a time?

No!

I didn't tell you that? The house entrance was up a dozen steps, and the entrance fee, at the Oyster Bar, was – if you could get up the steps you were allowed in.

If you were too drunk, you couldn't?

Yes, we didn't want them – "Go home!" They'd come through into a second room on the ground floor, which led into the back garden.

It was just like the downstairs room of a house?

Yes. We had all these crates and crates of Guinness or brown ale against the wall, and as they walked in the room, they'd be confronted by George and I, with our backs to all these crates. We'd say: "What d'you want?" They'd say: "– much for that?" – and hold a ten-bob note out. You'd say: "Four." They'd nod their head – yes. You'd pull four bottles out the crate, pull the tops off and give them these four bottles; then they'd walk over into the corner. Then the next guy would come in and he'd have two, and the next guy would have – whatever. When the crate was empty, you'd pull it down and put your foot on it. That was your first stock-hold: your foot on the crate.

So why were they buying it that way? Was it much cheaper than going to the pub?

Because we were horrible people – that's why. We didn't serve glasses. If we didn't serve glasses, they couldn't throw them; glasses broke a lot easier.

When did they come to you?

After the pub.

In those days pubs used to close at 2 o'clock in the afternoon, then 10 o'clock in the evening. Pat and George gradually build the crates up into a counter; any empty bottles went back in the crate – to avoid having them kicked all over the floor! The height of the counter increased in stages. Once they had this added protection – out came the whisky! At that time Sparkhill had a large number of Irish immigrants.

Did they walk back home after? I mean – they could hardly be arrested for drunken driving, because in those days they wouldn't own a car.

No, no, no. They'd go to the pub afterwards! If it was the afternoon drinking session they'd go back in the pub. Then, by the time we got them back at 10 o'clock at night – God, they were in a state!

They couldn't get back upstairs again!

Because Monday night was 'Paddy's' day off! It was well known that 'Paddies', in the building trade, never went to work on a Monday. They all got drunk: the funniest thing you ever saw! They tended to be the single men, with no family commitments.

So there wouldn't be any work on the building sites that day?

No, they used to go afternoon drinking in Sparkbrook: in the pub by 12, in the afternoon they'd come to us, then back into the pub – can you believe this? Then back to us – oh terrible! Terrible state to get into! If they could get up the steps they could get in. Occasionally they used to come round the back. We didn't want them to do that, because we wanted some form of control.

George and Pat spent an entire day, with '4 by 3' and '3 by 2' timbers. They built a fortress of a back door using all the timbers, and drilling into the wall. They didn't want to spoil the appearance of the house, as it had quite a smart exterior. Some time later, they walked across the road to admire their handiwork.

As we were doing that, we saw a 'Paddy' walking down the road, staggering on the pavement. He sidestepped into the very small entranceway up to the door, and bounced off the door – because it was shut! He proceeded to try to claw his way through the door! So I said to George: "What a barmy bugger! What's he trying to do?" George said: "Leave him alone." So he starts clawing at this door. George said: "If he gets in, he gets a drink."

Anyway, 20 minutes later, he'd battered the door down – he just tore it down. We went up the entry, up the steps, opened the door – before he battered the big French windows in. We opened the door, gave him a beer, and sent him home. A true story!

Where was the first car place you owned?

Down a passageway off Broad Street, which had an antique shop in it. I sold off the first of the garages when I was in my 20s. Eventually I sold Gordon Fewtrell my car pitch 'Pat Roach Cars' in Washwood Heath. Gordon's still there. It's next to the Swan pub. Johnny Kirkbright worked for me. He opened about 25 gambling clubs – all affiliated to Mecca Dance Hall, across the country, but they robbed him blind; he went skint – sold all his clubs.

When Pat opened his Washwood Heath car business in the early 70s, the local press was on hand for a publicity shot, of fellow television star Les Kellet and Pat, in a wrestling hold. In the accompanying text, Pat said that he'd bought the business as a second source of income to fall back upon, in case of injury.

Our canal boatman, George Smith, recalled an occasion when he bought a spare part from Pat's present scrap yard in Winson Green: "A friend of ours had the fan belt go on his boat, when we took it out for a day trip. Who should serve me but Pat Roach? Although I didn't know it was Pat until afterwards."

His friends from the *Auf Wiedersehen Pet* days related their memories of Pat the businessman, in previous chapters. Here, he tells a similar tale about himself and the scrap metal business..

We were filming at the East Midlands airport, Castle Donnington – inside an aircraft. It started to rain. I went 'walkabout' and found an old machine that was once used to start the propellers on an aircraft. I gave them six hundred pounds for it and moved it to my Winson Green yard. Some time later, I remember the taxman saying to me, in all seriousness: "OK Mr. Roach, where's your aeroplane?"

Chris Fairbank, a master of accents, describes this story as 'the ultimate'. His version is even more hilarious, re-told in colourful, 'brummie' vernacular! He was at Castle Donnington when Pat discovered the machine, and heard the *Customs and Excise* sequel to it later, when the two actors literally 'bumped into' each other, at Watford Gap Service Station.

A certain grammar school games mistress used to yell at us, as we belted puce-faced up the hockey pitch, that all that vigorous activity was doing us good: stimulating our brain cells via the extra oxygen being pumped into them. Pat, on the other hand, has maintained a *self-motivated* daily exercise regime throughout most of his life; sharpening his brain for business deals, helping him to focus on the next tricky stunt routine or acting role.

On the 1st of September 1980, just a few months before work on the first *Auf Wiedersehen* series began, he became the proud owner of the *Pat Roach Health Club,* ideally situated in Birmingham's Piccadilly Arcade, New Street. The week that Pat left to make *Raiders* coincided with the club's opening. He regards the event as a cautionary tale for would-be entrepreneurs:

I had over 400 people at my reception the first day it opened; we had a 'wine and cheese' actually at the club. About 400 people turned up. The only one of the 400 who joined us was everybody's friend Big Al – Alan Wilson.

That's amazing isn't it. Did they just come for the wine and cheese?

Oh yes. I'd advise anyone who's opening a club in Birmingham – don't throw a party! You're wasting your time! He joined just to give me support; he never ever came to the club. It was like being given a hundred quid to wish me well; I've never forgotten him for that.

So all of your members joined after that?

Yes, almost no one I knew came.

Just four years later, the club, with its mirrored walls, was described in the press as 'the biggest private gymnasium in the Midlands'. It had a wide range of activities, catering for most health and fitness requirements, and ran the length and breadth of the first floor of the arcade. The Bond Machine provided a unique feature, not least because Pat's character had tried to crush Connery beneath one of the weights; he still has it to this day!

The club was my 'baby'. We set up an oasis upstairs, with palm trees, a pebble beach, deck chairs, a fountain, sunlamps – a really relaxing ambience. It was a very popular place, with a cross-section of membership.

Pat's mother Dolly recalls: "A lot of the celebrities used to go to his club. I've been going to the *Body Shop* down New Street and I've seen the youths – 'Are you coming to Pat's? I'll see you in Pat's just now!' And they've little known – I don't tell anyone who I am.

"Pat used to come and see me, and took me and Evelyn for a drink in a little pub. The barman said, 'Excuse me, those two girls over there in the other smoke-room want to know if you're Pat Roach, because they've spoken to you. They've been to your club – Piccadilly – New Street.' They came round – the biggest mistake they'd made in their lives. 'You're Pat Roach, aren't you?' He could afford to deny it again and say, 'No, I'm the model of him – I'm taken for him,' because they weren't quite sure. When he finally convinced them, they went. I said: 'Oh Paddy' – I've got a story about his nickname but – I'd be here for a month! 'Oh Paddy!' He said: 'Mother, our night would have been ruined. I've proved it, over the years.'"

The club was open seven days a week, and was particularly useful for those working in the city centre. It eventually closed in May 1990. He later opened a smaller health club in Erdington, which is now also closed.

Although he has been involved with on-going work for charities for most of his adult life, he is reluctant to publicise the fact: "Deal with the subject very lightly," he advises, "don't make a big issue of it. I consider myself a 'free thinker', rather than a religious type of person. Helping charities is my way of saying thank you and putting something back." He recently helped to raise money for a young boy suffering from terminal cancer, but is unlikely to mention the fact.

Just a few of the charities and other causes that he has helped over the years are the former Children's Hospital in Birmingham; the Birmingham Mail Christmas Tree Fund; Birmingham Dogs Home; a Drugs Crusade – with his friend, Billy Sutton; a new Jobs Bureau for the city, and the Samaritans.

He and Arnold Schwarzenegger, have been involved with the *Special Olympics*, for many years. In May 2001, he raised £1000, by having his hair shaved off, then presented the cheque to Maria Lyttle, chairman of the *City of Birmingham Special Olympics*, before the start of the regional athletics championships at Alexander Stadium. Pat is honorary president of the charity.

Unbeknown to most people, he used to visit patients at Moseley Hall hospital who were brain-damaged, and would simply spend time talking to them: as they found it difficult to make intelligent conversation they were unlikely to get many visitors. He also helped to raise money for the hospital.

Eddie Fewtrell and Pat remain friends to this day. Seated in the office of his Birmingham nightclub, *XL's*, in Auchinleck Square Eddie explained: "We've seen each other in nightclubs quite a lot, and had a drink and a laugh together. I've watched him progress in his wrestling and then on to films. I've always considered him a good friend of mine." It's been like that from day one, when they first met: "He's a big guy, a nice guy – an easy guy to get on with."

Eddie hired several entertainers in the early stages of their careers. Shirley Bassey is one such example, Tom Jones another. According to Eddie, Tom and his band, the *Squires,* used to play together in the early days; at this particular time he'd just released *It's Not Unusual.*

"Pat was in the *Cedar Club* – very late – into the morning," explained Eddie. "Tom Jones and his wife were there, and Chris: the guy who used to be Tom Jones' 'Roadie' – his Road Manager. I always remember his name because of my brother Chris, you see." The club had an unusual 77-foot circular bar.

"Tom was there and he'd got a Minder. As you'll appreciate, all the women would try to pull his hair out and get a piece of him! Tom used to come back to the *Cedar Club* because he felt easy there. He could leave all the big lights and was happy to just play with the band – what you'd call a 'Blow'."

Tom Jones shared the same Christian name as his Minder – Thomas Paddy Hallet – sometimes referred to as 'Big Paddy'. He lives in Newcastle, so he and Pat were able to meet again recently, during the Middlesbrough-based filming of *Auf Wiedersehen Pet*. Paddy has led an eventful life is his own right, and has been Minder to several stars, including Engelbert Humperdinck. These jobs were assigned to him through the *M.A.M.* company, which was owned by the man who was also manager to these celebrities, Gordon Mills.

Back in the 60s, Paddy's employer was still under contract to Eddie. "I let him do his own shows, then come back late at night to do mine. On this occasion he'd got a Minder with him and there was a bit of an argument. I never actually saw it myself, but I learned about it afterwards." According to Pat, a fight ensued outside the club, between himself and Paddy, but ended in an unexpectedly friendly way.

When Eddie and Pat appeared together in a show in aid of charity, at *Liberty's* nightclub, they discovered that, as poverty-stricken boys, they'd both been allocated Daily Mail boots. It was rather ironical, because until that point, they hadn't realised that they were from such similar backgrounds. Like Pat, Eddie's life is a classic 'rags-to-riches' story.

"I was born in Mansfield Road, Aston. After that we went to 144 Albert Road by Six-Ways, Aston. My background is that I'm one of eight brothers and two sisters – a family of ten: born very poverty-stricken. I can remember getting three halfpence ($1\frac{1}{2}$d) for bacon bits and going to school with a piece of bread and lard."

His mother had a full-time job caring for all the children. "Starting with the youngest, there was Roger, Chrissie – who's just died – Gordon, Johnny, myself – Edward, Donald, Frankie, Kenny, Violet and Phyllis. That's ten."

He owns five clubs at present: "The *Exposure Rock Café*, which is at the centre of Birmingham, down there, *Zig-Zag*, in Auchinleck Square which has 'Tabletop' dancing – and *X-L'S*. I built and own the *Millennium Bar* and the *Millennium Nightclub*, in Merry Hill." His previous City Centre clubs include *Edward's Number 7*, which was at ground level in Lower Severn Street, and *Edward's Number 8*, the upstairs section of the same building.

"*Zig-Zag's* was part of *XL'S* but I separated them," explained Eddie. "The first time in all the years that I've been in the business – at least 45 years – for the first time ever, women in Birmingham are allowed to take their clothes off in nightclubs, and it's perfectly acceptable. We are licensed to do it now: it's tasteful."

Just a stone's-throw away from the Rock Club ambience of *Zig-Zag*, and Tabletop dancing at *X-L's* is the newly-completed Richardson Building, with a three thousand capacity. It includes a bowling alley, nightclub, shops, restaurants and car park, and in Eddie's view, represents a distinct business asset: "If they want to put three thousand business people next to my nightclub I'm not bothered. Someone's got to like Rock. I should imagine they'll *all* want to come to the Tabletop Dancing!"

Pat has attended the openings of all of Eddie's clubs. Having known him most of his life has given Eddie a reliable insight into his friend's personality. "His strongest qualities are being the big guy – but the Gentle Giant. Always polite, always very nice, never takes liberties: a peacemaker, rather than aggressive. If you are a friend of his, you can rely on him to watch your back, if you've got any problems."

Eddie was hardly surprised to learn that, despite the fact that they'd just been fighting one another, Pat still had the sharpness of wit to take Tom Jones' Minder home, in the early hours of the morning and put him to bed. This became another case of Pat turning a disaster into a triumph – like the time he sold spare parts to a taxi driver – who'd just smashed into him!

Only two or three weeks later, Pat was 'on top', which means taking on all-comers, at one of showman Ronnie Taylor's boxing booths. Pat's friend Ronnie Callow, having boxed in the navy, tried fairground fighting in Tiger Bay, Cardiff. "I met Ronnie Taylor, but didn't fight for him. I had 32 fights on Patterson's fairground. I stayed on there for about seventeen weeks, got my brains punched out, and packed up: found an easier way of earning a living!"

We tracked Ronnie Taylor down in September 2000, at a fair in Redditch town centre, in company with his wife Lily. Still going strong as an entrepreneur, at the age of ninety, he recalled that 'Big Paddy' used to keep his money in a sock! A month after our interview, he made history by closing down the last boxing booth in Britain, and was featured in a *Sunday Times Magazine* article about this, the following year.

'Ronnie' is a nickname: his Welsh name is Rhys Rowland Taylor. There was no need to ask him about his background because I'd taken notes from his autographed copy of *Fair Fight – an illustrated review of boxing on British fairgrounds* by Vanessa Toulmin.

He has known some famous boxers over the years. "The most famous we've had on the show was Mohammed Ali – Cassius Clay as he was in those days. In 1977, when he was Heavyweight Champion of the World, he came to South Shields, in the North of England, on behalf of some boys' clubs – he was on a kind of sponsored tour, to get money for them. He came on to the boxing booth. One of my old boxers – Johnny Walker – used to spar with Mohammed Ali in his younger days. He went to America, to get him to come over."

Ali's appearance cost Ronnie £500-00. "He was supposed to be on for eight minutes, but we couldn't get him off – he was on for twenty minutes!"

194

There was a surprise bonus, inside an envelope: an invitation for Lily and himself to attend Ali's mosque wedding!

Jackie, Dick and Randolph Turpin also boxed on the show. "They travelled with us, the three brothers; the sister used to come along and the brother-in-law as well: a man named 'Stack'. But Randy, even when he packed the boxing in and turned to wrestling, came up to the North of England with me. He was a lovely man."

Ronnie explained that he and Pat originally met at the annual fair in Gloucester. "I think Gordon Corbett brought him to me, because Gordon used to travel quite a lot with me, as well. At the time, Pat was boxing for Jack Solomons in a championship competition. If I remember rightly, when he got to the finals they tried to bar him, because he wouldn't shave his beard off." Paddy Hallet confirms that Pat 'stepped down' from the finals, because of his beard. It was against the regulations because if an opponent was injured, rubbing a beard into his wounds could result in serious infection.

According to Ronnie Taylor, "When Pat travelled with us, everywhere he went he was practically top-of-the-bill and everybody liked him, because he wouldn't take advantage of anybody. In fact, if he had someone who wasn't much good, he'd carry him and he'd make him look good.

"Gordon Corbett was the first with him – in wrestling and boxing. The crowd used to love them. They'd stand boxing one another, and go down on their knees, still hitting one another. It was so realistic. They had the best 'nobbins', as they call it, that we've ever had in boxing booths. He used to be on the front of the show, as something called 'The Men On Top', with three or four others. They used to challenge anyone; and don't kid yourself – there used to be some tough ones out of the crowd." Paddy Hallet and Gordon also knew each other well, and were regular opponents on the booths, during their tours with Ronnie.

Pat worked for Ronnie, on and off, for ten years. "We wouldn't see Pat for two or three years, then all of a sudden he'd decide to get in touch. Because when he was on TV or filming we wouldn't even bother to ask him, because it wasn't fair to expect him to. And of course, he had his business. He was so full of energy – he never stopped!

"I don't think I can ever remember Pat grumbling. Even when boxers came up and said, 'Take it easy', then tried to take advantage of him, he never lost his temper. He came to my 80th birthday party – ten years ago – and it's surprising the number of people who came up talking to him: people that recognised him when he used to be on the show. They couldn't make it out, because he was a star by then – how he'd come to my party. I was very proud to see him. He brought his wife and son with him. We got on very well with Pat's wife. She's never ever objected to him boxing on the shows, for as long as I've known her." Ronnie and Lily have met Doreen on several occasions.

Ronnie had *another* celebrity working for him, following her title role, alongside Diana Dors and Donald Sinden, in *An Alligator named Daisy*. "We had a half-cast girl, Gina, who used to go in a sideshow with it, as *Beauty and the Beast*. We went to a pub in Pembroke one night. The landlord said: 'Look Ron, is there any chance of you fetching the alligator up one night?' So he put the signs up, 'Famous film-star to visit the pub.'

"We put the alligator on the counter. She's about fourteen years old, and very, docile, until she knows there's a stranger. A fella went up there and hit her on the snout. When they hiss, it's just like a tyre going down. As she did that he said: 'Oh it's not a real one – it's stuffed!' Lil' used to carry it about. We got rid of it was when we had our little girl – the alligator was jealous of her. We used to let it run around the caravan. It was the best watchdog you could ever have!" They kept her for eight or nine years. As I remarked to Lily: "It's not everyone who's had an alligator in her kitchen!" Pat, meanwhile, was in for a 'close encounter of the snapping kind'!

We stayed one night and I sat on this box, changing, and all of a sudden, I noticed that the lid on the box, which wasn't held down very well, began to move. When you think about it, it had been put on loosely so that the alligator could breathe. As I moved, the lid moved a fraction, and dropped down, so I dropped into the box with the alligator! The funny thing was we were changing, so I was stripped off – with me bare bum. So it bit a right lump out of me bare arse, didn't it?!

Pat's skills as a boxer, wrestler, businessman and actor, exemplify my games teacher's point – that this exercise-and-mind combination really does work! Latin, for example was so much easier to digest following a games lesson, rather than before it. And so it is that even years later, I can *effortlessly* produce that famous quotation from the Roman satirist, Juvenal: 'Mens sana in corpore sano' – 'a sound mind in a sound body'. D'you think – possibly – he knew Pat's Roman counterpart?

Chapter Seventeen –

ROOTS

If neither foes nor loving friends can hurt you,
If all men count with you, but none too much;

So many of my friends have been lenient and generous in their description and opinions of me. I think you, as my co-author really ought to make clear the fact that I have a lot of arrogance about me. I'm quite blunt. I think you should recognise all those traits in me, because they're obviously there. I'm very conscious of my faults. A lot of people say that I'm very arrogant, but people who know me realise that my bluntness isn't meant to be rudeness.

I don't volunteer any information to anybody whatsoever. I keep my tongue between my teeth, keep my own counsel and don't suffer from verbal diarrhoea. You wouldn't go far wrong if you regarded everyone out there as your enemy. However, as my dad used to say: "Treat them with the iron hand, but be sure to wear a velvet glove."

Pat has never been keen to adopt gimmicks or fancy trademarks, preferring to "just stay fit and work hard." In the same down-to-earth manner, he likens the line about no one counting too much, to his experience in the film world.

When you walk onto a film set and maybe Sean Connery or Harrison Ford says, "Morning Pat – how are you doing?" Or Spielberg, Kubrick or George Lucas say, "Morning Pat" – it's all very wonderful. But then the Special Effects and stunt guys wish you good morning too – and the film wouldn't work without them.

Then 'wardrobe' might wish you good morning, and the film wouldn't work without him either – or is it her? Well anyway, it wouldn't work without 'wardrobe'.

It has been said, almost 'ad nauseum', that many people in the entertainment industry are there because they have something to prove. Search many of the showbiz magazines, articles and profiles, and you will discover that somewhere in that person's childhood, they were deprived of the unconditional love and approval of their parents.

197

They develop a neurotic drive, so the theory goes, which motivates them to prove their worth and boost their self-esteem by seeking public approbation. Although in Pat's case, there are undoubtedly elements of truth in this, substantiated in some detail by the very first chapter, it overlooks the fact that a significant percentage of the population, in professions not necessarily media-related, have similar problems.

When someone says the word 'childhood' to you, what do you think of?

Dis-jointed, totally dis-jointed. The immediate thing that springs to mind is that children shouldn't be brought up that way: they should be brought up with love in the family.

But they can't choose, can they?

The answer to save civilization – and it needs saving (repeats this) is that every child should have a father, a mother, and if possible two grandfathers, two grand-mothers.

At least their parents?

People that love them and tell them they love them – let them know that they love them – and give them hope – very, very important. I'm afraid it's missing from a lot of families: single-parent families.

It gives them security doesn't it – right from the start?

Absolutely. You grow up dis-jointed. You don't know what the measure of love is. You don't know the difference between love and whatever. You just don't know.

Dr John Gray explores this situation in *Men are from Mars, Women are from Venus*. 'If you were helped by parents' attitudes to feel that everyone is 'worthy' of love from the time they're born, you won't be weighed down by the burden of feeling that any love that you receive has to be 'earned'. Many of us are not fortunate enough to have been taught the first of these two attitudes. As a result we feel an almost frantic need throughout our lives to prove how worthy we are. The tragedy is that we will never really believe this ourselves, and are hampered by an obsessive need to be forever proving ourselves, in one way or another.'

The positive side is that often, it is the really creative individuals who feel driven in this way. This in turn may lead to exciting new discoveries, which can benefit their fellow human beings. Pat, Spielberg and Kubrick, like many other creative individuals, have been similarly unconventional in their own fields; each has believed in 'doing things his own way'. Determined individualism seems to be an important feature of this particular brand of creativity.

Pat once remarked to Michael Burke, then a journalist for the *Saturday Mail*: "Most people quit Birmingham when they make a name for themselves, particularly on screen, but I was born in the old Jewellery Quarter and I want to be buried there." He reinforced this view in an article dated Tuesday 10 February 1983, written by Barbara Henderson, for the *Birmingham Mail*:

> ... *a friend of mine, Tony Green, now has his business on a site where I spent some of my earliest years – in Tenby Street. There's no better place to live than Birmingham. It is a friendly, small community and if you can't get a living here, you can't get one anywhere in the world. I'd like to think I could be buried in St. Paul's churchyard in the Jewellery Quarter, but of course, that's impossible now.*

The Quarter, otherwise known as the 'Golden Triangle', is just a few minutes walk from the city centre. It owes its origins to an 18th century sale of land by the Colmore family. Plots of this land were used to provide housing for Birmingham industrialists, such as the toy makers. The boundaries, strictly speaking, consist of Great Hampton Street, Great Charles Street, Summer Hill and Sandpits Parade and Icknield Street, although in practise, nearby streets in Ladywood are sometimes referred to as being within the district. During the 19th century, a second area of land was released. Additional residences were built, then converted and extended into small business premises. This in turn led to 'pegs': small workshop areas, which were rented out to craftsmen.

The family trees, at the front and back of the book, show how the families of the two authors, the Thompsons and the Roaches, are linked by marriage. Ironically, recent research by the writer's cousin, Dennis Wareing, has produced documentary evidence, showing that Pat's family history and my own, overlap in four additional areas; these involve a different branch of the family tree, and the ancestors of the writer's father, Harry Wareing.

Dennis has discovered that Bernard Wareing had his own business in the Jewellery Quarter for fifty years, from 1877 to c1927. His premises, *Bernard Wareing Ltd*, were at 70 – 76 Northwood Street, off Caroline Street. Bernard was the son of James Wareing, one of a dynasty of New Street and High Street tailors, originating in London.

He married Emela Mewis, whose father owned a large rope-making business, in the Quarter. According to the 1881 Census, Bernard employed three craftsmen and two sales representatives. His business was situated on the right-hand side, just past the Caroline Street junction, and occupied six units.

The second family link is that two Wareing families lived in Ladywood. Bernard lived at 189 Monument Road, a century before Freda and Bill Bevis moved into the same street; the writer's grandfather, Harry Senior, spent part of his childhood at 43 Morville Street, close to Sheepcote Street, where Amelia was born, and was just three years older than her. Great-grandfather, William James Wareing was manager at a pen factory in the Jewellery Quarter. Harry's two sisters, Una and Elspeth, later had tailoring businesses in Deritend and the Great Western Arcade, off Corporation Street.

Thirdly, there is the Saint Chad's connection. Pat's father, Frank Roach attended Saint Chad's School, together with his brothers and sisters. We know that several of the Roach family attended services there, and may sometimes have been in the same congregation as the Catholic branch of the Wareing family, who were regular churchgoers, and wealthy benefactors. Norah Roach's husband, 'Harry' Mulroy, was a member of the choir. Cathedral records dating back to the Victorian era show that both families were baptised there. George Wareing, the New Street tailor, his wife Mary, and their son, James, are buried in the crypt, alongside the Poncias, the Hardman glaziers and the Pugin architects. Bishop Wareing, one of several churchmen in the family, conducted Pugin's funeral. George and James are commemorated in stained glass windows, in the cathedral.

Finally, there is the Birmingham entrepreneurial link. Just as there have been several Roach entrepreneurs, such as Pat's grandparents, his father and himself, the Wareings, tailors, jewellers and later solicitors, became a successful Birmingham business dynasty. They were more fortunate than the Roaches, as their wealth enabled most Wareing males to enjoy a grammar school education; Bernard's son, Eustace Wareing, graduated from Birmingham University and became a celebrated war and foreign correspondent for the *Times* and *Daily Telegraph*. The Roaches, however, had to run their businesses without such advantages, through wits, determination and sheer hard work.

Two decades after Bernard's demise, some factory owners still lived in Monument Road or Hagley Road, as Tom Arneill, one of the younger 1940s residents recalls. Often there were no managers because the places were fairly small. Tom's mother made badges in a Warstone Lane press shop, with a woman supervisor.

Tom left the neighbourhood at the age of ten, but Pat spent a much larger proportion of his youth in this area, which covers 265 acres to the north west of the city centre. His club, *The Rendezvous*, described in the previous chapter, was at 31 Hockley Street, by the top end of Spencer Street. A copy of his business card is shown in the illustrations.

Denis Wood's wife, Cynthia, worked at the *Sheffield Smelting Company*, from 1939 – 1964. "My dad died in 1939 and left mom a widow, and she got me a job where she worked. I was 12 years old when war broke out." She made necklaces, bracelets and ear rings. "I worked on a hand press, stamping out the settings for gold and silver things – and I made the screws that fasten ear rings."

Prior to becoming a production manager at *Lucas's,* in Great Hampton Street, Albert Townsend, mentioned in earlier chapters, worked for the company as a sheet metal worker. As a member of their maintenance staff, he recalls the laborious task of opening an enormous, abandoned safe at a works in Vyse Street, on to Hockley Street. Disappointingly, it contained no jewellery! "I'm sure a lot of those Jewellery Quarter factories, although they looked a bit decrepit, had enormous safes inside. The factory was built around the safe, which was right in the middle of the building."

The frontages of Warstone Lane and Vyse Street have the Chamberlain Clock at their junction. Nowadays, some of the streets in this area, including Spencer Street, are dominated by the respectable image of jewellery retailers. However, readers may recall the disreputable 'goings-on' of the previous century, within this same district. For example, the 'Direct' and the 'hookie gear', associated with the Summer Lane mob, over which Frank Roach presided; in later days – the *Fighting Room* at his son's club: all just tips of a very large iceberg. The city's canal system passes nearby – drawing us back, once more, to Amelia's early years.

Pat has been involved in several programmes based in or around his home city. In the 1970s, he worked on *Gangsters* – filmed alongside the canals. His female wrestling friend Mitzi Mueller, had a role in the series: "I came into the studio to see him, which I thought was fabulous."

The Birmingham canal system also featured in a *BBC* television programme, in which Pat took a barge trip, visiting familiar landmarks. In 1984, when film and television offers were pouring in, following the first series of *Auf Wiedersehen Pet,* he portrayed the famous Black Country bare-knuckle boxer, and one-time national champion, known as *The Tipton Slasher.* It was part of a new *Central* series about the Black Country called, *Gi' it some 'ommer.*

Pat's character lost his last fight against Tom Sayers, and all his money, in the 1850s. Although the make-up was pretty gruesome, in reality it was a friendly fight, because his boxing booth friend Gordon Corbett, a former professional light heavyweight from Birmingham, played Sayers. The *Slasher* received the thrashing of his life from a smaller opponent.

Bill Bevis, Pat's maternal grandfather, may have lived somewhere in the vicinity of Broad Street before marrying Amelia, although the exact address is unknown. "He was a Brummie, I believe," explained Dolly. "He had a sister – Auntie Lou."

Pat explained that Freda later lived in Monument Road with her father. When he died, she moved to Roderick Road, Sparkhill, where she and Dolly lived opposite each other, from 1981 until 1995.

Amelia and Bill may have met through Mrs.Gill's family. According to Dolly: " Momma used to go to Mrs Gill's. She lived opposite Bingley Hall by the Old Crown pub, in Broad Street." Amelia was a friend of Mrs. Gill's niece, whose surname was Greenhill, when they were teenagers, in the early 1900s. The Gill and Bevis families became near neighbours later, when members of both families including Bill and Amelia moved to Garbett Street.

Aunt Freda, Dolly's sister recalls that the two of them visited the Crown: "now and again, to meet friends, and that." This same pub was Alan Goodwin's second canal project, in the early 1990s. "It's very close to the James Brindley," he explained, "just on the other side of Broad Street, and is now alongside the canal. It's only separated by the driveway or service access into the ICC. So part of that space is the yard now, to the Crown." There had been plans to demolish this historical building, but it was successfully restored instead.

Its origins are quite surprising. In 1866, two Midland men, Henry Mitchell and William Butler opened a brewery at Smethwick. As their business expanded, Mitchell found a new site at Cape Hill whilst Butler was becoming famous for his home brew at the Crown Inn, as it was then known – in Broad Street. They formed the M&B firm in 1898.

Alan explained: "The Crown originally had two frontages – an L-shape: one into Edward Place and one on to Broad Street: we restored those. On the canal side it didn't have an elevation, because it was blocked in by another building, which was subsequently demolished. So we had to make a pastiche elevation to match the Broad Street elevation. At the back of it, against the ICC, was just a yard with some old lavatories in; it was all pretty run down. Essentially, the building was in two parts."

Our illustrations include a copy of Alan's original design for the front elevation of the pub. Structurally the *Crown* was an easier proposition than the *Brindley*, because the canal was sufficiently far away and it already had a basement. However, a few surprises lay in store for them!

"When I first went down there it was a maze of passageways, and we found an old engine in a partly bricked-up compartment. One of the intentions was to try and get this caste-iron engine out and restore it. I don't really know what it was for, but it *may* have been something to do with drawing up ground water. The pub was a front for the brewery that stood behind it: they could retail stuff straight out of it."

The cellar had been built in different sections – at different times, and was quite extensive. "Another complication," explained Alan, "was that it abuts the ICC at the back, and their foundations are quite deep underneath the concert hall. They'd built right up against our cellar wall; we had to be very careful in building that back wall, right the way up the height of the building."

Earlier memories of one particular Ladywood location were revived, when Pat featured in two local newspaper articles, about rebuilding the same area.

We went to a wedding in the old Morris 14.9 – called Bess One: an old red one. We were going down Ledsam Street. There was a cinema down there called the Ledsam. My old Granny used to take me round there. It used to be seven pence and 1/6d.

Amelia sat in the front, because she couldn't see too well. I'd sit half-way up the back, and at half-time she'd shout up the back: "D'you want an ice-cream Paddy?"

Not with me – I don't know her!

A friend of mine, Georgie Homer, owns half of Ledsam Street now. I knocked one of the first flats down, which was a new, big thing, when all of the people moved out of Shakespeare Road, in that area of Ladywood. All those years later, I was asked to sit on board a big crane, and knock down what had been the first of this new accommodation – where they moved us to – from Ladywood.

Dolly saved two 1980s newspaper cuttings relating to this event, entitled 'It's Flat Out For Pat' and 'Bring on the Bomber', which described how Pat struck the first blow in demolishing the Ladywood flats, knocking a hole in the side of six-storey Allensmore House, with a giant ball-and-chain.

A photograph from the *Central Library* collection, shows Ladywood, c1954, prior to demolition, and illustrates graphically the urgency for providing new housing at that time, although the new flats eventually proved unsuccessful

Meanwhile, back in the 21st century, Pat continues his story about the area:

So we were going down Ledsam Street, coming back from the wedding. The car was full of people – God knows how many! I must have forgotten to switch the offside light on. Do you remember the old black torches that you used to put on bikes – and you used to switch it on at the top?

Yes.

Well I'd forgotten to switch it on. I'd taped it onto the headlight. In those days, the sidelights used to stick up on the old cars, at the back; they were either chrome or back – hence the nickel/chrome. Anyway, I'd taped it on, or fastened it on with string – whatever it was.

Driving down the road – I'd forgotten to switch it on, and a policeman stepped out of a side road. He flashed his torch at me. I slowed down in the middle of the road and he walked up to the window and said: "Do you know you've got no front

offside light sir?" Before I could say anything, my mother said: "Oh officer," (I can't remember verbatim), "he's forgotten – it's a shame. The reason he's forgotten is he's drunk!"

Just to help you!

Yes. "He's forgotten – he's drunk: he's had too much to drink!"

What did the policeman say – "Would you mind stepping out of the car sir?"

The policeman switched the light on for me and waved us on.

Really?

The funniest thing – it's a true story!

At one stage, his agent, Peter Charlesworth, suggested that Pat should move to Hollywood. His acting and wrestling career was going particularly well at the time, taking him to the four corners of the world.

We'd hit the right note; Peter said we should go on to do bigger and better things. I got to the stage where we just never stopped: I just went from one thing to another; things were looking better and better.

However, Pat decided against the move, and to this day feels that he made the right decision. It coincided with a period of some years, when many American actors were coming to Britain to work on high quality films. The fact that he was in eight films that were Royal Premieres seems to vindicate his decision.

I think that as hard as you might look for deep and difficult reasons for not wanting to go abroad to work, it really is quite simple. It depends what you're locked into, if you're self-employed of course, on this side of the water; leases, commercial leases and immediate family: your mom and your immediate family. You would worry about your poor old mom if you went away. You can't just shake off commercial leases – they take a lot of shaking off nowadays.

The other thing is that I was born, and grew up in Birmingham, within a stone's throw of the clock in the Jewellery Quarter. My granddad – Granddad Bevis – is buried there. And I like Birmingham – I belong in Birmingham. I actually belong to Birmingham and I suppose that's the reason I didn't want to leave. I just wanted to be here: I didn't want to leave my memories. I have no regrets about not going to Hollywood – no regrets at all: it's as simple as that.

Ironically, following this decision, Pat worked on two movies in a row that took huge chunks out of his life, but ended up on the cutting room floor: "*Prince of Thieves*, which was a 14-week movie, and *Indiana Jones 3*. I had tremendous parts in both films – it knocked a hole in me – it really did!" When asked about his greatest achievements, Pat is at something of a loss:

> *Everything fades for me – about business, careers. It all fades into nothingness; I think it means nothing. I think you've got to survive and you've got to eat. But I always get stuck with 'the height of my achievements' – and that sort of thing. I think everything is so different.*

Throughout his career, he has had to be ready to leave Birmingham at very short notice. Just a fortnight ago, he received a telegram to fly to New Brunswick in Canada, for a guest appearance as Goran, in Episode 10 of the science fiction series, *Star Hunter*, and was away for two weeks. He explained this type of situation during an interview with Michael Burke, some years previously:

> *I've been in a lot of films, but I never know what I'll be doing next. The 'phone rings and I'm off. My mum, Doris, should take the credit for any acting talents I've developed, because she's always had a theatrical personality, which inspired me.*

Pat's strong motivation to succeed was partly due to his determination not to allow his initial, secondary modern education to hold him back.

> *I knew that – what's the word the police use? Without 'endeavour' and without drive, a lot of luck, and some good judgement, I wouldn't get anywhere – and that's what drove me on. And of course, my background: seeing my poor old gran working until she was 72 – and then she was retired from work – and within three or four months she was dead.*

So you were *determined* that would never happen to you – whatever it took?

> *Yes. My background of somewhat depraved – or was it deprived –*

A bit of both – maybe!

> *Yes – is what inspired me to go – it really did! My dad was more 'laid-back'. He'd drift out of the house at nine and have a bacon sandwich in the coffee house. Then they'd go and have a 'mooch' or a 'Toby'.*

Why a 'Toby'?

I don't know. They'd get a few quid together for ferrous – scrap iron – and have a 'weigh-in'. The intention was to be finished in time to get to the 'Bookies' before the first race, which in the winter was one o'clock – because of the dark coming in about four o'clock. So it was essential that you were back in the coffee house – or the 'corfee house' – by one o'clock – in time for the first race.

I think those first few years with my father, when we started work after nine – got it all done between having our bacon sandwich and the first race – one o'clock in the winter, 2.30 in the summer, set a pattern. We never struck a blow after that time; as soon as racing started we'd be in Harry Davis' bookmakers shop, just off Great King Street, Hockley.

Two of his favourite stock phrases, dating from those days, are: "If it moves, buy it, and if it doesn't sell the f... thing!" Also – "If there's room for improvement – you're fired!" Pat's philosophy on life seems to be based on a sardonic brand of humour, which has proved useful when dealing with a host of difficult situations.

His mother Doris has a similar approach: "When I wake up of a morning I say: 'Thank you dear God for this beautiful bed' – well it isn't beautiful – I'm dead povvy. 'Thank you for the beautiful room with the fresh air in' – that's why it's beautiful – because I've opened three windows! 'Thank you for this beautiful day' – no rain – another day. 'Thank you for keeping us safe through the night and from terrible fires, and from everyone else' – I mean, look at the flats that have been burnt. 'Thank you dear Mother Mary, for beautiful sleep in a lovely, warm, solid bed' – it hasn't sunk or anything! Our Pete bought me a solid bed and *Age Concern* have 'highered' it so that I don't have to go down – 'cause I can't get up!"

The golden rule in life is this: one thing you do every day of your life is to clean your teeth. And when you do, you have to look in the mirror. What you write on the mirror is: 'ego, vanity, greed'. And the secret of leading a successful life lies in the Japanese saying: 'Jhita Kii'. I could be wrong – it's in very old Japanese. The translation of that is 'the understanding of oneself within the realms of the universe'.

So seeing yourself in relation to the universe – you'd be tiny – like an ant on an elephant's proverbial!

Exactly, not even an ant – a flea on an ant!

Or if you measure mankind in terms of the time we've existed in the universe, it's a tiny fraction of time, like a blink?

Well that's exactly how I see myself.

In terms of his showbusiness career, he is concerned not to be egotistical, but is proud to have worked with such dynamic personalities as Stanley Kubrick, Steven Spielberg and Sean Connery.

What's lovely, is to meet a 'filmstar' – to meet someone who you know is a very genuine person. Then to meet him or her at a later stage, when they've become really big, and they still give you the same smile – and the same 'hello': that gives you a great kick! Every time I've been on a film where Connery's been in it, my golden rule was – always leave them alone. But Connery's always gone out of his way to say: "Hello Pat." You must make a point of saying that I'm not saying this for my ego: it's complimentary to him; I'm saying, credit to the man.

The other thing is that Spielberg and George Lucas sent me that lovely jacket, which is one of only three, I believe, in existence. I must show it to you. We'll take a photo of me wearing it: he gave one to the only three supporting actors to be in all three movies; Vic Armstrong and Billy Horrigan also have one. George Lucas and Spielberg, with all their ultra-success and all their billions of dollars, thought of little-old-me and sent me the jacket. But again, stress that particular point. We must stress that the idea is not: 'I've got the jacket', but that 'they've sent it to me', so the compliment is squarely at their feet..

Pat explained that he doesn't single out 'high points', because he finds more pleasure in situations that occur naturally, rather than those which are contrived.

I drove down to London last night and it was daylight, and every time I drove past a field of bright yellow crops, I swear, I lifted an inch off my seat! It was so beautiful; when I see daffodils, I get the same feeling. When I see those fields, I elate so much that there's no room for anything else. So if someone rang me up and said, "Pat, you're in a movie tomorrow," I'd feel great about it. But if there was a scale to measure feeling great about that, and looking at this beautiful field, I don't think that there's any comparison. I get a terrific kick when I see an oak tree. I get a kick out of looking out of a window and seeing a wild plant growing out of a piece of brickwork.

One of his most endearing qualities is that behind his large frame lies great sensitivity: he isn't afraid to express his emotions: a very useful trait for an actor – one might almost say – a pre-requisite! Pat also feels an affinity with the wildest aspects of nature – perhaps not surprising in view of some of the roles he's played!

When I was in New Street, I'd look out of my window, and there were all the buses, and there was a plant about that big (indicates) growing out of the wall – and it flowered. I used to look at it every day in wonder! The same way that I look at an aeroplane flying through the air: a totally different thing – but look at it. I have to say that I don't want to sound 'mushy'. What about skies? What about cumulus nimbus, or stratus? I'll stop a car and look at a sky – I will!

Although writing a couple of centuries ago, poet and artist William Blake's explanation about this way of looking at the world is hard to beat:

... to the eyes of the man of imagination Nature is imagination itself. As a man is, so he sees.

(From Blake's letter to the Reverend Dr. Trusler, 13 Hercules Buildings, Lambeth, 23 August 1799).

You know what else grabs me – if I can stop and do it? If ever the time comes when I do retire, I'm going to take up photography, because I have to capture some of this. Do you know what else I see? It's a bizarre beauty – it's there: dead trees, you see a tree that's dead. The thing is, it's obviously there; it's not under the ground, no one's burnt it – that's what's beautiful about it. You have to use the phrase 'bizarre beauty'. I just love to see wild flowers, much as I love roses.

Pat is very clear about the fact that, "I'm not *proud* of anything, I've just been lucky." He seems to have a personality that combines three elements: shrewd business sense, a street-wise instinct for survival, both physical and emotional, and a natural instinct and affection for those elements that make human beings 'tick'. Like Kubrick, only ten years his senior, Pat also did it 'the hard way', with no established role models and no well worn paths.

Chapter Eighteen –

TRUE COLOURS

If you can fill the unforgiving minute
With sixty seconds worth of distance run...

But what are we running away from – and what is the 'unforgiving minute' – in your particular life?

Although some negative characteristics have emerged, our book has largely emphasised the positive aspects of Pat's nature. Everyone has a positive and a negative side: darkness versus light. If we examine these grey areas, we are much more likely to discover his 'True Colours'; for the key to doing so lies in the realisation that Pat is a person of contradictions, with many hidden aspects to his personality.

To aid this investigation, we're about to employ a little déjà vu; imagine, *if* you will, Arnold Schwarzenegger as a *Conan-type* hero, sealed once again, sword poised for action, within the icy heart of a Crystal Palace: searching the circular hall of mirrors for the treacherous wizard.

There is a sound of splintering glass as Arnie smashes the first mirror, discovering, perhaps, the mercenary side of Pat? Well ... wait just a minute ... I don't think it is. Nor is it Goran, the gorilla-type monster, featured in **Conan II** *stills. The haughty figure who steps forward from the shattered mirror, appears to be a rather arrogant version of the wizard – or maybe it's just Pat in disguise?*

Let's face it, he *must* be arrogant, to suggest, as he did in the previous chapter, that his friends are being far too lenient in their description of him – I mean, how arrogant can you get? To dare to suggest that your friends have not described you fairly!

Vic Armstrong recalls an aspect of Pat that could easily be *interpreted* as arrogance: "I always remember listening to Pat Roach's theory on various things. Pat always had a 'theory'. Very much like Steve Kesten – he always had a theory. I sent him your regards the other day: I e-mailed him. It was quite funny – I always remember that!" Steve is a producer who Pat and Vic worked with in the USA. Vic has 'done a lot of shows with him'.

What's nice is that so many people remember something I said 25 years ago: I've always thought about, or lived by, or taken it into consideration. People say I'm arrogant because I won't stand for their f- - - nonsense!

In Chapter 22 of *Orley Farm* (1862), Anthony Trollope extols the virtues of a *similar* trait: 'As for conceit, what man will do any good that is not conceited? Nobody holds a good opinion of a man who has a low opinion of himself.' He takes this one stage further: 'Never think that you're not good enough yourself. A man should never think that. My belief is that in life people will take you very much at your own reckoning.'

Arnold raises his sword, smashing a second mirror – disturbing an impatient Pat, or the wizard – or whatever.

One irrefutable fact is that Pat is something of a 'bulldozer': you can take that any way you want to. Possibly, he's cultivated this approach over the years, in order to become a success in life; whether it be in a domestic or commercial situation, or within a corporate body. Let's face it, it's not easy to take kindly to a bulldozer in your front or back garden, the kitchen, or indeed in one's life!

Chris Fairbank, talking recently about the making of the original two *Auf Wiedersehen Pet* series, described certain events that seem to substantiate the impatient side of Pat. "Every time there was a free moment, Pat would be on the phone, and it was always to do with the health club, because there were always problems. It usually centered on staff not being up to the mark, not doing what they should do, and generally giving him aggravation and problems.

"So it was like this 'Pat Roach Health Club' soap opera. Every time he came off the phone there'd be another tale of doom and disaster. He was always firing people: that was the problem. He was always bemoaning the fact that you couldn't get staff any more, and when he got somebody they lasted about two days, then they were fired. That's the recollection I have of events, twenty years in the past.

"But it was great: we just used to wait for the next episode really. Whenever Pat would say: 'I'm just off to make a quick phone call, tell David, Roger or whoever, that's what I'm doing if I'm needed,' then we'd just wait for Episode 34 to emerge, when he returned."

Arnie loses his footing; stumbling backwards, his sword smashes into the mirror behind him. A bent and furtive version of the grotesque, red-cloaked wizard creeps out from between the shards of glass – maybe, his secretive side:

Tim Spall makes an important point, which Pat confirms, that in order to cope with the uncertain environment of his youth, he had to be particularly adept at keeping secrets; so the habit was formed from an early age – until it became second nature. Tim puts it succinctly when he says: "Pat has got a bit of a mystery about him. He's got that kind of 'gypsy' thing that is quite interesting. Although he's a very personable, gentle, amiable man, there is something a bit mysterious about him." The majority of Pat's friends and colleagues have mentioned this characteristic. With no prior knowledge of Amelia's background, Ian Sandy describes it as "... a bit Romany."

Arnold continues to search with each blow, for Pat's character. Perhaps he doesn't actually realise it, but he is helping us with the quest that this book has become. The next wizard to emerge from his shattered refuge, lingers for a while, uncertain of his next move. When he finally moves, he steps first to the left and then to the right. But is there an unpredictable side to Pat – or is it sometimes the public perception of him? Take the following example:

After *Auf Wiedersehen Pet*, its leading actors were very 'hot', as they say in the business. Pat made a tender – a closed bid – for a piece of property in Yardley Road – the gatehouse to the cemetery. He bid fourteen thousand pounds, but believes that it was sold to someone else for six thousand.

It quite clearly says, in all council dealings, that the property will be sold to whoever they think is a fit person, or has a better reason, and has nothing to do with how much you bid. Just before the bids were opened, it leaked out – somehow – that I was to come by this property, open a pet cemetery and was going to call it 'Auf Wiedersehen Pet'. That was in the Birmingham newspapers. I don't know how the rumour started, but it completely ruined my chances.

In each mirror lurks a distorted fraction of the grey areas of Pat's personality. As Arnie shatters the fifth mirror, a desperate figure leaps out, then rushes around the circular hall, examining everything that remains; Arnie retreats into the shadows.

Jim White is very familiar with this energetic side of his friend: "That's his life – interesting people. In fact I don't think he can stand 'ordinary' people, quite honestly! He likes a bit of character in people. He likes to be where it's going on: he's always been like that. And he *never* stops trying; I've never known him to stop trying. He'd get up early in the morning, and be knocking on me door saying: 'Come on Chalky!' That's my nickname by the way – Chalky White. He'd say: 'Come on Chalk, time to get up. Let's out and away!' And that was it – off we'd go!"

Kevin Whately confirms this: "He's a 'driven' man, with a very strong work ethic. My overall memories of him are that he was always exercising, or doing something. He has more energy than anyone I've ever met."

There are times in my dim and distant past, referring to what Kevin is saying about me being a 'driven man', where I would be possibly wrestling at a different seaside resort every evening, in the summer. I would drive there by myself, every single night – there and back – never told anyone else. I would do like – oh – so many miles in a week. I'd come back and be in the yard the next day – nine o'clock – and I'd have to leave at three.

But time is running out. We must break down these mirrors – destroy these images – and find the real Pat. Arnie is tiring, but manages to smash another mirror. A figure steps through the gap, clutching six bags of gold coins. He wears a broad grin and a smug, self-satisfied expression. He turns to Arnie:

First of all, I'm a mercenary bastard! Having admitted that, and got it out of the way, because of my commitments to what I'm trying to do: I'm struggling to make sure that none of my businesses go into liquidation, but even before that, I never really could afford to work on the stage. But I have to say, and you can quote me in this book, I wouldn't give two-bob to the Church. Whenever I go to a birth, a death or a marriage, I always take a cheque in an envelope with me, made out to a charity. Rather than embarrass anyone else there, I put the envelope on the plate face downwards, with a stamp on it. The church could be a non-profit-making bank – lending money at x% on a non-profit-making basis; as 1 in 3 businesses may fail, they've got to cover that aspect.

Four images of Pat remain, for Arnie to release. This time, a particularly disreputable wizard lies waiting – one might almost say – gloating!

Well as long as you're successful it doesn't matter if you're a scoundrel. It's as simple as this: If you're a successful scoundrel, then you're respected. If you're a scoundrel who's not been successful – everyone thinks you're low life.

Kevin recalls that sometimes, when he and Madelaine visited Birmingham, certain people would say, "Oh Pat Roach, we know all about *him*!" – as if to hint at something disreputable. But, as Kevin says, "they were never people who actually knew him well – just people who thought they did, because he was a celebrity."

So are we any closer to discovering Pat's real persona? All that Arnie's done so far is release a series of distorted images. But wait – someone is hammering furiously on the inside of the mirror – desperate to be let out – to begin the day's business:

This restless side of Pat gives Dolly cause for concern. "He's a glutton for work and it worries me to death, because he takes far too much on, and I think he'll have a brain attack. I don't know how he does it. He goes to London twice a week and he goes here, there. One minute he says: 'Mother, I'm off to so-and-so. I shall be back tomorrow.' They send him a telegram and he never, never refuses – off he'll go. He says: 'Mother, you never get the chance again – if you refuse to go when they send you a telegram.' That's what happens when they send for him to go for films, ooh yes."

Maybe the real Pat is still there – undiscovered – behind one of the remaining mirrors? Is he a man of mystery – or just a plain, ordinary person? A giant of a wizard is heading for 'Conan'. His appearance alone is enough to intimidate anyone!

Aunt Freda remarked: "When he comes in they all gasp you know. There they are down there, and there he is – up there! Very strong – fine big fella." So why is he is generally cast as Mr. Nasty? Perhaps Pat can explain? "You get down to basics; here is a big man – therefore he is bad. But not only a big man, here is a big *bearded* man, which is even worse." When asked about the amount of time he spent at his former health club, he replied: "… not a lot, because I tend to intimidate people – I pop in."

Chris Fairbank, recalling the car accident involving Tim Healy and Pat, comments: "I think, without doubt, he's the strongest man, physically, that I've ever met. No question about that; his physical strength is just *unbelievable*. He basically took the full impact of a head-on smash, within his body. The steering wheel was bent back at right angles to himself."

Although we had no idea earlier in the book, 'Conan' has become a conduit for us, to finish what we have to say about Pat's characteristics. But Arnie has done more than enough; thinking that he's released all the negative aspects of Pat, he escapes from the hall of mirrors. As he sails away across the wine-dark lake, the Crystal Palace gradually recedes into the distance.

Everything grows still once more and the night descends. A shaft of moonlight, shining through a casement window, suddenly reveals the image of one more remaining wizard, trapped behind the glass – biding his time. A red hood obscures his face. He can wait… There is absolutely no hurry…

We don't have to smash the glass to release this final side of Pat's personality. There is a diamond-shaped button on the inside frame of the mirror, which the wizard simply presses; the glass lifts and this monk-like figure steps forward, in dignified silence. His entire body, apart from his huge hands, adorned with rings, is concealed by a crimson robe. All the other slain wizards have vanished into thin air – as though they count for nothing. If this is the real wizard, maybe he is smiling, because only he knows his true nature…

Plato used a very graphic analogy for describing a person's soul, his true personality. He likened it to a chariot, with two horses pulling in opposing directions. Reason is the driver, trying to control Spirit, a horse representing man's nobler emotions, pulling against rival steed, Appetite, which represents our baser instincts. Despite so-called progress, human nature has probably changed little since the time of the Ancient Greeks.

The components of Pat's personality are similarly diverse and sometimes, although not always, contradictory. At any given time therefore, he can be the streetwise 'ducker and diver', or an active supporter of charities; action man and 'man-of–the-world', or loyal, home-loving person, who prefers Birmingham to Hollywood. One moment a competitive wrestler and sportsman of exceptional strength, then by contrast, a 'Gentle Giant'; someone who appears very arrogant – or simply an honest man, standing firmly by his beliefs: not wishing to deceive.

Is he perhaps the actor and man of many disguises – often impossible to recognise, or a considerate friend, who will 'watch your back'? By his own admission, a bluntly spoken man, or natural storyteller – a weaver of fascinating tales? A person who has experienced and coped with all manner of situations, including the exotic and extremely dangerous, or someone who considers his most important achievement to be keeping his feet firmly on the ground?

The man who finally emerges from the pages of this book is in fact, a highly complex, but very accomplished person, with a unique and engaging personality: a man of many talents – a 'polymath'. He thinks that he is arrogant and to external experiences, this may appear to be the case. But in some ways he isn't. He's a dichotomy – a person of contradictions – like so many of us. It takes a certain amount of arrogance and self-confidence to achieve his level of success. But does that mean that every successful person is arrogant – or just focused?

One thing is certain however, to John Baxter's assertion that Kubrick was sure to be Kubrick 'to the end', it can be added, with equal confidence, 'and so will Pat Roach' – whichever aspect of his enigmatic personality that may be – at any given time! But believe me, that's definitely not the end of the Pat Roach story. How can it be, when there is still *so* much more to tell?

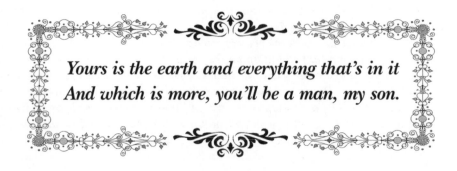

Yours is the earth and everything that's in it
And which is more, you'll be a man, my son.

APPENDICES

APPENDIX A

DARA SINGH OF INDIA AND THE 'BIRMINGHAM BULL'

(alternative title: 'Hanuman and the Harvest')

In the Uttar Pradesh, near Delhi, is the city of Brinda Bhan, where the ancient story of *Ramayan* is regularly re-enacted. A grey-haired actor, clad in magnificent costume steps slowly towards the light – and the cameras roll. His voice and bearing are distinguished – almost regal. He is the Hanuman, disciple of the great god Ram, whose temples abound in India.

Sixty years before, there was nothing to distinguish the thirteen-year-old Dharmuchak farm worker from any other village youth, except perhaps his dark good-looks, reflected in the face of the younger brother working beside him. For five hundred years Dara's family had worked the land in this impoverished, wheat-growing region of the Punjab.

Although other family members had wrestled to amuse the villagers, Dara and his younger brother, Randhawa, were particularly talented. Their dedication to the sport eventually paid dividends, providing a passport away from the agricultural community, and into the world of professional wrestling.

In 1954 Dara became 'Rustom-E-Hind', when he defeated Tiger Jaginder Singh in Bombay. Greater prizes lay in store in 1957, when he fought Lou

Thez in the finals of the World Heavyweight Championship. "We fought each other twice. In London it was a drawn match. We had a re-match in Bombay in 1968 – where I won the World Championship, and retired unbeaten in 1983." He also won the Commonwealth Heavyweight Wrestling Tournament in Calcutta, in 1959, from George Gordienko.

Pat first met Dara, who was by then World Champion, in India, during the 1970s. Pat made two tours of the country, with two or three years separating each tour. "Pat was very famous in India," explained Dara. "He was much younger than me. He's the best wrestler of the high class, because of his action: his body is very flexible. There are so many wrestlers who have stiff bodies, and they are strong, but they cannot show their skills subtly." When asked to choose just one or two words to describe Pat he replies: "A 'gentleman wrestler' – you can say."

The *Birmingham Bull*, as Pat was often referred to, and the *Rustom-E-Hind*, have wrestled one another on four occasions: "In Bombay, Guhati, Canada and in Birmingham," Dara recalled, at a recent London interview. "I came to England in August 1957 and was here until May 1958, wrestling all over the country, but especially in Birmingham, because on a Sunday there was no other place to wrestle except Birmingham." The venue, on that occasion, was a small stadium at Bingley Hall in Broad Street, but he wrestled in larger stadiums as his fame increased.

Dara returned to England in 1966 and 1972. "Pat was too young to have wrestled with me at that time. I wrestled with him in Birmingham in 1978 or 79. I wrestled with *Big Daddy* – his name was Shirley Crabtree!" He took on opponents too numerous to mention. In Bombay he wrestled *Giant Haystacks*.

He regards Pat as a "...very loveable person – and very straightforward. When we meet a new person, we make an opinion about him in our mind. So in my mind he is very straightforward... just like... I call him a 'farmer'. He's not *really* a farmer, but he looks and *behaves* like a farmer! We were very friendly, and had fun together."

Pat has always held Dara in very high esteem, "particularly after he had the courtesy to stop the match which took place two days or so after I was stabbed. The wound was giving me problems and Dara stopped the fight to save further injury."

There is a striking similarity between the careers of the two men in one other respect. A 'sea-change' in Dara's career occurred in 1961, resulting in the film, *King Kong*, released the following year. "The producer of the film approached me while I was wrestling in Bombay. At first I hesitated, because I hadn't done any acting before. I said: 'I don't know if I can act.' But he said: 'My director has seen you wrestling. Don't worry.' That film became a hit. It was more like a stunt, – you could say – fighting."

Just a decade later, Pat was approached under similar circumstances, when Kubrick provided his key to the world of films, via *Clockwork Orange*. By sheer coincidence, both wrestlers made similar transitions, at the age of thirty-three. However, Dara makes the point that, unlike India, to the best of his knowledge Pat is the only English wrestler to have become a fully-fledged actor. Both men had a ready-made audience, in the form of their wrestling fans!

Details of just some of the many films in which Dara has been involved, both as an actor, and then a director, may be found at the end of this section. Unlike Pat, when Dara first entered the film world he had cope with language problems. "For the first few films I had difficulty pronouncing the correct language. My pronunciation was not good in Hindi, because I'm from the Punjab. We have so many languages in India. Being a Punjabi from the village, I didn't pronounce the proper Hindi language."

He learned the language by working on the films. "After three or four I became perfect. Then I directed my own productions." *Nanak Dukhya Sab Sansar* was the first of these. He has directed eleven films: 6 in Punjabi, 5 in Hindi, and also produced and acted in another Hindi film in 1966.

Seated in the Hounslow restaurant of their mutual friend, ex-wrestler Paul Mann Singh, I am privileged to be interviewing Dara, following a conversation between himself and Pat. In six days' time he will be jetting back to India, to direct a film about a Punjabi family who come to live in Bombay. He explains: "They've just produced a 'pilot', which both channels have approved. It will come on TV at the end of the year."

It is July 2001 and Dara has been invited to England to be Chief Guest at an Asian family festival in Greenwich on 22 July, called *Asian Mela*, meaning *Asian Festival*. His comment: "I came a few days earlier to meet my friends and go around," is something of an understatement. During the short time he is here, he will have fulfilled a string of other social engagements, visited Wolverhampton and met Ken Livingstone, and will also spend time in London filming a religious Punjabi film. He was due to meet the director that afternoon. The *Whirlwind of India* could quite conceivably be an alternative title for him!

Such is his disposition it seems highly unlikely that he will retire in the foreseeable future. Meanwhile, back in India, his 95-year-old father still lives in the farming community where he was raised. The occupations of Dara's substantial family are firmly rooted in the modern world. One of his sons, Vindu Singh, works at the same TV studios where his father acts in two series. His other son, Amrik Singh, runs a web site for him. Dara's brother Randhawa has now retired, although he too was involved in the film world at one time. The two brothers live in close proximity to each other, and maintain regular contact.

My overall impression of Dara, without wishing to appear sycophantic, is that he is a gentleman philosopher, deep thinker and an excellent communicator. A creative person with an easy-going, laid-back manner, underpinned by a shrewd, perceptive nature, and undoubtedly, a very sharp business brain.

Dara classifies the films he directs and often writes, as historical, with an underlying, philosophical message. Unsurprisingly, there appears to be a strong autobiographical element in them. He explained several of them, two of which are included here. "*Rustom* (1982) was about the career of a wrestler. We showed that when the wrestler is on top everybody followed him. But when he gets older, people don't bother." Feeling unloved, the hero resumes his wrestling in old age; sadly, he dies in the process.

In 1974, he directed *Kisan Aur Bhagwan (Farmer and God)*. "Kisan, the farmer, sows the seeds," he explains, "and God grows it up. They are similar. Kisan puts the seed in the land, God makes it big and eatable."

Although his own farming background undoubtedly provided him with the necessary insight for making the film, his present world is, inevitably, light-years away from the one that his father still inhabits. The family sometimes journey to the north-west to visit him – the only remaining link to the youthful origins of the famous *Rustom-E Hind*: the wrestler-turned-actor-turned-film director, Dara Singh.

Further details about Dara Singh:

Birth name: Dara Singh Randhawa, born 1928.
Location: Dharmuchak, Punjab, India.
Occupation: Wrestler, Actor, Director

Actor Filmograph (in reverse order – does not represent the complete list):

1. Dillagi (1999)
2. Prem Deewane (1992)
3. Har Har Mahadev (1974) ...aka Hail Lord Shiva (1974)
4. Mera Naam Joker (1970) ...aka My Name Is Joker – (title role – Raj Kapoor)
5. Apna Khoon Apna Dushnam (1969)
6. Jung Aur Aman (1968) ... aka War & Peace (1968/II)
7. Chand par Chayadee (1967) ... aka Trip to the Moon (1967)
8. Do Dushman (1967)
9. Daku Mangal Singh (1966)

10. Jawan Mard (1966)
11. Boxer (1965)
12. Khakaan (1965)
13. Raaka (1965)
14. Rustom – E – Hind (1965)
15. Sikandar – e – Azam (1965)
16. Tarzan comes to Delhi (1965)
17. Aandi Aur Toofan (1964)
18. Hercules (1964)
19. Samson (1964)
20. Brave Bhimsen (1964)
21. Faulad (1963)
22. First screen appearance – King Kong (1962) directed by Babuhai Mistry.

Films Directed by Dara:

PUNJABI FILMS:

1. 1970 – Nanak Dukhya Sab Sansar
2. 1974 – Bhagat Dhana Jat
3. 1975 – Sawa Lakh Se Ek Laraun
4. 1978 – Dhyanu Bhagat
5. 1982 – Ankhili Muttiar
6. 1995 – Rab Dian Rakhan

HINDI FILMS:

1. 1966 – PRODUCER – Nasihat (Dara also acted in this – double role).
2. 1972 – Mera Desh Mera Dharam
   … aka – My Country My Religion
3. 1974 – Kisan Aur Bhagwan
   … aka – Farmer and God
4. 1978 – Bhakti Main Shakti
   … aka – Those Who Pray Get Their Strength From God
5. 1982 – Rustom …aka Champion
6. 1994 – Karan

APPENDIX B

Hudson Shaw, aka Andy Townsend, provides a 'fan's eye' view . . .

ALL WHAT I KNOW ABOUT BOMB!

Pat's been my hero since I first saw him on TV in my childhood (that'll make him feel old)! My earliest memories are of being in a smoke-filled living room (mum always smoked too much) and watching a black and white TV set, tuned to *ITV's World of Sport*, ready for the wrestling to come on at four

o'clock. It seems funny, but Saturdays even *smelled* different when I was a kid (no, it wasn't mum's smoking)!

It was my mother who was the wrestling fan in our house – knew all about it. I wasn't into every little detail or every match or even the moves as she was, but right from watching the wrestling in the 60s, to its assassination by Greg Dyke in the late 1980s (when Pat was the last wrestler we saw) I had my favourite.

To this day, I can't figure out why audiences never took to him. To a kid like me, he looked like all the statues and paintings I had ever seen of Hercules, so why has no one ever asked him to play that part? Hephaestus and Atlas are the closest he's ever got. And yet as soon as he got in the ring and was announced, he would be getting booed. The look on the poor bloke's face! No wonder he'd get frustrated, lose his temper and wind up being disqualified, due to a tally of public warnings. Even my old Nan, in later years, when due to a certain TV drama, Pat went from heel to 'blue-eye' overnight, still called him a 'dirty fighter'; although after a long pause she would add: "But hasn't he got nice teeth!"

I think part of the problem was the 'Bluto Effect': if someone's big, beefy and bearded he *must* be a villain – which hasn't done Pat's TV and movie career too badly: for a while in the 80s he was 'Rent-a-villain'.

Sadly, wrestling was taken from its regular slot, shortened, and eventually killed off. Saturdays were *never* the same again. A vital fixture was missing. Face facts, the *Flintstones* wouldn't be the same without Fred getting locked out and calling for Wilma at the end of each show, would it? To me, now, Saturdays don't even smell or seem different anymore.

Although he'd turned up on various TV shows and films, it wasn't until *Auf Wiedersehen Pet* that the British public really realised that they loved the Big Guy after all. People who had never seen him act before were pleased with his performance. From then on, everyone took to calling him 'Bomber'. It's just sad that the only time one sees him fighting these days is when he uses his wrestling skills in re-runs of movies. I always try to see him in his various roles, although you sometimes *really* have to look to recognise him.

And of course, he may not be on screen for very long (bad guys tend to perish easily at the hands of heroes). Even so, I always try to catch and treasure these moments. From Pat's turn at the start of *The Big Man* (punched on the nose) – to the times in various guises where he's tried to kill Indiana Jones and got burnt, sliced and squished, and sadly left on the cutting room floor – in one case.

I always get upset when I either miss Pat in something, or find that parts of what he did have been left out (the Celtic chieftain he played in *Robin Hood – Prince Of Thieves,* also suffered that fate). However, the times I watch something and know he's there on screen are worth it, especially when I can hear the audience reaction. When his name came up in the credits for *Conan The Destroyer,* it was great to hear everyone going, "Isn't he a wrestler?" I recognised him as the wizard and the man-ape he conjured up. The girlfriend who saw the film with me cried when the man-ape got killed: she loves gorillas you see! But did *you* know he was also Dagoth?

There's no denying the unintentional laughs I got from seeing Pat as emotionless, machine-like trained killer Lippe, in *Never Say Never Again.* Trying to 'do-in' James Bond to audience comments of, "Oh look – it's Bomber!" And "Oh no – he's trying to kill him! Bomber would never do that!" Full circle I suppose, 'blue eye' to heel.

One of Pat's movie appearances – his second – caused problems, due to his resemblance to something else: a huge plaster maquette of Hercules and a nymph, to be found in the *V&A* does cause comments of: "It's Bomber!" and "Oh look, it's Pat Roach!" A small statue of Hercules I once saw in a garden centre caused the same reaction, as well as – "He's forgot to put 'is trunks on!"

224

No, remember Sergeant Toole, from Kubrick's *Barry Lyndon*? Well, just after the fight scene where Pat as Toole gets practically flattened into the mud, again, inspiring audience comment, this time: "Hasn't he got huge bare feet?" (Well of course Pat's got huge great plates, how else is a 6 foot $4\frac{1}{2}$ inches heavyweight giant, with a big 53-inch chest going to stay upright)? Well, directly after that scene, we see some soldiers raiding a farm, and one is leading away a Hereford bull – and I always mistake it for Pat!

I know, once Pat used to be billed as the 'Birmingham Bull'. I used to look after a Hereford bull when I had a holiday job as a teenager, and seriously, the physical *and* facial similarities were amazing. The bull was named Henry, after another British Heavyweight fighter presumably? He was big and strong like Pat – OK? But he also had curly hair on his big chest, big pink feet, a thick neck, a mop of curly hair, sad little blue eyes, a big pink squidgy nose,

and big red hairy chops! I'm quite sure that if most farmyard bulls (in particular the Hereford, Sussex and Devon Red breeds) could talk, they would most likely sound like Pat as Bomber; a bit like if Bengal tigers could talk, they would all sound like Windsor Davies!

Which brings me on to my last piece. In 1986, I was doing a monthly comic strip for the late-lamented fantasy magazine *Adventurer*, and although I wasn't paid very much, and indeed, had chosen a character a little too difficult to draw, at least I was doing what I wanted – a strip about funny monsters. The main character was a Bull-Man, as in Greek mythology, who wore black wrestling trunks, had an operation scar on his left arm, and spoke with an exaggerated Bristol accent. The name of the strip – *Bomber the Minotaur*, of course!

He was quite popular at the time. If I gave the strip over to one of the supporting characters one month, we would get letters the following month asking, "Where is Bomber?" I still think the concept has lots of life in it, if only we could do an animated version, with Pat doing the voice … After all, you *know* you're famous, when they start basing cartoon characters on you!

Andy Townsend, aka Hudson Shaw, June 2001.

APPENDIX C

SELECTED FILMOGRAPHIES –
IN CHRONOLOGICAL ORDER:

<u>A CLOCKWORK ORANGE</u>

1971: *Producer/Director:* Stanley Kubrick. *Production Company:* Warner Brothers/ Hawk Films. *Line Producer:* Bernard Williams. *Script:* Stanley Kubrick, based on the novel by Anthony Burgess. *Lighting Cameraman:* John Alcott. *Editor:* Bill Butler. *Production Designer:* John Barry. *Art Directors:* Russell Hagg, Peter Shields. *Electronic music:* Walter Carlos. *Costume Designer:* Melina Canonero. *Assistant to Producer:* Jan Harlan.

Music: Ludwig von Beethoven, Edward Elgar, Gioacchino Rossini, Nikolai Rimsky-Korsakov, Henry Purcell, Terry Tucker, Arthur Freed, Nacio Herb Brown, James Yorkston, Erica Eigen.

Cast: Malcolm McDowell (Alex Burgess, alias Alex DeLarge), Patrick Magee (Mr. Alexander), Michael Bates (Chief Guard), Warren Clarke (Dim) John Clive (Stage Actor 'Lardface'), Adrienne Corri (Mrs Alexander), Carl Duering (Dr Brodsky), Paul Farrell (Tramp), Clive Francis (Joe the Lodger), Michael Gover (Prison Governor), Miriam Karlin (Miss Weber, the Cat Lady), James Marcus (Georgie), Aubrey Morris (Mr. Deltoid), Godfrey Quigley (Prison Chaplain), Sheila Raynor (Mum), Madge Ryan (Dr Branom), Pauline Taylor (psychiatrist), John Savident (Conspirator), Anthony Sharp (Minister of the Interior), Philip Stone (Dad), Margaret Tyzack (Conspirator), Pat Roach (Bouncer in Korova Milkbar), David Prowse (Julian), Steven Berkoff (Constable), Michael Tarn (Pete).

Length: 137 minutes
Distributor: Warner Brothers.

BARRY LYNDON:

1975: *Production Company:* Hawk/Peregrine Films for Warner Brothers *Producer/Director:* Stanley Kubrick. *Script:* Stanley Kubrick, from the novel by William Makepeace Thackeray. *Lighting Cameraman:* John Alcott. *Editor:* Tony Lawson. *Production Designer:* Ken Adam. *Art Director:* Roy Walker. *Costume Designers:* Ulla – Brit Soderlund, Milena Canonero. *Executive Producer:* Jan Harlan.

Music: J.S.Bach, Frederick the Great, W.A. Mozart, G.F. Handel, Franz Schubert, Giovanni Paisiello, Antonio Vivaldi, tradional Irish music played by The Chieftains. *Musical Adaptation:* Leonard Rosenman.

Cast: Ryan O'Neal (Redmond Barry) Marisa Berenson (Lady Lyndon), Patrick Magee (Chevalier Balibari), Hardy Kruger (Captain Potzdorf), Marie Kean (Mrs. Barry), Gay Hamilton (Norah Brady), Murray Melvin (Rev Runt), Godfrey Quigley (Captain Grogan), Leonard Rossiter (Captain Quin), Leon Vitali (Lord Bullingdon), Frank Middlemass (Sir Charles Lyndon), Diana Koerner (Lischen), Andre Morell (Lord Wendover), Arthur O'Sullivan (Captain Freny), Philip Stone (Graham), Steven Berkoff (Lord Ludd), Anthony Sharp (Lord Hallum), Michael Hordern (Narrator), Norman Mitchell (Brock), Pat Roach (Toole).

Length: 185 minutes.

Distributor: Warner Brothers.

THE SPACEMAN AND KING ARTHUR:

(AKA *The Unidentified Flying Oddball*)

1979: *Production Company:* Disney. *Producer/Director:* Russ Mayberry *Script:* Based on Mark Twain's 'A Connecticut Yankee in King Arthur's Court'.

Cast: Dennis Dugan – dual roles – (Tom Trimble) and (Hermes the Robot) Sheila White – Alisandy (Sandy), Kenneth More (King Arthur), Ron Moody (Merlin), John Le Mesurier (Gawain), Jim Dale (Sir Mordred), Rodney Bewes (Clarence, a page), Robert Beatty, Pat Roach (Oaf).

Length: 93 minutes.

CLASH OF THE TITANS:

1981: *Production Company:* United Artists/MGM. *Director:* Desmond Davis. *Production:* Charles H. Schneer, Ray Harryhausen. *Script/Screenplay:* Beverly Cross. *Cinematography:* Ted Moore. *Editor:* Timothy Gee. *Music:* Lawrence Rosenthal. *Art Director:* Frank White.

Cast: Laurence Olivier (Zeus), Claire Bloom (Hera), Harry Hamlin (Perseus), Judi Bowker (Andromeda), Sian Phillips (Queen Cassiopeia), Maggie Smith (Thetis), Burgess Meredith (Ammon), Ursula Andress (Aphrodite), Flora Robson (one of the three Stygian Witches), Jack Gwillim (Poseidon), Neil McCarthy (Calibos), Pat Roach (Hephaestus), Susan Fleetwood (Athena), Tim Piggot-Smith (Thallon), Donald Houston (Acrisius).

Length: 118 minutes.

RAIDERS OF THE LOST ARK:

1981: Paramount/Lucasfilm. *Director:* Steven Spielberg. *Screenplay:* Lawrence Kasdan (from a story by George Lucas and Philip Kaufman. *Producer:* Frank Marshall. *Cinemat.Editor and Music:* as above. *Production Design:* Norman Reynolds. *Visual Effects Supervisor:* Richard Edlund.

Cast: Harrison Ford, Karen Allen, Paul Freeman, Ronald Lacey, John Rhys-Davies, Alfred Molina, Wolf Kahler, Anthony Higgins, Denholm Elliott, Vic Tablian, Don Fellows, William Hootkins, Bill Reimbold, Fred Sorenson, Patrick Durkin, Matthew Scurfield, Malcom Weaver, Sonny Caldinez, Pat Roach.

Length: 118 minutes.

INDIANA JONES AND THE TEMPLE OF DOOM

1984: Paramount/Lucasfilm. *Director:* Steven Spielberg. *Screenplay:* Willard Huyck and Gloria Katz (based on a story by George Lucas). *Producer:* Robert Watts. *Cinematography:* Douglas Slocombe (Panavision). *Editor:* Michael Kahn. *Music:* John Williams. *Production Design:* Elliot Scott. *Visual Effects Supervisor:* Dennis Muren.

Cast: Harrison Ford, Kate Capshaw, Ke Huy Quan, Amrish Puri, Roshan Seth, Philip Stone, Roy Chiao, D.R. Nanayakkaru, Dharmadasa Kuruppi, David Yip, Ric Young, Chua Kah Joo, Rex Ngui, Philip Tann, Dan Aykroyd, Pat Roach.

Length: 118 minutes.

INDIANA JONES AND THE LAST CRUSADE

1989: Paramount/Lucasfilm. *Director:* Steven Spielberg. *Screenplay:* Jeffrey Boam (based on a story by George Lucas and Menno Meyjes). *Producer:* Robert Watts. *Cinematography:* Douglas Slocombe (Panavision). *Editor:* Michael Kahn. *Music:* John Williams. *Production Design:* Elliot Scott. *Visual Effects Supervisor:* Michael J. McAllister.

Cast: Harrison Ford, Sean Connery, Denholm Elliott, Alison Doody, John Rhys-Davies, Julian Glover, River Phoenix, Michael Byrne, Kerork Malikyan, Robert Eddison, Richard Young, Alexei Sayle, Alex Hyde-White, Paul Maxwell, Mrs Glover, Vernon Dobtcheft, J.J. Hardy, Bradley Gregg, Pat Roach.

Length: 127 minutes

NEVER SAY NEVER AGAIN

1983: Taliafilm. *Distributor:* Warner Brothers. *Director:* Irvin Kershner. *Screenplay:* Lorenzo Semple, Jnr. *Producer:* Jack Schwartman. *Cinematography:* Douglas Slocombe. *Editor:* Michael Kahn. *Music:* Michel Legrand. *Production Design:* Ken Adam. *Visual Effects Supervisor:* Michael J. McAllister.

Cast: Sean Connery, Klaus Maria Brandauer, Max Von Sydow, Barbara Carrera, Kim Basinger, Bernie Casey, Alec McCowan, Edward Fox, Pamela Salem, Rowan Atkinson, Valerie Leon, Pat Roach, Ronald Pickup.

WILLOW:

1988: Lucasfilm. *Director:* Ron Howard. *Screenplay:* Bob Dolman *Producer:* Nigel Wooll. *Cinematography:* Adrian Biddle. *Editor:* Daniel Hanley, Michael Hill. *Music:* James Horner. *Production Design:* Allan Cameron. *Visual Effects Supervisor:* John Richardson.

Cast: Warwick Davis (Willow), Val Kilmer (Madmartigan), Joanne Whalley (Sorsha), Jean Marsh (Queen Bavmorda), Patricia Hayes (Raziel), Pat Roach (General Kael).

Lensed in England, Wales and New Zealand. 1988: *Nomination:* Best Sound Effects, Editing, Visual Effects.

Length: 125 minutes.

THE BIG MAN:

1990: *Production Company:* Palace/Miramax/ BSB/British Screen. *Director:* David Leland. *Producer:* StephenWoolley. *Screenplay:* Don MacPherson, based on the book by William McIlvanney. *Cinematography:* Ian Wilson. *Editor:* George Akers. *Music:* Ennio Morricone. *Art Director:* Caroline Amies.

Cast includes (not the complete list): Liam Neeson (Danny Scoular), Joanne Whalley-Kilmer (Beth Scoular), Ian Bannen (Mason), Billy Connolly (Frankie), Maurice Roeves (Cam Colvin), Hugh Grant (Gordon), Pat Roach (Billy), George Rossi (Chauffeur).

The fight, when it comes, is one of the most gruelling ever caught on film. Top marks go to the makeup team, which provided the battered and bloodied faces for the actors.

APPENDIX D

FILM AND TELEVISION:

CURRICULUM VITAE – PAT ROACH

Films

(Including eight Royal Premieres)
Raiders Of The Last Ark
Indiana Jones – The Temple Of Doom
Indiana Jones – The Last Crusade

Willow (Kael)

A Clockwork Orange – (Stanley Kubrick)
Barry Lyndon – (Stanley Kubrick)
Never Say Never Again – (James Bond)
Conan The Destroyer
Red Sonja
The Monster Club
Clash Of The Titans
The Portrait Of A Lady
I Love You Love Me – (working title)
Flash Gordon

The Spaceman and King Arthur
The Return Of The Musketeers

The Big Man
Kull The Conqueror
Three Robin Hood Films: Prince Of Thieves,
    The New Adventures Of, and

Television and Radio

Ellington – YTV Ltd
The Bill – Thames
Space Precinct
Last Place On Earth –
    (P O Evans)
Auf Wiedersehen Pet –
    (Bomber 26 episodes)
Juliet Bravo
Give Us A Kiss, Christabel
Hazell
The Lenny & Jerry Show
Saturday Starship
Casualty
Coasting
A Roller Next Year
Heartbeat
Jack And Jeremy Police 4 –
    (pilot) Ch.4
The Detectives – Celador
Marlene Marlow Investigates
    (2 series) BBC
Gangsters
Minder
Telly Addicts
Jim Davidson Show

The Zany Antics/Adventures Of
Wings of Fame
Crust

Bullseye
Three Wishes for Jamie
True Tilda
Sea Dragon
Pirates
First Midnight – (radio)
Auf Wiedersehen Pet –
    new series, expected in
    March or April 2002.

SELECTED BIBLIOGRAPHY

HISTORICAL

A History of Greater Birmingham – down to 1830 – Victor Skipp (1980).

A Walk Down Summer Lane – John Douglas (1977).

Birmingham – John Sanders (1969).

British Economic and Social History 1700-1982 Fifth edition – C.P. Hill (1986).

Discovering Birmingham – An Introduction to the City – by Jonathan Berg.

Handsworth, Hockley and Handsworth Wood – compiled by Peter Drake (1998).

Handsworth Remembered – Victor J. Price (1992).

Old Ladywood Remembered – Victor J. Price (1987).

Streetwise – Vivian Bird (1991).

The Avery Business (1730-1918) – L.H. Broadbent (1949) – W & T Avery Ltd.

Soho Foundry – W.K.V. Gale, F.R. Hist. S. (1948) – W & T Avery Ltd.

THE CINEMA

Acting For The Camera – Tony Barr (1986).

British Cinema History – Edited by James Curran and Vincent Porter (1983).

Film Making in 1930s Britain – Rachel Low (1985).

Harrison Ford – Minty Clinch (1987).

Major Film Directors of the American and British Cinema – Gene D. Phillips (1999)

Movies From The Mansion – A History of Pinewood Studios – George Perry.

Sean Connery – John Parker (1993).

Sean Connery – Michael Freedland (1994).

Stanley Kubrick – John Baxter (1997).

Stanley Kubrick – A Narrative and Stylistic Analysis – Mario Falsetto (1994).

Stanley Kubrick – Vincent LoBrutto (1997).

Steven Spielberg – Andrew Yule (1996).

Steven Spielberg A Biography – Joseph McBride (1997).

Halliwell's Film and Video Guide 2002.

International Motion Picture Almanac 2001, 72nd Edition, Editorial Director Tracy Stevens.

Variety Movie Guide '97, Edited by Derek Elley.

SPORT:

The Mick McManus Wrestling Book – Charles Arnold

Fair Fight – an illustrated review of boxing on British Fairgrounds – Vanessa Toulmin.

LITERATURE:

Orley Farm (1862) by Anthony Trollope (Penguin UK)

William Blake, English artist and poet (1757 – 1827):

Quotation for Chapter 17, regarding Nature and man's imagination. This is taken from Blake's letter to the Reverend Dr. Trusler, 13 Hercules Buildings, Lambeth, 23 August 1799.

The Poetry And Prose Of William Blake, edited by Geoffrey Keynes (1967).

SOCIAL PSYCHOLOGY:

Men Are From Mars, Women Are from Venus – Doctor John Gray (1992).

The Integrity of the Personality – Anthony Storr (1977 reprint)

NEWSPAPER ARTICLES AND MAGAZINES:

The Sunday Times magazine

The Sunday Telegraph newspaper

The Birmingham Post and Mail

The Birmingham Post

The Sunday Mercury

The Sutton Coldfield News.

First Down (American Football publication)

HISTORICAL RECORDS AND MAPS:

<u>Local Studies Dept. Birmingham Central Reference Library:</u>

Register of Electors for Ladywood Division (number 313, Polling District LA.):

a) Spring 1920; b) register in force 16 October, 1933 to 14 October 1934.

Ordnance Survey maps for the Ladywood, Balsall Heath and Handsworth areas of Birmingham: early 1900s and 1950s.

A range of other resource material relating to the book.

<u>Birmingham Archdiocesan Archives, Saint Chad's Cathedral:</u>

Baptismal records; log book of Saint Chad's School.

<u>Archives Department of Sutton Coldfield Library:</u>

A range of material relating to the Wareing family.

INDEX

A SECTION OF THE ROACH/

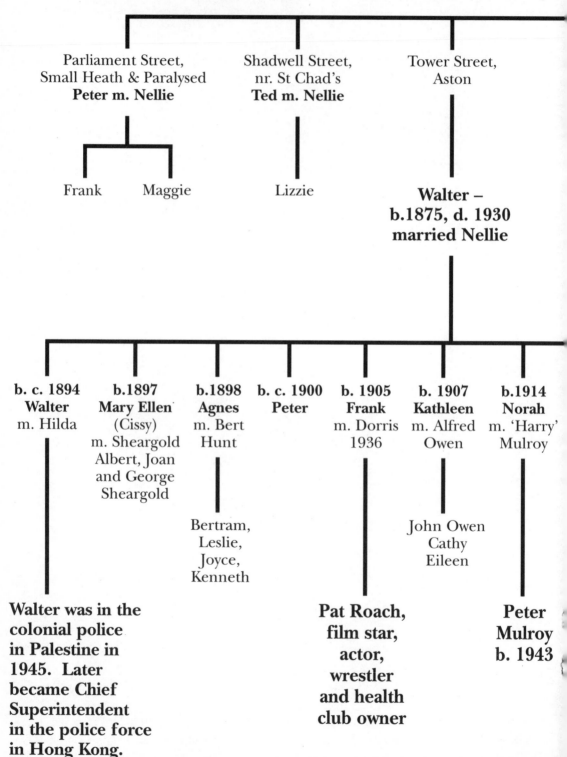

Parliament Street,
Small Heath & Paralysed
Peter m. Nellie

Shadwell Street,
nr. St Chad's
Ted m. Nellie

Tower Street,
Aston

Frank   Maggie

Lizzie

**Walter –
b.1875, d. 1930
married Nellie**

**b. c. 1894
Walter**
m. Hilda

**b.1897
Mary Ellen**
(Cissy)
m. Sheargold
Albert, Joan
and George
Sheargold

**b.1898
Agnes**
m. Bert
Hunt

Bertram,
Leslie,
Joyce,
Kenneth

**b. c. 1900
Peter**

**b. 1905
Frank**
m. Dorris
1936

**b. 1907
Kathleen**
m. Alfred
Owen

John Owen
Cathy
Eileen

**b.1914
Norah**
m. 'Harry'
Mulroy

**Walter was in the
colonial police
in Palestine in
1945. Later
became Chief
Superintendent
in the police force
in Hong Kong.**

**Pat Roach,
film star,
actor,
wrestler
and health
club owner**

**Peter
Mulroy
b. 1943**

ROCHE FAMILY TREE

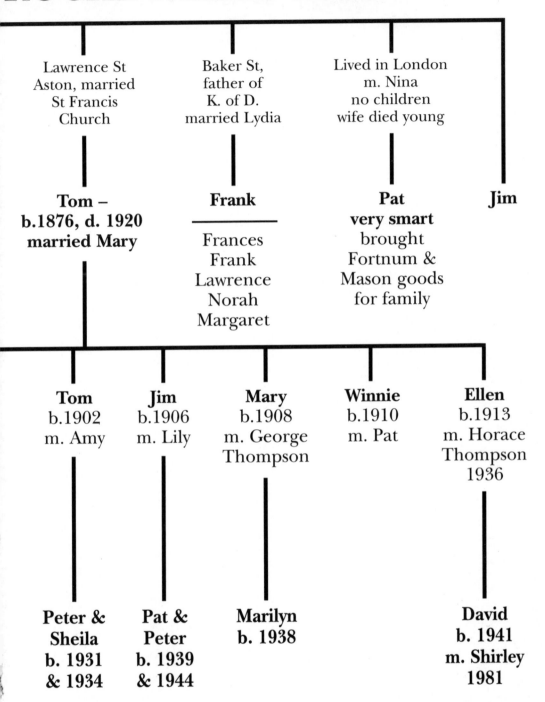

Lawrence St
Aston, married
St Francis
Church

Baker St,
father of
K. of D.
married Lydia

Lived in London
m. Nina
no children
wife died young

**Tom –
b.1876, d. 1920
married Mary**

Frank
————
Frances
Frank
Lawrence
Norah
Margaret

Pat
**very smart
brought
Fortnum &
Mason goods
for family**

Jim

Tom
b.1902
m. Amy

Jim
b.1906
m. Lily

Mary
b.1908
m. George
Thompson

Winnie
b.1910
m. Pat

Ellen
b.1913
m. Horace
Thompson
1936

**Peter &
Sheila
b. 1931
& 1934**

**Pat &
Peter
b. 1939
& 1944**

**Marilyn
b. 1938**

**David
b. 1941
m. Shirley
1981**

This is a partially completed family tree, compiled from information
supplied by Ellen Roche, Peter Mulroy, John Owen, George and
Norma Sheargold, Joyce Taylor, Stan Ballard, Dolly Roach and Pat
Roach. Our apologies to any family members who are not included.